T0110959

Conforming TO HIS IMAGE

A Fascinating and Easy to Understand Commentary on the Book of Romans.

REV. WILLIAM BURK

WestBow Press books may be ordered through booksellers or by contacting:

WestBow Press
A Division of Thomas Nelson & Zondervan
1663 Liberty Drive
Bloomington, IN 47403
www.westbowpress.com
844-714-3454

Scripture taken from the King James Version of the Bible.

ISBN: 978-1-6642-1354-8 (sc)
ISBN: 978-1-6642-1353-1 (hc)
ISBN: 978-1-6642-1355-5 (e)

Library of Congress Control Number: 2020923378

Print information available on the last page.

WestBow Press rev. date: 12/10/2020

If you are a true Christian, you have a deeper responsibility than just going to heaven one day. You have a responsibility today and every day to become more like the One in whom you say you follow. The technical term for this is sanctification, and it means to be holy or set apart. Therefore, our salvation is just the initial start of the journey. The daily sanctification process is now what is of greatest importance, and we need to know this fact and surrender to the process. The question isn't why we should do this; it is how?

Jesus came to show us the pathway of sanctification through the knowledge of the truth, repentance of sin, and practical application of the principles of His word to our daily life. The Holy Spirit works in the believer's heart to transform him or her into the image and likeness of Jesus, who is sinless. It is a process of transformation that requires some time; it does not happen in one day, or after praying a prayer of commitment to God. As stated above, that is merely the beginning of the believer's walk with the Lord and the first step into the sanctification process. When you make a decision to follow God, you join yourself to Him and are adopted into His family, but to experience the family dynamics and benefits in being in His family, you have to be faithful to Him all your life.

We conform to the image of Christ in holiness; we are being changed into His image from glory to glory, namely from victory over sin to the next victory over sin, little by little, as the Holy Spirit leads us. God has provided us with a plan to successfully accomplish this in His Word.

The book of Romans is a powerful book of the Bible. In this letter, Paul goes into great detail about the deep theological issues facing all of us. Paul tells us about the person of Jesus, the power of the Holy Spirit, God's plan for our lives, and what conforming to the image of His Son looks like. What stands in our way from this process is often our own complacency and apathy towards change. When it comes to a believer's walk, there is a battle between ordinary and extraordinary, and too many choose to settle for ordinary. This is not what God has intended nor what glorifies Him.

Unfortunately, The concept of "ordinary" or "average" is seemingly acceptable in many other things people do, but in my mind it must not be acceptable in the Christian life. I have met hundreds, if not thousands, of Christians who struggle with mediocrity in their walk of faith, and they seemingly are content to believe this or mediocrity is normal. It is neither normal nor biblical! So let's do something about it!

The Book of Romans is a phenomenal book; it can absolutely change your life! It is, in my opinion, the key to understanding the extraordinary life we are all meant to live. It is absolutely the high water mark of Christian doctrine. But we must understand the truths contained in this book at its basic level, which means we need to study it verse by verse in a way that is understandable to the average reader. When I study this book, I realize just how tired I am of ordinary Christianity! I bet you are too! I have written this book for this reason.

What you hold in your hands is an easy-to-read-and- understand commentary on the biblical book of Romans as found in the New Testament. This book is written in a conversational style as if I were speaking to my Sunday school class, commenting on each verse. Upon completion of this book, I believe one should have a much better understanding of the great doctrinal teachings of Romans.

The Word of God will be more powerful and enlightening than you can imagine as you discover its truths. Your thoughts, ideas, attitudes, and life can radically change. I have to warn you though, some of you may get angry or upset with what the book of Romans really says. All I ask of you is you would continue on as the Spirit reveals truth and remember God wrote the book. I'm just the messenger!

Reverend William Burk

The Holy Spirit wrote the Book of Romans through the apostle Paul's pen. As the human instrument God used to write the book, Paul ultimately wrote to all people who search for truth and theological depth. As you join me on this journey, seek truth and depth! Let's get started.

Chapter 1 Verse 1

In Romans 1:1 Paul states, "*Paul, a servant of Jesus Christ*" Paul challenges us immediately by letting us know that no one is a true follower of Jesus Christ unless he or she is *enslaved by Christ*! A person may or may not be saved, but a true follower is totally surrendered to Jesus. Paul teaches it is impossible for a person to belong to Jesus unless he or she is enslaved by Jesus. This is a shocking message to most people!

The word "*slave*" means *"a servant bound to serve.*" Paul was saying he was totally willing and desirous to serve Christ completely. Nothing came before Jesus in Paul's life. Nothing! I can honestly say I have met few people who had this attitude about serving Jesus. Jesus must have meant a great deal to Paul. Does He mean a great deal to you? Or is He your method of escaping punishment? Isn't that kind of selfish and one sided? Maybe Paul knew something the average Christian seems to have missed. All I know is if more "followers" of Jesus were willing to serve Him unconditionally, we'd have more Paul's in our midst! And more Paul's in our midst would be a game changer, friend!

"Called to be an apostle" Paul continues on and says as a bond-servant of Jesus he is called to be an apostle, or one sent out or sent forth on a mission because God sent him or her and Paul was willing to go! Can I share a great, immutable truth with you? There is no greater calling on a person's life than to be called to serve Jesus. Greater than being the chief executive officer of General Motors or the president of the United States! And all true followers are called to be sent forth. Are you answering the call? It doesn't mean you have to go evangelize Spain. It simply means you are willing if called to do so.

"*Separated unto the gospel of God.*" Paul challenges us to step it up! If you're a servant of Jesus, you're called to be something. If you're called to be something, you're separated from something! All true believers are separated from man-made religions, denominations, and cults. We're separated from unrighteousness and ungodliness. We're separated from antagonistic worldviews and emotional temper tantrums. We are called and separated to the gospel of Jesus!

Servant, sent, separated. Paul starts off by bringing the truth boldly. He's bringing the heat!

CHAPTER 1 VERSE 2–3

In Romans 1:2, God puts in a parenthetical phrase to establish the fact that the gospel of Jesus mentioned in verse 1 was not something new or different. No, the gospel Paul mentions was the same one foretold in Old Testament prophecy going all the way back to Genesis 3:15!

"*Which he had promised*" A promise from God is a sure thing, friend. A promise from God never fails. A promise from God is secure and steady. A promise from God is verifiable, and Paul is letting his readers know they can verify it simply by searching God's Word. You can too! Are you living your life on the full promises of God? Paul sure did! Paul knew God was trustworthy!

"*Concerning His Son Jesus Christ.*" The gospel is concerned with only one thing or, better yet, one person - Jesus. It's not concerned with social justice. It's not concerned with utopian endeavors. It's not concerned with humanistic worldviews. It's not concerned with people's physical or emotional well-being. It is concerned with people's spiritual well-being! It is concerned with the birth, life, vicarious death, and resurrection of Jesus Christ. Nothing is more important than that, at least not to God or Paul. Is it to you?

"Our Lord …" That's the main issue with so many people. Is Jesus Lord? Paul doesn't say "his Lord." he says "our Lord" because the culmination of the gospel is not getting you saved or out of hell. It's getting Jesus to be Lord of your life! If Jesus is God, then He at least ought to be Lord, right? Paul wasn't satisfied with just being saved. He wanted more, and he had more! Much more!

"*Made of the seed of David.* " Don't overlook this or important principle. The fact that Jesus is "born of the seed of David according to the flesh" establishes a Jewish context for Paul's gospel, but also a material context; he was born as a man with a physical, human body. Both concepts are equally important as the rest of the book of Romans develops. Jesus would have to be able to trace his genealogy back to David. And Jesus can! This is vitally important!

"*according to the flesh.*" Look out. Paul is describing the Incarnation of Jesus here! An act of grace! That act of grace where Christ took your human nature into union with His divine Person, and became human like us. Want to learn of a mighty act of grace? How about how a divine Person was united to human nature! That's grace, folks! What you study becomes what you think about. What you think about becomes who you are. Who you are becomes who you'll be.

Chapter 1 Verse 4

Paul is still bringing the heat, folks! But it's a good heat. It's a necessary heat. We need to be heated up. Paul is still talking about the gospel.

"And declared to be the Son of God" Notice how Paul has taken the names and titles of Jesus and stacked them together. God's Son. Jesus. Christ. Our Lord. Paul goes from top to bottom, from heavenward to "heart-ward". Do you think there's a message there or a purpose? Jesus is the subject and the author of the gospel. He is the embodiment of the good news! It's not that the good news is good news; it's that the good news is Jesus! Jesus is the good news from God to us!

"*With power …*" This is a strong word meaning power to perform. It implies ability or capacity to perform. Our English word *dynamite* comes from this Greek word. Paul is saying Jesus was dynamite, friends! He has the means and wherewithal to take on the title Son of God because He was and is! He has the ability to command and control! There is no power more powerful than Jesus. No, the devil *is not* His equal. The devil is a wet firecracker compared to Jesus.

"*According to the spirit of holiness"*- Jesus is the very spirit of holiness. He was the very embodiment of holiness, purity, morality, and justice. His life upon earth proves this fact. If we live in a world of un-holiness, impurity, immorality, and injustice, doesn't it stand to reason we need more Jesus? We don't need less Jesus, we need more! We need all of Him. Not just a slice on Sunday. The world has been doing a pretty good job of getting rid of Jesus for the past fifty years. Consequently, there's not much spirit of holiness in the world anymore. All it takes is a quick look at the current situation in our country and one can see the truth in that statement.

"*By the resurrection from the dead*" Look out; Paul is rolling up his sleeves. The resurrection from the dead proves Jesus is the Son of God, the Messiah, and the good news. All other people are dead. Want proof? Ask yourself where are they? They're all in some cold grave somewhere. But not Jesus! He died, rose again, and walked amongst over five hundred eyewitnesses, according to the Bible. And that has never been refuted.

We have only covered the first four verses of the first chapter of Romans. I sometimes feel I'm drinking from a fire hydrant! But then I realize just how powerful and important this book of the Bible truly is.

CHAPTER 1 VERSE 5

After the first four verses, are you ready to keep going? That's what I thought! C'mon!

"*By whom …*" By whom? That's right! By Jesus! It's all about Jesus, friends. Paul was becoming more like Jesus, which is what God wants from you and from me, too. "But I can't be like Jesus," you say. Well, you can sure be like Paul! Paul didn't have anything spiritually special about him that you don't have if you're a true follower of Jesus. If you have Jesus, you have the "by whom." All you need to do is let go and let Him have you! Look, this weak, mediocre Christianity we see and live is not what we read about in the Bible! Folks, we got it all wrong!

""*We have received grace and apostleship.*" Notice the word "we." Paul speaks of all believers, not just himself. If you read too fast, you'll miss it. But because he uses the word "we" he includes you and me. This is a personal letter God has written to all of His true believers. We have all received God's grace for eternity; and His salvation, forgiveness, and redemption, among other things. But in this context, Paul is saying we have received grace as God has called all of us to separation from all unrighteousness and called us to the gospel of Jesus. Why? Paul tells us in the next phrase!

"*For obedience to the faith*" God didn't give us His grace so we could live any way we thought was right but to live obediently in faith in what God says is right! We're not saved to live "our" way but the way God describes in His Word! So God is teaching us that we are "saved" for two primary reasons. One is to obey Him and His Word. The other is to lead others to obey Him too! Are you living in obedience? Are you leading others to? One can't take someone to a place one has never been. Have you been there? Do you stay there? Obedience will either make or break you.

"*among all the nations*" We are all called to be missionaries in our mission area. If more "followers" would be obedient and missional in their own mission areas, the world would change! Nation by nation! If you are saved, you are, like Paul, a missionary. Are you missional in your mission area? If not, why not?

"for his name." All for the glory of Jesus! Not your glory. Not my glory. Not the church's glory. His glory!

Friends, we haven't even gotten through Paul's introduction and into the deeper parts of the Book of Romans, and it's already amazing, challenging, and convicting!

Chapter 1 Verse 6-7

"Among whom are ye, also the called of Jesus Christ" Remember, Paul is writing to believers, and verse 6 tells us plainly that if you have ever made a decision to accept Jesus as Savior, you also should accept the calling He will put on your life; the calling of obedience to Him, and being used by Him to lead others to obedience. You see, your salvation isn't the issue anymore once you're saved. Once you're saved, you're saved! Move on to what's next. Look, to believe your salvation is just something that keeps you from going to hell sometime in the future is really pretty self-centered, isn't it? No, your salvation is a calling to obedience. To understand this concept changes the "get out of hell free" mediocrity thinking you may have to a life which is dynamic, passionate, fired-up, and obedient as a servant of the Most High God! Kind of changes things, doesn't it?

"To all that be in Rome" When this letter was written, it was written to the believers in Rome. But the bigger picture is it is written to all believers throughout the centuries, including you and me.

"beloved of God" God loves all people, but remember, Paul is writing to believers. So believers are referred to as "beloved". How amazing is that? The word means *"esteemed"* or *"worthy of love."* As a believer, you are "worthy of God's love!" The world teaches you are not worthy of anything or worthy only of being used. Honestly, in essence the world

often teaches, for the most part, you are worthless. God says He loves you as a believer because you are worthy of His love. How can that be? You guessed it. Jesus! Oh what a Savior! Do you know Him? Really know Him? You are ever so close to God's heart because of your heart for Jesus.

"called to be saints" Believers are called to be set apart and holy, which is what the word *"saint"* means. It is part of your obedience as described earlier. We've fallen for the partial truth that we're all just sinners saved by grace. To believe only that puts us in a weak position of making excuses for our lack of obedience, for we can say, when we sin, we are just poor old sinners. God's Word says because of grace we are now made saints! And saints don't act the way sinners do. Saints are separated from the sin; maybe not perfectly, but certainly obediently. It's what you believe about yourself that gets you past the excuses.

"grace to you and peace from God the Father" God offers all of us His grace to become saints of God. There's peace in sainthood. Not so much as mere sinners using grace as an excuse to sin.

"and the Lord Jesus Christ." It's all about Jesus, friends. It's all about Him. And He is Lord. It's all about His power to deliver you from what you do (sins) and who you are (sin). Notice the difference in the two words. It's about to get real good.

Chapter 1 Verse 8

Paul now shifts his writing from his own credentials (and the credentials of all true believers) to the discussion of his great interest in the local church to which the letter is written. Paul never visited the church at Rome, but he wanted to let them know how important they were to his kingdom work. Many of you reading this commentary have never met me, but I write this because you are important to my kingdom work too!

"First, I want to thank God through Jesus Christ for you all" Paul is grateful for the testimony of the church at Rome. Wherever Paul travelled, he heard of the great testimony of this church. I would love to find a church like that today! Wouldn't you? A church beyond average and mediocre!

What made them so great? First, the believers there were living pure lives in the midst of an immoral, base, and unjust society. The citizens of Rome were known for their ungodly worldliness, but the believers at Rome were known for their firm stance of their biblical convictions. Standing for Jesus and His Word in spite of the moral decline in their culture was making a huge difference! Standing for Jesus always makes a difference. But the believer must know the truth and stand for it! The true believers were not getting caught up in the world or the culture; they were serving Christ faithfully and ministering to people. Christians in a local church living this way openly and vocally will change a mediocre church into a powerhouse of deliverance!

"that your faith is spoken of " Notice it wasn't their beautiful church or their outstanding ministries or their wonderful fellowship that Paul mentions. No, it was their faith! Faith in what, Rome? No way. Faith in Paul? No way. Faith in the pastor? No way! It was their faith in the risen Lord Jesus Christ and their calling to be obedient to Him and to lead others to be obedient too! In the very midst of the most decadent place on earth at the time, there were faithful and obedient church members who cared more about Jesus than trying to fit in with society. And it made a huge difference. Honestly, it always does.

"throughout the world." This faith was so strong they had a worldwide testimony! In the middle of a horribly nasty society, a people of faith stood out to the whole point that their testimony was worldwide, or at least empire wide. Is your church like that? Is my church like that? Are you like that at your church? Am I? No good reason not to be. You really can make a difference; you just have to stand.

Chapter 1 Verse 9

"For God is my witness" Paul is making a bold statement here! He is verifying his constant prayer for the believers at Rome. He is calling out God as his witness. I doubt Paul was telling a lie. Paul was subject to Jesus to the point where he was praying for believers constantly! Do you pray like that? I don't, at least not always. When a person considers, like Paul has done, that he or she is either enslaved to sin or to Jesus, it is foolish not to accept salvation through Jesus. But even beyond that, it is more foolish to not subject one's life to serve God each day, certainly by at least praying for other believers!

"whom I serve with my spirit" It's a spiritual thing, friends! And it's a serving thing! The word *"serve"* means *"labor of hire"* and Paul says he serves from his spirit in the gospel of Jesus. Why? Because the true believer's labor and service is bought and paid for by the blood of Jesus! Once a believer has surrendered to the gospel, he has no choice but to labor and serve spiritually, unless he was just trying not to go to hell. And it's a joy, not a burden. Does that describe you?

"in the gospel of His Son" Again, the point of the believer's life while here on earth is to be obedient to Jesus and His Word. The believer is to serve God physically, emotionally, and spiritually. He or she is to keep his or her spirit strong by feeding it. He or she is to keep his or her emotions in check by conquering them. He or she is to overcome his or her weaknesses by strengthening his or her body. When a believer does this, he or she can serve God to the fullest extent possible. I don't know about you, but I'm feeling some conviction!

"that without ceasing" Paul's daily habit was to pray constantly. Paul was a faithful prayer warrior. Often, when someone says they'll pray for me, I think: "that's good! I need the prayers, and you need the practice!" Paul likely didn't need the practice, but had the discipline to pray constantly. If you want to be conformed to the image of His Son, or at least be like Paul and experience God and be used by God in a great way, you're going to have to pray a lot. There's a direct correlation, friends.

"I make mention of you always in my prayers." This was the best thing Paul could do for the believers. If you read Ephesians 3:14-21, you can learn the specifics of what Paul prayed for. Here's the interesting thing: Paul didn't even know these believers! Yet he prayed for them constantly! So the takeaway is that the Bible charges all of us to pray for believers all around the world and to pray for believers constantly. When's the last time you did that? Don't know who to pray for? Pray for me! Because I need the prayers, and you need the practice. And I do too!

CHAPTER 1 VERSE 10-12

"Making request, if by any means now at length I might have a prosperous journey by the will of God to come unto you." Paul is still in prayer mode, and he is so stirred by the gospel that he sought a personal relationship with people. Remember, this is the same guy sending Christians to prison and their deaths just a short time before he wrote this letter. Paul has changed! He's gone from murderer to missionary! From accuser to apostle! From darkness to light! He's gotten a lot more friendly and personable. Why? Well, the gospel is personal, friends! Paul did not leave the ministry and evangelism to others. He didn't expect others to do the work he was called to do, the work we're all called to do. Paul was, and we should be, stirred to reach people for Jesus!

"For I long to see you, that I may impart unto you some spiritual gift, to the end you may be established." Paul wanted to reach people, but to what end? Well, to *"impart some spiritual gift"* to those he reached. Why? So the people would be better established in their faith and hopefully obedient to their call. The term *"spiritual gift"* means *"a gift of grace"* and refers to Paul's desire to lead people to salvation in Jesus and to teach those who already are in order to strengthen them for obedience, and nothing has changed! I am following the same pattern as I write this commentary. I want to reach out to as many as I can to disciple and encourage true believers to truly follow Jesus, and for those who are struggling with a decision to accept Jesus as Lord to be better informed. God's spiritual blessings were overflowing in Paul's heart, and he was always ready

and willing to be proactive in reaching and teaching others about Jesus. May I ask you some personal questions I must also ask of myself? Do we have the same desire to live for and share Jesus? If not, why not? If we have the same Holy Spirit in us that Paul had, shouldn't we have the same desires? If God never changes, why aren't we being more like Paul? I think we should be.

"That is, that I may be comforted together with you by the mutual faith both of you and me." The word *"comforted"* means "*to be encouraged"* Paul needed other believers to encourage him and share their faith with him and others. God expects all of us to share and encourage to the point of bearing fruit! Are you? Have you? Will you?

As a pastor, when believers neglect their spiritual growth and obedience, it greatly discourages me. I'm sure it discourages your pastor. I bet it causes Jesus some grief too.

Chapter 1 Verse 13

"Now I would not have you ignorant, brethren" "Ignorance is bliss" is often quoted and I suppose with some things that makes sense. But when we're talking about eternal things and our own eternal destination, we better have a good grasp on what we need to know! Paul's heart was to inform them and keep them out of ignorance. This is why we should attend church and pay attention, even after we're saved. Why? Remember, the audience was believers in Rome so it wasn't just to get them saved because they already were! Paul was trying to get them "*sanctified*" or "*set apart*" for their successful, obedient daily walk with the Lord. You can't live in spiritual ignorance friends! You shouldn't be "*born-again*" and remain a baby the rest of your life content to be spiritually ignorant. You must know what you're to know and grow how you're to grow! That makes sense now, doesn't it? Who enrolls in college, becomes a college student, and then never attends classes? Who becomes employed but never goes to work? Who becomes a Christian but never goes to church? Who accepts Jesus then remains in spiritual ignorance for the next sixty years?

"that oftentimes I purposed to come into you" Paul longed to be with these dear saints, but never made it. I think I know how he must have felt. He was providentially hindered and could not visit them. That's sad. But sadder still would have been the believers in Rome not going to the church to grow spiritually because of excuses. And I know, because I've used all the excuses in the book when I was younger and I missed out on all the things Jesus wanted to show me and do with me during those years. I regret it to this day!

"that I might have some fruit among you also, even among other gentiles." Here's Paul's motive for his desire to visit and to teach, even if it was teaching from his writings. He wanted to bear witness, plant seeds, and reap a harvest of souls from both the Jewish and Gentile population which the church was ministering to. Paul's worldwide vision, which is to say God's worldwide vision, was to evangelize and disciple people who were in spiritual ignorance. That same need exists today. It's my heart too. It's why I do what I do. It's the call on every true believer. Do you faithfully attend classes? Do you faithfully go to work?

Look, going to college is just organized training to grow you, and if you don't study and attend, you get kicked out. Going to work is just organized activities to accomplish a goal, and if you don't show up and work you get fired. Going to church and serving, for the true believer, is simply training and serving opportunities to accomplish a goal too. But if you're not there, you don't grow and you miss out also.

Chapter 1 Verse 14-15

"I am debtor both to the Greeks, and to the Barbarians; both to the wise and to the unwise" The gospel stirred Paul with a deep sense of indebtedness and a readiness to reach all people. We have the same gospel Paul had and should have the same passion. If we don't, we need to find out why. No, seriously, we need to. If the answer to eternal life is now known, it must be proclaimed. Since Paul is no longer with us, it's going to have to be us.

The word "*debtor*" means *"bound by duty"* and Paul certainly demonstrated by actions his sense of duty to the Lord. God has done two major things to Paul that He does to all true believers. First, God saved Paul from the penalty of his sins. Second, God called Paul to preach and thereby gave him something to do that was kingdom work related. It's the same with all believers. If God has saved you, it's not just to keep you from going to hell. It's also to give you kingdom work that you'll be obedient in doing to help keep others from going to hell!

Notice Paul said he was indebted to the whole world. He caught the vision of Jesus concerning world evangelism. He was a missionary to the Jews, the Greeks (Gentiles) and the Barbarians which symbolizes all uncivilized and primitive peoples. Paul has come a long way from his early years as a Pharisee set out to eliminate all Christians. He is now involved in world evangelism and he isn't making any more excuses. So, if the same spirit lives in us, can we possibly make any valid excuses for not being missional? You might be thinking, "Well, that's good for Paul, but I'm not called to be a missionary." Yeah, I used to think the same thing. But, oh yes you are, friend. And I am too! You and I are called to world missions and the support thereof.

"*both to the wise and to the unwise.*" Paul is still *"indebted"* to reach and teach everyone, including, in this case, the learned and unlearned, the educated and uneducated, the motivated and unmotivated, the seeking and the complacent. Titles are meaningless; the work isn't.

"So, as much as in me is, I am ready to preach the gospel to you that are at Rome also." When Paul says he is "*ready*" he is saying he is urgently willing. Paul has a sense of urgency to accomplish his kingdom work, and therefore we should too. He says "*as much as is in me*" which describes him being sold out to the Lord and His mission. He allowed no hindrance to enter his life that would affect his capability to accomplish what he was called to do. He was possessed and obsessed with his Lord and his call, and he would not allow anything to slow him down. Are we anything like this in our own walk and service? If not, why not? This is what being conformed to His image looks like!

Chapter 1 Verse 16a

"*For I am not ashamed of the gospel of Christ:*" Verse 16 and 17 contain one of the greatest summaries of the gospel ever written. It is a clear declaration of the power and desire of God to save all who will believe, no matter their nationality, social status, financial standing, or any other condition. It is a clear explanation of why Paul was never ashamed of the gospel, because it was good news about Jesus and His plan of salvation for all those separated from God, and that's everybody!

I've noticed that today many people seem to be ashamed of the gospel, or at least of sharing it. They are ashamed because they fear ridicule, rejection, and the loss of recognition, position, and/or livelihood. But there are two things in particular they fear: intellectually shame and social shame

First, there is fear of intellectual shame; the fear that the gospel does not measure up intellectually to modern science. It is deemed to be not for the scholar or the philosopher. It's only for the weak-minded or those who need some sort of crutch to get through life. Well, I must confess that Jesus is not my crutch; He's my life support system! But I digress.

This attitude of the "learned" is from a misunderstanding of the philosophy of the gospel. No greater philosophy exists. No greater reasoning has ever been worked through. No greater thought has ever been processed. No greater truth has ever been told. The issue is a person either holds to the philosophy of the world or to the philosophy of Christ and His redemption. Upon looking at both philosophies open-mindedly, there is no question which philosophy and intellectual thought is greater.

The second issue is fear of social shame. Many fear if they accept and proclaim the gospel, they will be ridiculed and mocked by society, and they're right. But if the gospel is truth, then not standing for it is mocking it ourselves. We don't need anyone's help to mock it. We're guilty too. Slow down right now and think about that.

Are you ashamed of the gospel of Jesus? Well, if you struggle with the lordship of Jesus in your life, if He's not Lord to you, then do you really believe? And if you struggle here, is it because there are things in your life that are more important to you than your relationship with Jesus? If that's the case, is it because other things bring you more comfort than the gospel? Yeah, you may be ashamed and not even realize it. I know; I've been there. Paul isn't ashamed of the gospel because he knows the power and majesty of the One he believed in. Paul really knew Jesus and had real faith in Him. That's nothing to be ashamed of!

"For therein is the righteousness of God revealed from faith to faith: as it is written" God has revealed His very righteousness in the gospel! The world and the flesh and the devil are constantly fighting against God's plan of saving men by convincing all of us we are righteous without Him, or at least righteous enough. Nothing could be further from the truth. If we were, or could be, righteous enough, why did Jesus die on a cross? The answer to man's problem is Jesus. The road to Jesus is faith. The vehicle which takes us there is hearing the Word of God.

"The just shall live by faith." The righteous (or just) man will "live" (because of the gospel and his faith in it) in that he will not face God's judgment; rather, in return for his faith in God, he has been given eternal life. Do you know Jesus? Or do you just know some facts about him? Eternity hinges on how you and I honestly answer this question.

Chapter 1 Verse 16b

"For I am not ashamed of the gospel of Christ: ... for it is the power of God" Paul is not ashamed of the gospel because it is the power of God to save! Only the message of Christ's death, burial, and resurrection can deliver sinners from the dominion of sin and Satan, and impart the gift of everlasting life to those who believe in the person and work of the Lord Jesus Christ. There is nothing more urgent than proclaiming the Gospel, and nothing more transforming than walking in its truth! Why? Because it is the power, or the strength that is within God; it is of God!

God could wipe us all off the face of the earth, and quite frankly, I don't know why He doesn't sometimes. But He chooses to be powerful and offer us a different way.

*"unto salvation to everyone that believet*h" God's power is so powerful He can create everything that has been created by just speaking the words. But His focal point regarding His power is our salvation. This is a tremendous truth. He speaks, and worlds come into existence. He declares, and galaxies are formed. He communicates, and universes are established. He voices, and everything comes to order. That's beyond power, friends! Yet His focal point is saving you basically from yourself. I know it's incredible, but it is true. But you must believe! Belief is the one condition for salvation, but it's not just mental agreement. Even the demons believe, and they're certainly not going to live with God for all eternity! It's committing yourself to what you believe. It's getting saved then living saved. It's believing the truth and demonstrating your belief by living in truth. Look, we're not saved by good works, but our salvation produces good works, and the work is to be obedient! Starting to make sense? If you made a profession of faith but you're living in sin, or you haven't changed, or you could care less about God and His Word, or serving Him, or loving His church, there's something fundamentally wrong!

"to the Jew first, and also to the Greek." God's offer to be united with Him forever (definition of heaven, folks) is for everyone and anyone. The word "first" in this phrase doesn't mean favoritism, it means first in time. The gospel was simply carried to the Jew first. They were the people from whom His Son would come from according to Old Testament prophecy. But everyone is included. No one is left out from His offer, including you and me. Where are you with God? What has been your answer to His offer? If you haven't given Him an answer, your answer by default is no. If you've said yes, but your living is saying no, you've said no! If you're under some conviction, work out your salvation! It's the most important thing you can do!

Chapter 1 Verse 17

"For therein is the righteousness of God revealed from faith to faith " Your salvation reveals the righteousness of God. Your faith reveals the righteousness of God. This addresses the two issues of people being ashamed of the gospel. First, many people think they are good enough on their own to be acceptable to God. Why do they feel this way? Because they use the wrong benchmark! If you use me as God's benchmark, you probably stand an excellent chance of being with God and me being kicked out. But I'm not the benchmark. Neither is your heathen neighbor. Or your heathen spouse. No, Jesus is the benchmark. Now, you and I have both failed miserably and have come up short when compared to Jesus. So, we need someone's help who has made the cut, and there's only one person who has. You guessed it! Jesus.

See, the only way a person can be made righteous enough to live in the presence of a righteous God is to have the righteousness of God! The only way a person can be made holy enough to live in the presence of a holy God is to have the holiness of God! We can never get there on our own because we are neither righteous nor holy. We need help. God has sent us help. His name is Jesus. Why do so many people fight this? Spiritual blindness, that's why.

The answer to our problem is not our faith but the object of our faith, Jesus. When a person truly believes that Christ is who He says He is and has done what He says He's done and that He saves those who truly confess and repent and believe, God counts His righteousness as our righteousness. The person (you and me) is not righteous and still imperfect, but God honors the death and resurrection of His Son so much He counts us as being righteous because of Jesus and our faith in Him. What an incredible offer! Folks, that's power! That's as good an offer as you'll ever get. What God has done and offered everyone is absolutely phenomenal. But, you must make a decision, and putting the decision off for whatever reason is effectively saying no thank you. And that's incredibly and phenomenally sad.

"as it is written, the just shall live by faith" But understand something. If you accept, you must continue to believe! A true believer must live by faith from the moment of belief to the last moment on this earth, for it is a person's faith God takes and counts as righteousness. Said another way, the whole life of a believer is to be a life of faith, from beginning to end, from faith to faith. The just (saved) shall (you must do this) live by faith. Continuously. Tenaciously. Passionately. Fully.

Mediocre living, for the Christian, is ridiculous. It is ludicrous. It is absurd. Yet it is the reality in the vast majority of us. Is it the reality for you? Why? Do something about it by making a decision to be conformed in the image of His Son.

Chapter 1 Verse 18

The message of this passage is perfectly plain. It explains why God reveals and executes wrath upon men. But we must see it from God's perspective. The issue with us is we don't want to be confronted with all the truth, just the parts that are comfortable to us. This passage is most uncomfortable, but it is necessary for us so we can understand the earlier verses we have already discussed and God's desire to have us come to Him through His love offering, Jesus.

"The wrath of God" God has the right to demonstrate wrath when disobedience is flaunted in His face. Do you get upset when someone breaks the law and it affects you? Do you get angry when you have done everything right yet someone else does something wrong and messes it up for you? Do you get mad when someone is mean to you or your child? Don't you feel like you have a right to be wrathful when someone takes something precious from you? Shouldn't God be given the same respect? Shouldn't He be angry when we disobey Him or ignore Him and His Word? Of course He should! And He tells us He is! The concept that God is love and you can disrespect Him all you want is baloney! And He tells us up front He reserves the right to have and demonstrate wrath to those people and situations which mock Him and His wishes.

Friends, He's only doing what you and I do and take for granted, albeit in a much more holy and honest way.

"The wrath of God is being revealed from heaven against all the godlessness and wickedness of people." The wrath of God is a reality. That's not debatable. God's wrath is revealed from heaven. In verse 17, Paul explained how God's righteousness was revealed; he went on in verse 18 to explain how God's wrath is revealed. This wrath of God is a universal indictment, as we shall see in future verses. However, there is hope as we shall also see. But we must realize an important truth: God does not view sin passively. God's love does not preclude His wrath. I want you to think about this: the opposite of love is hate, not wrath. While God hates sin (because of what it does) He does not hate those who sin. To be fair and impartial to His word, He must show His disapproval, and He must judge sin; otherwise, what good is His love? To let everyone sin in every manner they want and God just wink at it is not love; it is indifference, and God is not indifferent. God does not hate, but He does and He will reveal wrath. Now we need to know something else: God's wrath is not loss of self-control for selfish reasons. He never loses His temper. God's wrath is His opposition to anything contrary to His nature. His wrath, therefore, has a personal dimension. That is why forgiveness is not cheap from God's viewpoint; the cost of forgiveness was the Cross. And it was huge and very painful for Him. People who see the love of God without a proper emphasis on the wrath of God are out of balance biblically. We should never leave the impression that sin does not matter to God. God is not gentle about sin. He does not tolerate it. It brings forth His wrath!

God directs His wrath against two areas: (1) ungodliness and (2) unrighteousness (wickedness). He points His wrath not against men *per se* but against their sin. God hates the sin but loves the sinner, but sin walks on the wrathful side of God. It's just the way it is, friends!

Earlier, I mentioned the concept of "sins" and "sin". Do you remember? Can you connect the dots to come to a conclusion and tie this all together? Yes you can!

"since what may be known about God is plain to them, because God has made it plain to them" It's as plain as the nose on our faces! God has been abundantly truthful and clear to us all. For centuries! He's given us a love letter we call the Bible. He's given us the ability to reason and read. But do we read it? Do we study it? Do we try to master it? If His revelation to us is contained in His Word, why aren't we getting serious about learning it? Well, hopefully you are as you read this book. And I hope it is helping you understand God's Word better.

Chapter 1 Verse 19-20

Paul is about to bring hard truths, and I'm afraid most people nowadays don't want to hear it. Truth is the aim of real belief. People need intellectual and physical truth about the world in order to thrive. Therefore, truth is important. I want you to think about something: believing what is not true typically spoils everything and is very costly. Telling what is not true may result in legal and social penalties. Conversely, a dedicated pursuit of truth characterizes the good physician, the good scientist, the good historian, and the good detective. These occupations cannot succeed operating on half-truths or full lies. Neither can the Christian when it comes to spiritual truth, which is why we have a Bible in the first place. God has communicated to us His truths, but many people fight against it. Always have, always will I guess. So the question is why? Paul addresses that in the coming chapters. So please, please, please stay with me!

"Because that which may be known of God is manifest in them; for God hath shewed it unto them." Our knowledge of God is certainly partial at best, but we cannot plead complete ignorance because He has told us what we need to know. Paul says His creation reveals enough of Him to make a major difference in our lives. And it does! Jesus said the most important thing we can ever do with our lives is to love God with all of our heart, and with all of our soul, and with our entire mind. Honestly, the failure to do this is the major reason why this world is in its current condition. Had mankind kept Jesus's words, the natural, spiritual progression

would have led him to be better because he would then, at the very least, have had the correct source of law and morality. Without keeping this commandment, the best that man can do in establishing standards is by his own experience, and that leads him directly to Satan! We've been fooled with the idea that truth is relative. Truth is truth, and lies are lies, and the highest truth the world will ever know is biblical truth. I hope we can all agree with that, and we can if we all think about it correctly.

"*For the invisible things of him from the creation of the world are clearly seen*" God can be understood because of His truths He has given us, even in nature! Honestly, even the unconverted can comprehend enough things about Him to realize there is a God, and many do. Despite these verses in Romans 1, the opinions of "learned men" say that God is incomprehensible, yet Paul is saying that there is a clear testimony everywhere. In fact, it is so evident that even the invisible things reflect His truth. It is a constant and natural revelation of God's power and nature, and that revelation is sufficient for God to hold these people responsible for their conduct.

"*being understood by the things that are made, even his eternal power and Godhead; so that they are without excuse.*" Remember, the subject matter is God's wrath. God is saying He has given everyone ample evidence of His existence through the life and historicity of Jesus. He has given us His written Word. He has given us His creation. He has given us this world and all the natural things in it. When a person looks at such evidence and reasons with an honest spirit, he or she will clearly see the world was made by a Creator. God has warned us all; we are all without excuse to believe anything other than what He tells us. The evidence is there. Man has many "theories" trying to explain things, but they are just excuses people use to reject God's truth. I have a Bachelor of Science degree from a secular university and three Master's degrees from seminary, and I am telling you the evidence for God far outweighs man's "evidence" for other "theories." I'm just asking you to think beyond man's theories.

Whatever your view of God, the Creator of the universe and the Father of our Lord Jesus Christ, if it does not include a healthy confession that He is holy and righteous and will pour out wrath and judgment on those who persist in their rejection of Him, it is an unbiblical and unrealistic view. In fact, it is an unloving view. For if you communicate to non-Christians that they should repent and believe the gospel, but if they don't, "Aw, don't worry about it, God will figure out a way to embrace you in spite of your unbelief," you are treating that person with contempt. You are leaving them vulnerable to eternal damnation with the false hope of a God who is too loving ever to consign anyone to hell.

Chapter 1 Verse 21

Let's remember that the subject matter is still God's wrath, and willful and habitual sin stirs the wrath of God. He made the rules, folks. And they're fair rules as far as I'm concerned. The teaching so far can be summarized into three points: first, people who willfully and habitually sin bring upon themselves the wrath of God; second, all people have enough evidence in nature alone to know there is a God if they are honest and seek truth with an open mind; and third, because of the first two points, the guilty need God's righteousness (and we're all guilty). In this verse, Paul is building the reason why people do what they do. The next couple of verses help us understand the problem.

"Because that, when they knew God, they glorified him not as God" God shows wrath when men disrespect Him and/or His Word. How can God be God and men treat Him as if He's a "nobody"? Well, non-believers find that easy to do, as do fence-sitters. But those who say they are "saved" and "followers" of Christ do it too! How? Just like Paul said: they know God, but they don't glorify Him as God. The word "*glorified*" means "*to be of the opinion God is worthy to be praised continuously*'. Daily. Minute by minute. We want God to save us from hell, but we don't want to respect Him daily while we're alive here on this earth. That would make me mad too, wouldn't it you?

"*Neither were thankful*" the word means "*to be grateful*". Like grateful enough to obey Him because He has saved you from hell, if He truly has. If we're just going to use Him as a spiritual credit card, we've missed the whole point!

"*but became vain in their imaginations*" Why would intelligent, sane, and decent people do this? Well, the word *"vain"* means to *"become morally wicked."* It means to "have one's thoughts brought to folly" which is what the world is trying to do every day. The world attempts to bring your thinking to folly by convincing you to become, accept, and practice moral wickedness. And it's not our opinion about morality that matters. It's God's opinion! When a person becomes vain in their imaginations, it is easy to not be thankful for what God has done and not glorify God the way He should be glorified. That's so sad. When a "believer" gets there, it's tragic! It's horrible! I pray you're not there, but if you are, repent and return to Him! Get under the word of God with a pastor who is serious about your spiritual health!

"*and their foolish heart was darkened.*" Oh my! This means a person is spiritually blinded because they are without understanding. This is what happens when we know God, but we don't glorify Him as God. We start to go spiritually blind. Lies start to become truth, and truth starts to become lies, and we can't tell the difference! I have just described our country, folks, haven't I? Have I described anyone you know?

CHAPTER 1 VERSE 22-23

"Professing themselves to be wise, they became fools" One thing about God, He doesn't mince His words. Remember, Paul is discussing *why* God shows wrath, and how people bring it upon themselves. God is fair, but He's also firm. Here, Paul is saying that when we turn from God and accept lies, we think we're gaining wisdom, but we're actually becoming fools. What lies? Well, how about there is no God? How about all roads lead to heaven? How about all of man's "theories" that go against the clear teaching of scripture? How about I don't need to go to church? How about all truth is relative? How about it's all about

me? How about I know what the Bible says, but I'm not going to do it? Well, you get the picture. It's foolish to live in any other wisdom than God's. It's ridiculous to proclaim wisdom when it's not His wisdom you're proclaiming.

"And changed the glory of the incorruptible God into an image" Man swaps God, who never dies and has always existed, with all kinds of theories and beliefs which do die every time a new theory or belief supersedes the old one. People want to and have swapped God for man's philosophies, man's theories, man's religion, and man's technical advances, to name a few. And it's foolish. Why? Because it's always changing. But God never changes!

"made like a corruptible man, and to birds, and four-footed beasts, and creeping things." Man creates his or her own humanistic gods, whether mental images and thoughts or some grotesque image, because of pride and conceit. Men want to control their own lives and do as they wish, to be recognized and honored, and to receive the credit and acknowledgment themselves. Therefore they turn from God and make their own gods. Others just want to be left alone with their "gods" as they disrespect God by not giving Him the praise He deserves. I used to insist this wasn't me until I started to calculate the time God got from my week versus all the other things I was involved in. What do you "glorify" more than God? It's hard to face the truth, but the truth is I constantly put things ahead of God. And I'm a pastor! That's foolish, my friends! How are you in regards to this?

We're going to deal with more in the next several verses, friends. These next nine verses (Romans 1:24-32) are seemingly controversial, but only to those who are struggling with the issues we've discussed in the previous verses. Look, the verses weren't controversial for the first nineteen hundred years since they were written; they've only become controversial just recently. Why? Well, re-read the commentaries for Romans 1:18-23, especially verse 21. I'm going to tell you exactly what the verses mean. You'll have to determine for yourself if it's wisdom or foolishness, but please think with a biblical perspective and a heart to be obedient to God and His Word.

Chapter 1 Verse 24-25

To understand these verses, we must understand what is being said and what is not being said. The next nine verses (Romans 1:24-32) discuss the four ways God reveals His wrath. This is what is being said. *These verses describe what happens to people when God's wrath is upon them, not what they do to deserve God's wrath*! This is very important to understand.

"Wherefore God also gave them up to uncleanness through the lusts of their own heart" When sin is habitual and people are unrepentant, God shows His wrath! In the first case we see, it's by giving men up to do as they will. This is frightening and terrible for God says He gives up on them. Man chooses sin over God, and two things happen. First, man becomes enslaved to sin; sin actually stirs up more and more sin. It's a vicious cycle. Second, man abandons God. He actually turns away from God, just like Adam and Eve did. So, when people choose to live in sin and turn on God and do all the things I described in the earlier verses, God gives mankind up to their own uncleanness. The reason? The lust humanity holds in their hearts! We want what we want, not what God wants for us. Mostly out of ignorance, because God wants only what's best for us, and He knows what's best. Man has passions and cravings that if left unbridled will manifest into lusts, which if left unchecked will more often than not go deeper and deeper into perversions. Don't believe me? Let me give you an example.

In the early days of television, there were no sexual innuendos, no cussing, no perversions, no controversial scenes, etc. (or at least very, very little). A few decades later the broadcasts were much more sexual in content, and some profane words and perverse situations were allowed. Today, it's all sexual, profane, perverse, and no longer controversial. Additionally, God was honored in the early years. Today, His name is taken in vain, and His Son is ridiculed as well as His followers. You get the point. Music is the same too. Why? Re-read the earlier commentary on the verses.

"to dishonor their own bodies between themselves" Sin takes place in the heart before it takes place in the body. And as unrepentant sin has taken place

in so many hearts over so many years, God is allowing the sin to take place in the body now. It's a shame people long after things that displease God and dishonor their own bodies. But it's not just that dishonoring one's body is sin. It's proof that God is demonstrating His wrath towards us. How in the world could this have happened? Read on.

"Who changed the truth of God into a lie, and worshipped and served the creature more than the Creator" The result of living an unclean life is idolatry. The result of idolatry is God abandoning us. The result of God abandoning us is more idolatry. High price to pay for our stubbornness and ignorance, isn't it? When people live in uncleanness, they begin to serve and give their lives to one of two things: they serve themselves and their lust, or they serve the imaginary gods they dream up that will allow them to live as they wish. God just won't agree to participate with that, friends.

People will serve and give their time and energy to the god he or she imagines because this imaginary god typically serves them. People abandon the true God, so they can live the unclean life they want to live and the life they crave; even so-called "Christians". Therefore, God demonstrates His wrath by turning them over to those desires and abandons them to live in their uncleanness. Just the way it is. And it's fair too because God has been open and honest with us since the beginning. We're the ones with the issues.

"who is blessed forever. Amen." God's not going to bless our mess, regardless of how hard we pray and insist He does. Blessings will be held back. Penalties will be measured out. Abandonment will happen. We won't be admired by God like we assume we will be. But He will be blessed forever regardless of our actions, and that's the truth.

Chapter 1 Verse 26-27

The key to understanding these verses is to remember they are describing the ways God shows His wrath. It's not just that these particular sins cause God to be angry (they certainly do), it's that at some point

God has enough of the unrepentant sin, disengages from us, stops the conviction process, and leaves us to our own devices. If you're truly paying attention to our world, the signs are all around us that we are likely at this point in our country.

"For this cause God gave them up unto vile affections" This is the second way God shows wrath: by giving men (and women) up to vile, unnatural affections. The term *"vile affections"* means *"uncontrolled passions that lead to disgrace, dishonor, and shame."* And the benchmark is God's Word, not mankind's changing ideas of what's right or wrong. Look, God gives humanity over to their unnatural passions because mankind wants to be active in those passions and not active in being passionate about God! It is ultimately our choice, but boy don't we so often choose wrong! And when this kind of behavior is running rampant, and God's people are silent, then we get what we get; bondage. In this case, spiritual bondage for the Spirit is no longer bringing about conviction to people. Do you see this happening right before our very eyes?

"for even their women did change the natural use into that which is against nature: And likewise also the men, leaving the natural use of the woman, burned in their lust one toward another; men with men working that which is unseemly" You don't have to read this part too carefully. It says exactly what it says. Sexual perversions are a sign God has turned us over to our lusts and has abandoned us. I pray you see this. Sexual perversions are sin, but they are also indicative of God abandoning mankind in order for mankind to live the way mankind wants to live. When people want to live in sin, God will convict people. If people want to ignore the conviction, God allows them to suffer the consequences. It is ultimately mankind's choice, and since it is mankind's choice, God will eventually allow it to bear fruit and do nothing about it. God has to give humanity up to what he or she chooses.

"and receiving in themselves that recompense of their error which was meet." There's a payday someday, friends. The judgment for sexual perversions is within, not without, man. And the judgment is "meet" or exactly as it should be. God judges man; He shows His wrath by giving humanity

up to live in their vile affections. Friends, we're seeing it right before our very eyes. It's not on an individual basis anymore; it's on a national level now.

It's time to repent and turn back to Jesus. If you're a Christian and living in sexual sin, you are not in God's good grace. If you are not a Christian, you're not in God's good grace either. But you can be. You better learn all you can about Jesus and His offer of freedom from bondage. You need to think hard about it. And you need to choose wisely. Payday is coming, and we have checks we're going to have to cash. But I care; I really do. I hope you do too.

Chapter 1 Verse 28-30

"And even as they did not like to retain God in their knowledge, God gave them over to a reprobate mind" This is the third way God shows His wrath when people are unrepentant in their sins; He gives people over to a "*reprobate mind.*" This phrase means "*a mind that cannot hold up to the stress of truth.*" It is a mind that is depraved, disobedient, and degraded. Why does God allow a person's mind to become reprobate? Because the person has used their minds to reject God. Friends, God is very serious about serious things, and this is as serious as it gets. Many people do not approve of God. They don't want to recognize Him. They don't want to acknowledge Him. They don't want anything to do with Him. And this attitude is seemingly becoming rampant in Christian circles too. Do you see our country this way? It's because the average church is becoming this way. And that's because the average Christian is becoming this way. And God is saying, "Have it your way!"

"to do those things which are not convenient." God will allow mankind to do exactly as he or she chooses. People are enslaved more and more in their depravity and unsuitable behavior. I've been around for a little over a half a century, and I see it in this country and, honestly, the world. What do these things look like? Well, God answers that question too by listing a sample of these things. I'm going to define them for you.

"Being filled with all unrighteousness" means being filled with every kind of wrong doing. It's kind of a generic explanation to start off with. It is the opposite of righteousness. It doesn't mean a person does every kind of wrong doing, it just means they are capable of it. It also means self-centeredness or narcissism. That's pretty much everyone today, isn't it?

"fornication" means all kinds of immoral and sexual acts, including pre-marital sex, adultery, and abnormal sex. In my opinion, This is rampant in today's society too.

"wickedness" means to do mischief and cause harm. It's an active desire in one's heart to corrupt people. Again, this is everywhere.

"covetousness" means a lust for more and more. It's a craving for getting more and never being satisfied. This is everywhere too, isn't it?

"maliciousness" means having or holding a grudge. Not letting go. Know anyone like this?

"full of envy" is beyond jealousy. It is wanting what another has but also begrudging the fact that the person has it. Sound like anyone you know?

"murder" means to kill or take the life of another.

"debate" means discord, fighting, and quarreling.

"deceit" means to misguide someone. It means to give a false impression. It is twisting the truth.

"malignity" means to always look for the worse in a person. It describes a person with a mean or evil spirit.

"whisperers" describes gossipers or people who talk behind a person's back.

"Backbiters" means a person who will talk in front of a person and doesn't care.

"haters of God" means hating and being hateful to God.

"despiteful" means a willingness to attack and assault verbally or physically.

"proud" means arrogant and haughty.

"boasters" means someone who always brags.

"inventors of evil things" describes a person who tires of one sin and seeks a new and more perverse sin.

"disobedient to parents" means rebelling against authority (in this case parental).

"Without understanding" describes a person who is foolish or ignorant.

"covenant breakers" means an untrustworthy person. A liar.

"without natural affection" describes a person who doesn't care for others. No feelings for others.

"implacable" describes a person who is never sorry nor will admit guilt.

"unmerciful" describes a person unwilling to show mercy or be merciful.

I want you to re-read these words and their definitions. Do you see people you know described in any of them? Do you see our country as described by these words? I hope you don't see you in these words! If you do, you're seeing the wrath of God poured out already. It's not that these sins are going to bring the wrath of God. It's that allowing people to commit these sins freely *is* the wrath of God!

Chapter 1 Verse 32

We've learned a lot from verses 28-32, but it's hard teaching, especially for those on the wrong side of the Cross. When I read those verses, I see our country. We live in a time when these verses describe so many people. I pray they don't describe you. If they do, you need to recognize it and do something about it. That something is Jesus, friends. Because the fourth way God shows His wrath is by death, or eternal separation.

"Who knowing the judgment of God" Judgment is coming, friends. We all know it. We can feel it in our spirits. Even atheists know, I think. God's Word is saying the people who are described in the earlier verses *know* the judgment is coming. They may say they'd rather be partying in Hell than living with a mean, hateful god, but they're wrong on so many counts. God isn't hateful or mean. He has painstakingly told us the truth in written form. He has given us Bibles, churches, teachers, intelligence, and common sense to try to reach us. He's even using this commentary at this exact moment for those who will read it. He's not mean, folks. But He's not a pushover either. And the party in hell people think they're going to enjoy is going to be a huge disappointment. I'm just saying.

"that they which commit such things are worthy of death" That seems kind of harsh for such a loving God, don't you think? I guess it would be if God hadn't told us the game rules up front. He said the wages of sin is death, or permanent (eternal) separation from God. So those that commit the things we discussed in the previous verses are worthy of being eternally separated from God. You see, God tells us the truth and then has the backbone to do what He says, unlike so many others. I can appreciate that. I bet you can too.

"not only do the same, but have pleasure in them that do them." It gets worse. God is saying that there are some who not only sin, but they blatantly enjoy it in spite of being warned not to. In addition, they seek out those of like mindedness. Birds of a feather flock together, I suppose.

The issue is larger than personal sin. The issue is how personal sin tears at the world and destroys human life. A few people sinning is bad enough. Millions of people sinning is horrible. God must judge that. And He *will* judge that, and His wrath will be given. Some may even argue it's already here. But it's not too late. The offer of forgiveness is still valid. You and I must confess our sins, repent of them, turn to Jesus, accept His alternatives, grow in His truth, and show Him some faithfulness. If you need help, contact me. I care about you and your future, and I know you do too. Let's get things right with Jesus and move forward.

Chapter 2 Verse 1-3

Chapter 2 is an excellent study on judgment and criticism from the point of view of those who believe they live a clean life but judge others because they don't live the way they should, or they don't follow some sort of religious way. There's a lot going on in this chapter, so let's begin.

"Therefore you are inexcusable, O man, whoever you are who judge, for in whatever you judge another you condemn yourself; for you who judge practice the same things." This verse is describing the person who is moral, upright, good, decent, and honorable but judges those who aren't. The word "*judge*" means "*to criticize and condemn.*" The issue is that when a person judges others, they raise themselves up and lower the other person. It is being full of self-righteousness, pride, and arrogance. It makes a person judgmental and critical. We are all supposed to inspect the fruit of each believer; and to expect a certain lifestyle from him or her but we should be careful to not become a moralist in doing so. God's Word says the moralist fails to satisfy God's requirements just like the non-moralist does. In God's eyes, sin is a matter of the heart and mind, not just an act. Everyone stands guilty before God regardless of good, honest, and upright living.

"*But we know that the judgment of God is according to truth against those who practice such things.*" This verse is the proof of my last sentence. All sin comes short of God's glory, and God is letting us know. All stand guilty no matter how we live because sin is in all of our lives, God's not saying the judicial system should be abolished; we need discipline as much as we need forgiveness. God is telling us that we should reach out to each other with truth and see the big picture. Finding fault in a person is not as strong a position as speaking truth in love and helping that person see his or her errors so he or she may repent. Passing judgment is wrong. Speaking the truth in love is right. But we're all guilty, so we need to hear from someone who's not and see what He says about it. That's Jesus, folks. We can trust His judgment and truth. And He loves you just the way you are, but He doesn't want you to stay just the way you are. He offers forgiveness and change. And it's all good.

"And do you think this, O man, you who judge those practicing such things, and doing the same, that you will escape the judgment of God?" No one will escape God's judgment. No one will escape. No one lives "good" enough. No one is good enough. We can harden our hearts against God or surrender them to His truths. But no one escapes. We better have an outstanding helper when the day arrives.

Chapter 2 Verse 4-6

"Or do you show contempt for the riches of his kindness, forbearance and patience, not realizing that God's kindness is intended to lead you to repentance? Let's start by just saying, "ouch"! Ouch, ouch, ouch! Remember, Paul is addressing those who think they are good enough to earn God's forgiveness. He's already stated that's not true, therefore, that's not happening. Friend, when you or I turn down the gospel of Jesus, we're turning Him down. The reasons are numerous for those who do say no, but there are no good reasons, just excuses. Here, God is explaining it to us and asking us to realize it is much better for us to conform to the image of His Son.

We love saying "God is love" but it seems we don't love loving Him back. No, we use our excuses as our reasons to say no to His offer as if His love will allow us to live the way we want. We often treat God as someone we will get to eventually, but for now just chill. He doesn't operate that way, friends. No, God's "love", His attributes listed in this verse, are given to lead us to repentance. Not apathy. Not mediocrity! Not business as usual. No, He uses this to change us.

"But because of your stubbornness and your unrepentant heart, you are storing up wrath against yourself for the day of God's wrath, when his or righteous judgment will be revealed." Here's more of the "ouch" part. God has called us out, and I'm guilty. I bet you are too. Here's why we refuse Him as Lord. Here's why we don't learn His Word. Here's why we rarely attend corporate worship (church). Here's why we live mediocre and average lives. We are rebellious and refuse to truly repent. Ouch! I'm hanging my head as I write this. And the worst part is, God's diagnosis is spot on, but His prognosis is hard medicine, because we are rebellious and unrepentant, and because God has been truthful, but we dismiss Him, He will judge us in wrath. Not cool, friends. Not cool at all. And very, very convicting.

Who will render to every man according to his or deeds." And it's my own fault. I can't blame you; you can't blame me. It's not what I say that matters. I can say I'm a Christian. I can say I was baptized. I can wear the jewelry, have the bumper stickers, sport the "Jesus is my homeboy" t-shirt. But if my walk doesn't validate my talk, my talk is useless. And the day's coming when God will separate the walkers from the talkers. That day is one day closer than it was yesterday. Time is running out. You and I need Jesus. Not as our "get out of hell free" card, but as our Lord, who we love enough to serve daily. To get out of spiritual mediocrity is to walk the talk.

Chapter 2 Verse 7-9

"To them who by patient continuance in well doing seek for glory and honor and immortality, eternal life" God is contrasting those in the earlier verses with those who want to not just be saved, but live saved. God is saying those who just do it, just pull up their boots and tie them on every day to do well or do good works, are the ones who are truly seeking Jesus. The

word "*glory*" means "*to be full of perfect light*" and the word "*honor*" means "*to be recognized and esteemed by God.*" It means "*to be privileged and exalted to a position of responsibility and service to God*" The word *"immortality*" means "*living forever with God*". So let's look at this verse and say it the way we would say it in a conversation, using the definition of the words instead of the words. Here it is: "The people who live their lives biblically (continue in doing well) and openly by seeking Jesus and His truth (He's the perfect light) are recognized by God and exalted to positions of responsibility and service, forever." Now, just living good isn't good enough as we have already seen. But for those who are trying to live God's Word diligently, God's Word is saying they are probably saved. Makes sense, doesn't it?

"But unto them that are contentious, and do not obey the truth, but obey unrighteousness, indignation and wrath" But as for those who fight against, struggle with, or are belligerent to God, His Word, His Son, and His gospel, they are in trouble. For those who know the truth but refuse to surrender to the truth, they are in trouble. For those who are obedient to disobedience, who prefer their way over Gods, who are complacent and uncaring, are in trouble. Spiritual trouble. Eternal trouble. That's real trouble, friends. What does that look like?

"Tribulation and anguish, upon every soul of man that doeth evil, of the Jew first, and also of the Gentile" Well, the word "*tribulation*" means "*oppression, affliction, or suffering.*" "*Anguish*" means "*to be put in a narrow place; to experience supreme pain.*" The word "*soul*" lets us know the process may start here, but it's going to be eternal in duration. How can a person hate God when He is lovingly telling us the truth? Don't you want all the people you know, and especially your close friends, to just be honest, even if it hurts? Well, there's no friend like Jesus!

Our lives do not have to be mundane and mediocre. In fact, as we have seen already, a life like that is probably not biblical and may reflect a life outside of God's will. So the questions are, what will we do about it, and what can be done about it? The answer is Jesus. The answer is knowing, believing, and living in what He has done and will do. But you have to know the truth and make a daily decision.

Chapter 2 Verse 10-13

"But glory, honor, and peace, to every man that worked good, to the Jew first, and also to the Gentile" There's a difference in the lives of those who blatantly disregard God and His Word and those who strive to live obediently to Him, just like there's a difference between a lazy student who doesn't study and learn compared to a student who does. The studious student typically makes better grades and has more opportunities in life because of their obedience to master the subject matter they study. An employee, who works hard and is efficient, conscientious, and punctual, typically gets the promotions and opportunities the lazy employee doesn't. Well, God offers the studious and conscientious believer an exalted state (glory), makes him more valuable (honor), and provides tranquility between him and God (peace); a huge difference from the earlier verses and the commentaries explaining them, right?

"For there is no respect of persons with God." God is perfectly impartial to all people. He doesn't play favorites, but He draws the line at willful sin, no matter who you are. Just the way it is, friends! But at least He tells us the truth up front. Now, what He tells us may not be popular or what we want to hear, but at least we know what He thinks, and that we're all on the same playing field.

"For as many as have sinned without law shall also perish without law: and as many as have sinned in the law shall be judged by the law." The law of God was not given for salvation. Jesus was. The issue here is responsibility according to privilege enjoyed. The Gentiles didn't know the law; the Jews did, or at least they should have. Regardless, everyone will stand before God in judgment. Knowing or not knowing the law still carries the same sentence. You say that's not fair? If you drive 60 mph in a 25 mph zone and get a ticket, you can claim all you want that you didn't know the speed limit. Ignorance of the law is no defense. The judge will tell you that, as a driver of an automobile, you should have known the law. Well, you and I and everyone else should be aware of God's Word and willing to follow it. God will judge us in perfect righteousness. He must be impartial and judge according to the letter

of the law. Otherwise, why have the law in the first place? There's not going to be a barter system then. There won't be talking our way out of it. There won't be varying degrees of judicial verdicts. All will stand guilty, and all will be judged rightly and fairly. But without Jesus, it's going to be very bad.

"For not the hearers of the law are just before God, but the doers of the law shall be justified." God is so clear to us; if we'll just listen. You can sit under biblical teaching and preaching until the cows come home, but if it doesn't change you, if you won't assimilate the Word into your life, if you won't be a "doer" of the Word, there won't be any justification. Doing is a fruit of a true faith relationship with Jesus. Hearing only isn't.

The word "*justification*" means "*to declare or pronounce righteous.*" God is telling us hearing the Word and not doing anything with it is meaningless. No different than hearing the teachings on how to grow a garden but never growing one, only with infinitely deeper consequences. What good was going to the seminar?

Our only hope as we stand before God is to claim Jesus and to have demonstrated in our life that we were serious about Him. It's not that we can tell God we know Jesus. It's can Jesus tell His Father He knows us?

Chapter 2 Verse 14-16

"For when the Gentiles, which have not the law, do by nature the things contained in the law, these, having not the law, are a law unto themselves." Even heathen peoples, who know nothing about the Mosaic law but live rightly just because they know to do so, are expressing the magnitude of God's law, which supersedes even atheistic thought.

"*Which show the work of the law written in their hearts, their conscience also bearing witness, and their thoughts the mean while accusing or else excusing one another.*" The example is that the Gentiles did not have God's Laws written in stone like Israel did, but the Gentiles naturally had orderly societies that punish murder, theft, adultery, lying, etc. because the Gentiles had a conscience that leads them to govern themselves. That fact makes Israel unable to use the "we-are-not-as-sinful-as-the-Gentiles" excuse. If the Gentiles act more decently or better than the Jews, and the Gentiles do not have God's laws written down like Israel, then Israel is that more accountable because they had those laws written down in stone and broke them anyway. We Christians have the entire Bible. If we act like the world; or worse, are we going to be able to say God won't judge us because we've been baptized? That's not going to stand under scrutiny, folks.

It is written in the heart of every person, in the conscience, which beliefs and behaviors are acceptable and which are not acceptable. This very concept of conscience governs any and every society, whether the society is Christian or non-Christian. Conscience is what keeps law and order, even if it is in a very primitive form. The Gentiles know right from wrong by virtue of their conscience, even though they did not have the written laws of God in stone like Israel had. You and I know too, even if we've never seen a Bible. And most of us have seen a Bible!

"In the day when God shall judge the secrets of men by Jesus Christ according to my gospel." Romans 2:12-16 are very difficult verses to understand because Paul uses the term law quite frequently, but he also uses the word Gentile frequently too. But the two words are typically not associated with one another. The point isn't law or Gentile, or Jews for that matter.

The point is judgment of both Jews and Gentiles. Look, two powerful and eternally connected issues are here that clear everything else up. Jesus and the gospel. If you know the gospel, it will lead you to Jesus. If you know Jesus, He will lead you to salvation. If you don't, you're being led by the wrong things.

Chapter 2 Verse 17 to 20

"Behold, thou art called a Jew" Paul described the moralist in the earlier verses; he now discusses the religionist. Where the moralist thinks he can please God with being a moral person, the religionist believes he can

please God by being a religious person, or a person who thinks religion is the way to God. They're both wrong. Friends, a relationship with Jesus is the only way. Not a religion *of* Jesus. A relationship *with* Jesus. There's a huge difference. The Jews were known for their adherence to their religion, and it's the main thing that got in their way when Jesus walked among them. I hope it's not in your way.

"and restest in the law, and makest thy boast of God, and knowest His will" A religionist can know and rest in God's Word. He can profess God. He can know God's will; and be as lost as a golf ball. I know many people who own Bibles, take their Bibles to church, occasionally read it, can quote it, but are still lost. I know many people who profess God as their God, but God isn't so much interested in a person's profession as He is in their life, and quite frankly, many people talk the talk but few walk the walk. I know people who know God's will, but that's not enough. A person has to *do* God's will. These types of people who know and profess, and talk but there's no fruit in their life are religionists. This is what Paul is describing here.

"and approvest the things that are more excellent, being instructed out of the law" Paul continues by saying there are those who not only know God's will, but they actually know the deeper things of God's will, and they approve and proclaim adherence to it, but again, there's no visible proof. This religionist has had training in God's Word and understands it but refuses to live by it. They have no excuse. God expects a person to live what they have been taught. This is very difficult for many of us because it's so convicting. Why is it so convicting? Because we're so guilty!

"And art confident that thou thyself art a guide of the blind, a light of them which are in darkness, An instructor of the foolish, a teacher of babes, which hast the form of knowledge and of the truth in the law." Religionists are like the blind leading the blind, only they don't think they're blind. The religionist thinks he is leading people to spiritual truth with religion. The religionist is convinced they are the ones the immature need because they have all the answers, and their answers are found in religion. But that's just not true. The answer is found in Jesus. He is

your guide. He is the light. He is your instructor. He is your teacher. He is the ultimate knowledge and truth. You and I may need someone to help us learn about Him, but it's all about Him! Not religion. Not a denomination. Not a group. Just Jesus.

The religionist fails to live what he professes, as we will see. The person with a real relationship with Jesus professes Him and Him alone.

Chapter 2 Verse 21-24

Oh my! Paul keeps telling it like it is. But that's certainly appropriate, because it's God telling it like it is through Paul. Here's the deal: after affirming the privileges of the Jew, Paul now demonstrated their inconsistencies by asking five rhetorical questions. Well, maybe they're not that rhetorical. These questions do not charge individuals in particular but demonstrate the pattern or consistency of the reality of their experience.

"*Thou therefore which teachest another, teachest thou not thyself?*" First, Paul stated a general principle of the Jew's authority in teaching, and they did teach, but then he called them out in specific areas of inconsistency with their lives. Look, he's saying it is easy to teach something but not live it out. That's called hypocrisy. God is letting us know He sees us talk the talk, but He's not seeing the corresponding walk that should go along with it. And He has a problem with that kind of lifestyle. And we do too.

For example, when a person thinks they're above the law and lives outside of it, don't we get riled up? A politician is supposed to make and support the law. A policeman is supposed to enforce it. But if they think they are above it and break it constantly (or even once), we will get all belligerent and complain about it not being right. And it isn't. Well, God should have the same right to be the same way. And He is. They tell us one thing, and then do another. That's the issue here.

"Thou that preachest a man should not steal, dost thou steal?" Some Jews preached not to steal, but they were not as scrupulous about their own

honest dealings. They wanted to grade degrees of honesty. Let's get a little more personal. Do you steal little things from work? Do you cheat on your taxes? Do you borrow and forget to give back? Do you take advantage of others? It's all the same, friends. And if you tell people that people shouldn't do it, yet you do, well, you get the picture.

"Thou that sayest a man should not commit adultery, dost thou commit adultery?" Here Paul changed from the verb "preach" to the verb "say." This is a claim by the self-righteous. Those who teach have a greater accountability for how they live. Some Jews practiced the very thing they condemned in others. But let's get a little more personal. What are you watching and looking at? Soft porn? R-rated movies? Profanity? Do you dress in a manner exposing or aggressively complimenting your body? Do you look a second, third, fourth time? We're all guilty of this too. And if we're guilty, we're in trouble.

"Thou that abhorrest idols, dost thou commit sacrilege?" Jews prided themselves as monotheistic, or believing in one god only. Worship of idols was outside their realm of devotion (so they thought), but that's the thing about idols; they can pop up out of nowhere. In this example, they engaged with idols by robbing temples. I know it doesn't sound like much, but it doesn't take much. Their monotheistic religion forbade making personal profit from idols or their temples. So what's the big deal to us? Well, let's get personal again. Typically, when a person holds back their time, talents, tithe and energy from God and His work, they're doing the exact same thing. Why? Because all of that belongs to God!! God gives each of us time and talents and energy in order to be compensated somehow as we use these things. So to hold back from Him any of those things is to use Him for our benefit. To hold back our time, talents, tithe (money), and energy in serving Him is akin to robbery, because we're willing to give it to something else. He doesn't expect or ask for it all, but what He does ask for and require of us, we should be willing to give to Him, right?

"Thou that makest thy boast of the law, through breaking the law dishonourest thou God?" Many do not live or practice what they preach. Our lives

need to match our doctrine. Christians who sin dishonor God. Christian leaders who are hypocritical and inconsistent dishonor God in a very particular way. They stand indicted against their privilege. I'm not guilty, you say? Well, have you ever used God's name in a profane way? Have you ever mocked God, His church, or the pastor? Have you ever not witnessed? Have you held back from God (in any of the ways mentioned above)? Well, then you're guilty. I am too. We need a change of heart. We need to be conformed in the image of His Son Jesus.

"For the name of God is blasphemed among the Gentiles through you, as it is written." The issue for all the above is that it blasphemes God! If a "true" believer knows God's Word, but just talks about His Word or worse still breaks it, they dishonor God and His Word. Do we suppose He's just going to shrug that off? If a "believer" can and does do that, what will the unbelieving do? Look, all this does is cause people to withdraw from God. It causes people to not care about eternal things. When God's people act like the unsaved, the unsaved have no reason to live any other way than lost. And if they live lost and believers live lost, what's the point in believing in God?

Chapter 2 Verse 25-27

Who are the most difficult people to reach with the gospel? I realize that only God can save a soul and that nothing is too difficult for Him. But, from a human standpoint, some types of people seem to be more difficult to bring to a saving faith than other people. The Bible shows us that the most difficult people to reach are religious people who trust in their religion. This is what Paul is referring to here. He's describing those who relish their rituals and religious traditions. They don't see their need for a Savior from sin because they view themselves as pretty good people. They think they are right with God because of their religious performance. Paul is trying to get them to think!

"For circumcision is indeed profitable if you keep the law; but if you are a breaker of the law, your circumcision has become uncircumcision" God instituted the practice of circumcision (the removal of the male foreskin) as a sign of

His covenant with Abraham, over 500 years before He gave Moses the Law. It symbolized moral purity and separation from the world unto God. Under the Law of Moses, it became a sign of membership in the covenant community. So as a God-ordained ritual, circumcision was of value to the Jews as a reminder of their covenant relationship to God and of the need to be morally set apart to God. Not a sign of being in the men's club.

"*Therefore, if an uncircumcised man keeps the righteous requirements of the law, will not his uncircumcision be counted as circumcision?*" Paul is saying it's a heart issue, not a ritual issue. He means, "If a Gentile obeys the moral requirements of God's Law, God will count him as righteous, even though he is uncircumcised." So the religionist can't use religion as a means to say they're okay with God, because God is saying they are not. Look, our church attendance, while appropriate and necessary, doesn't impress God unless our motives are pure. Our religious lifestyle, while appropriate and necessary, doesn't impress God either, unless it's done in the right spirit and with the right heart. And rituals typically are not in the right spirit or heart.

"And will not the physically uncircumcised, if he fulfills the law, judge you who, even with your written code and circumcision, are a transgressor of the law?" And, even more shocking, "The obedient, but uncircumcised Gentile someday will condemn you who have the written Law and have been circumcised, but are disobedient to that Law." He does not mean that obedient Gentiles literally will act as judges against the Jews, but rather that they will be "a witness for the prosecution" in the sense that the Gentiles' obedience will be evidence of what the Jew ought to have been doing. In other words, the Jewish believer who assumed their ritualistic religion or religious pedigree was all they needed to be right with God was going to have an eye-opening experience when they stood before God to account for their lives. We will too, friends, and our church membership or our baptism or our better-than-you lifestyle will not be enough to satisfy God's holiness. All of us are going to need help. His name is Jesus. And we probably ought to start the process of conforming to His image immediately.

3

CHAPTER 3 VERSE 1-2

"What advantage then has the Jew, or what is the profit of circumcision?" Based upon Paul's case in Romans 2:17-29, it appears that the Jew has been reduced to a position of equality with the heathen (Romans 1:18-32) and the hypocrite (Romans 2:1-16). Why? Because they were acting as such. So, if a Jew stands under the condemnation of God, even as the heathen and hypocrite, in spite of his or her possession of the Law and his practice of circumcision, what is the advantage of being a Jew? Paul answered this objection by reminding the Jew that his or her greatest advantage was the possession of the Word of God. This great treasure was entrusted to him and her to share with the world. This great treasure told him or her of the coming Messiah. But the Jew failed to share God's Word and to obey God's will, thus he and she stood accountable to God. What's the point? We Christians face the same dilemma. What's the advantage of being a Christian if all we do is ritualistic worship or no worship at all? If we act like heathens and hypocrites, what good does it do to be Christian? If there's no change in us from when we were heathen and hypocrites, what good does a profession of faith make? Calling ourselves Christians but not truly following Christ is the height of hypocrisy. What good is that? It is mediocre living at best.

"Much in every way!" There was no advantage to works like circumcision or baptism, but there was to being a Jew who not only recorded but

preserved the Word of God. At least they had that. But here's the thing: their unfaithfulness didn't nullify the faithfulness of God at all. As you see in the wanderings in the wilderness, God was faithful even when His people were not. God is always true as He cannot lie like humans often do. We're the ones who are not true and lie, and God really doesn't appreciate it, no matter what we think. And there's a cost associated with all of that even though God is faithful.

"Chiefly because to them were committed the oracles of God." In these verses, we have Paul's case against the Jew and all mankind who count on religion to make them right with God. Religion cannot make a person right with God nor will it exempt a person from God's judgment. Assembly of God, Baptist, Catholic, Methodist, Non-Denominational, it doesn't matter. Religious people stand in need of the righteousness of God just as much as the worst sinner. The only hope for religious and irreligious people alike is a personal relationship with Jesus Christ. The Good News is not just for "bad guys," it is for all "good guys" too! But the good news must make a good change or what's the use? Has it made a good change in you? What has your life been like since you were baptized? Are you closer to God? Do you know deeper things about God? Are you serving Him in how you live and in what you do? Are you active in both attending corporate worship and kingdom service, or are you content to just barely get by? Are you consistent in your Christian walk, or are you happy to settle for mediocre living? Is Jesus worthy of more?

Chapter 3 Verse 3-6

"For what if some did not believe? Will their unbelief make the faithfulness of God without effect?" Does unbelief void God's promises? Does unbelief make God a liar? Of course not. Five hundred years ago, people believed the world was flat. Was it? No. The world is round whether we believe it is or not. A hundred years ago mankind believed if God wanted humanity to fly He would have given people wings. We don't have wings, but we can fly anytime we want to whether we believe it or

not. Two thousand years ago God made a way back to Him via Jesus on the Cross. Whether a person believes that or not doesn't change the fact it's true. Unbelief won't keep you out of hell, folks. God has clearly and plainly told us the truth.

"Certainly not! Indeed, let God be true but every man a liar. As it is written:"That You may be justified in Your words, And may overcome when You are judged." God never voids His Word or His promises. He cannot lie. Even if no one believed His Word, it still is true. Paul is saying here it is mankind who has the problem with truth. God deserves (and honestly demands) that mankind should obey and worship Jesus and live their lives biblically. But so many want to get baptized, go to church, buy a Bible, anything to ease their mind with an easier salvation, so they can be free to live the way they want. Sound familiar? Denying truth doesn't destroy it. Ignoring truth doesn't make it ineffective. That's just insane.

"But if our unrighteousness demonstrates the righteousness of God, what shall we say? Is God unjust who inflicts wrath? (I speak as a man.)" Do you see the insanity here? If our sin life, which blinds us and clouds our thinking to the point we are living a lie, and that in itself proves the Word of God to be true as it says, does that not demonstrate the righteousness of God? Our insanity proves God's sanity! He has told us what will happen. When it happens, we blame everything but the truth. Sometimes we even blame God as if He's to blame. Folks, is that insane or what?

"Certainly not! For then how will God judge the world?" Paul is saying, in the vernacular of today, "You've done lost your mind!" God's moral truth will always judge man's immorality. Truth will always trump lies! God has told us, in written form, His truth! It has been in existence forever. Humanity on the other hand, changes truth about every hundred years. Who will you go to for the truth today? What about thirty years from now? What about on your deathbed?

We've been at a pretty steady pace, so let's take a break and think about what we've learned so far in a different way.

I'm sure everyone has heard of Cinderella. "Cinderella" is a folk tale embodying unjust oppression and triumphant reward. But folks, it's really a picture of biblical salvation and sanctification.

Here's the deal: Cinderella is in bondage and treated like a slave by her own step family. In spite of these circumstances, Cinderella was a very hard working young lady. She was a very pleasant, sincere, and forgiving young lady. She was beautiful and sweet. But she was still in bondage! All of her great personal qualities only made her reality that more shameful. Her great personal qualities, all of her hard work, did nothing for her bondage.

All she really wants from life is a chance for freedom, and she finds this chance when she hears of the upcoming Royal Ball. The only problem is when Cinderella's cruel stepmother hears of her desire, she prevents her from attending the Royal Ball. Cinderella gets very sad and lonely. During this time, she gets some unexpected help from the lovable mice and from her Fairy Godmother.

As a person, you can be very pleasant. You can be very sincere and forgiving. You can work hard. You can be beautiful (or not so). But spiritually you are separated from God and in bondage to death. You have a wicked step-mother (your sin-nature) and three wicked step-sisters (the world, your "flesh," and the devil). All three are working against you to keep you from the Royal Ball (the presence of Jesus). You may want to go, but you're in bondage, and you can't make a way. But, God sends help in the lowly form of a friend, or a pastor (guess that makes me a mouse, lol), or parents to help you see the truth. The Holy Spirit (like the Fairy Godmother) comes to change you, to get you ready to see the Prince!

At the ball, you see the Prince, and you fall in love with him, but you know the real you is coming back, so you flee so He won't see the real you. What you don't know is the Prince has fallen in love with the real you already because you are actually a beautiful princess; you're just being kept in an ugly environment. The Prince searches for you and eventually finds you, shows you you're worthy of His love, and sets you up to be His Bride. You marry and live happily ever after.

Funny, we never hear about the three step sisters again, and the step mom is nowhere to be found. Why? Because the story is about the Prince setting Cinderella free, not the bondage. Look, the lies are gone, and the truth is given. Her life has been changed because she was taught truth and encouraged to live it and not to live in the lies of bondage anymore. She was allowed to be the beautiful princess she was born to be. All she needed was truth and a Prince. Now let me ask you a few questions.

After she was delivered, did Cinderella go back to her old life once she truly met her Prince? No way! Did she flirt with the other men at the ball? Nope. Did she go to the bars looking for more love? Nope. Did she sleep with anyone else? Not hardly. Did she talk bad about the Prince? No! Was her life all about pleasing her? No! Her life was about pleasing the prince. She loved Him for who He was and how He justified her and freed her from bondage. She didn't get attitudinal with the prince. She became His chaste and honorable Bride. And she never went back to her old self nor did she pay attention to yesterday's news.

If you've accepted Jesus as your Savior, He's your Prince; you're His Bride. You are justified and freed from the world, the flesh, and the devil. The old sin nature has been crucified. You are now kingdom royalty. This is the gospel truth. And if it is true, and it is, why in the world would you ever go back to bondage? Christians do it all the time with their worldly, carnal, sinful, mediocre living. There's a better way friends, and the Prince deserves better.

I'm not perfect, and I never will be. You aren't either. But I am concerned about being as obedient as I can be to the One who has saved me from spiritual bondage. If you are a true Christian, you should be concerned and obedient too. Contact me if you need to talk. I care about you and your walk with Christ.

Chapter 3 Verse 7-8

"For if the truth of God has increased through my lie to His glory, why am I also still judged as a sinner?" The question presented here is "If I sin and God overcomes it, and He receives glory by doing so, isn't my sin justifiable?" "Why not sin more if God gets more glory when I do so because He forgives me and shows His Grace? Utter nonsense, folks! Let's say a human judge showed you mercy and told you that you did not have to pay your speeding ticket. Will this human judge continue to let you get away with speeding habitually? Even if you think speeding demonstrates his mercy? Will he tell you his love for you will allow you to do as you want? No, he will tell you the law compels him to punish you! Well, God is the same way. Keep doing it, and sooner or later you're going to receive justice. It's just that simple.

"And why not say, "Let us do evil that good may come?" It's the same issue. Let's continue to break the law, so we can continue to receive forgiveness. You know, this is a pretty neat concept. I can do whatever I want, and love will get me through. This reminds me of a spoiled child. Look, God does love you, but you can't play the "God is my daddy" card and live like a spoiled child. You and I have to grow up and become responsible spiritual adults at some point. Doing evil that good may come from it is nuts! It's where spiritual mediocrity comes from. How about we do well as good may come from it. That world makes better sense, doesn't it? What's wrong with doing well?

"As we are slanderously reported and as some affirm that we say. Their condemnation is just." The word "*condemnation*" means "*damnation*." People wrongfully think a god of love cannot take vengeance. He is too good and loving. He will be denying his very nature of love if he judges me. What this argument fails to see is that His love is *just*! Love expressed unjustly is not love at all; it is a license for indulgence. God's love is not a license to indulge. It is completely and perfectly just, and it demands justice. God's justice is the demonstration of perfect love. The Cross was where God exacted His perfect justice upon His perfect Love. The Cross is the perfect demonstration of both love and justice.

You and I are found on either side of the cross. If we have accepted Jesus' sacrifice for our sins, we are on the side of love and we will not intentionally try to bring more shame to Jesus by living in indulgence. If we haven't accepted His sacrifice, His love is there; we're just not under it, and justice will be served, and soon.

Chapter 3 Verse 9-12

"What then? Are we better than they? Not at all." Not a moralist or a religionist? Think you're better than those who are? The whole point of everything written so far, according to Paul, was not to berate or belittle anyone, but to offer hope. The challenge is to see our need for help, find that help, and reach out to that help. It's okay to do this. But it's not okay to minimize sin! Nor is it okay to minimize the redeeming power of Jesus Christ. Don't hang your head in despair. Call out to Jesus and be changed. Don't fight the truth, surrender to it! Mediocre living is living in half-truths or partial truths but denying the whole truth. It's settling for what we want to believe instead of what God says. It's getting close to being turned over to a reprobate mind. I hope you see this. Seeing this is part of the process of conforming to His image.

"For we have previously charged both Jews and Greeks that they are all under sin." Jew or Greek. Rich or poor. Conservative or Liberal. Black or white. Young or old. Everyone is guilty of sin, according to the Bible. And we all know it too, don't we? We see the speck in the eyes of others, but we dismiss the log in our own eyes. Let's deal with our own sins, folks, and stop living in apathy.

"As it is written: There is none righteous, no, not one" A sinful nature is unrighteous by God's standard. And God says there's not a person dead or alive or to be born who isn't guilty. No one is righteous; no one. And all the good works we can do in a lifetime won't change the fact. Righteousness is a Person, not an activity. His name is Jesus. Do you know Him, or just facts about Him?

"There is none who understands" A sinful nature is also ignorant. Left to our own devices, we will struggle with understanding God and His purposes. We need the Holy Spirit to help us understand. When someone says they don't understand the Bible, there's a reason for that. When we don't fully grasp biblical things like real truth, there's a reason for that too.

"There is none who seeks after God. They have all turned aside" A sinful nature is indifferent and selfish. It creates selfishness. It makes us focus on encouragement only, and that of a worldly kind. We ask God to encourage us in our sins, but He wants to free us from them. That's the epitome of encouragement. Do you desire real joy and encouragement? Seek after Jesus and the understanding of His Word. There are no shortcuts. One must do this to truly understand. But be of good cheer, it's very simple to do. We just need to be disciplined.

"They have together become unprofitable; There is none who does good, no, not one." This is pretty self-explanatory. God is saying there is no one who does good, when compared to His goodness. And that's the issue: we want to be judged based on our benchmark. God judges on His. That's a real issue for all of us because His benchmark is the Cross, more specifically the One Who hung upon it. And you and I just don't measure up.

Chapter 3 Verse 13-17

To continue to understand these verses, we have to remember the context. As you might recall, God is making a case against all humanity and that case is all mankind has sinned. Some worse than others from our perspective, but the only perspective that matters is God's. This is what He's telling us. He's using not our benchmark, but His, and His benchmark is Jesus, and compared to Him all have sinned and are in trouble. The earlier verses described the case of a sinful nature (our attitudes), and these verses describe the case of a sinful tongue (our actions).

"Their throat is an open sepulchre; with their tongues they have used deceit; the poison of asps is under their lips:" A sinful tongue is full of corruption, like an open grave. A person with a sinful mouth is a person who is foul, dirty, obscene, profane, dishonorable, and offensive. Like the people on television we often idolize. Crazy, isn't it? The obscene mouth may range from off-colored jokes to dirty jokes, and from immoral suggestions to outright propositions. Like the movies we watch and idolize. Again, crazy, isn't it? The word "*deceit*" describes the person "*who's a smooth talker, a flatterer, a good liar.*" One who can lie and keep a straight face. The asp is the cobra. The idea is that some people's tongues reveal a diabolical nature. And the less we watch and glorify it, the easier it is to see what God means.

"Whose mouth is full of cursing and bitterness:" Cursing is sin which comes from a bitter heart. The more a person curses, the deeper the person's bitterness typically is. We live in a society where it's generally accepted and in fact desired. It shouldn't be this way for the Christian. Cursing is just mediocre living with some mascara on.

"Their feet are swift to shed blood:" Sinful acts include murderous intentions. Now, I know we probably won't actually murder anyone, but what about when we use our tongue to gossip and defame someone? Don't we hurt them? Don't we "murder" their reputation and their spirit? "Sticks and stones may break our bones, but words will never hurt us" is baloney. Words have consequences. Words from people with corrupt minds and tongues can be devastating. The idea here is many people run to find and cause trouble, usually at the expense of someone else. It's wrong and God knows it. We know it too.

"Destruction and misery are in their ways:" Here's one of our main issues: we are all bent towards destruction. Some of us focus on self-destruction. Others focus on destroying others. Some are blatantly open with it; others hide it very well, but we are all guilty to some extent. And God is calling us out. Destruction will always lead to misery.

"And the way of peace have they not known:" People do not experience peace because they are so often pursuing everything that is not peaceful. Why? Because we're self-destructing; we don't know how to find it or where to look. Fortunately, God has written us the how and where. We call it the Bible, a book describing His story. This commentary is my effort to help people understand it better and conform to His image.

"There is no fear of God before their eyes." If there's no respect for God in our vision or how we actually see Him, there will be no respect for God in our speech, our actions, and our attitudes. Why is our music becoming so profane? Why is our television becoming so inappropriate? Why is our communication becoming more and more vulgar? Because we've lost our respect for who God is.

Chapter 3 Verse 19-20

We're laying the groundwork for some amazing theological teaching in the next five chapters. The type of teaching that will absolutely change your life. And if your life has changed, but you find yourself living in mediocrity as a Christian, you can get back to bold, passionate living for Jesus just by mastering the teaching in this book. It's that important.

"Now we know that whatever the law says, it says to those who are under the law, that every mouth may be stopped, and all the world may become guilty before God." Notice this verse starts with "we know". We know, don't we? Obvious truth cannot be missed unless we have our heads buried in the sand, or we are preoccupied with mediocre things. But we know, and because we know, we all stand guilty before God. The earlier verses describing the tongue are now being laid bare that every mouth may be stopped. God has the final word, friends. No one escapes His Word. Everyone is subject to His power and authority. Rolling our eyes to that truth is like rolling our eyes to gravity. We can assume it doesn't exist, or we're not subject to it, but we're wrong, right?

God's Word speaks to all of us. The entire world is guilty according to the Word of God. We all stand before God imperfect, unholy, unrighteous, and unworthy. The amount of sins we commit, their severity, and their duration is not the issue. Sin is the issue, and we're all carriers of a deadly spiritual virus. We need a cure. The cure is Jesus. He was proclaimed guilty according to man's law. He is declared innocent by God's law. And God's law and philosophy supersedes man's laws and philosophies. Boom goes the dynamite!

"Therefore by the deeds of the law no flesh will be justified in His sight, for by the law is the knowledge of sin." Look closely at what is being said here: No law or no deed of the law will ever justify a person, or make him acceptable to God. Being good or doing good will not work, my friends. Nothing that you do will get you right with God. God has spoken.

Let me illustrate with the same example from earlier. Speed limit laws don't make you acceptable to anyone. They're just laws. They have no effect on who you are. Keeping the speed limit just means you didn't break the law. Still doesn't mean you're acceptable to anyone. You're just "good" at keeping the law. Breaking the speed limit is breaking the law. Now, you're a lawbreaker because you broke the law. There's now a penalty to pay, and a costly one too, typically. You stand before the judge. He knows you're guilty; you know you're guilty. There's another person there shaking their head at you, you the lawbreaker. But if you were to ask the judge if everyone in the courtroom were guilty of speeding, he may say no, but he'd know they're guilty of something. So it is with our God. You may not be as bad as your friend or your neighbor, but you're guilty of something. And all it takes is one sin to get you in hot water with God. And we're all guilty, including me. I need help. You do too. Everyone does. Jesus is standing by to help us if we'd just allow Him to. How? Just admit you're who you are, a sinner. I am too. Believe Jesus died for your sins, so you could be in a relationship with Him for all eternity. Confess your sins to Him (He knows already, but it does you a world of good), repent from those sins, and allow Him to disciple you. Work on keeping your relationship with Him fresh and dynamic. Then buckle up and watch Him work in and around your life! Boom goes the dynamite on mediocrity as we conform to His image.

Chapter 3 Verse 21-23

God is sharing something really magnificent here, but you have to think about what's being said. As we have seen, there is a great difference between what we wish and hope God may do, and what He tells us He's going to do. Don't be fooled. Study His Word and be biblically informed. You're going to need it.

*"**But now** the righteousness of God without the law is manifested, being witnessed by the law and the prophets"* Look out everyone! Righteousness refers to the justice and perfection which God possesses and shows. The opposite would be a lack of godly character. The point is God is righteousness; man is not. But God provides man with righteousness through His Son, Jesus. God has now revealed how man is to get right with Him. The word "now" may be easy to overlook, but don't! It is describing a cataclysmic breaking point in the book of Romans. It points to a pivotal point in man's history. Before Jesus, God had great patience in that He put up with man's attempts at self-righteousness through the law. God has already made the case that self-righteousness is impossible, and the law proves it. But now righteousness is available in Jesus. Jesus came to demonstrate God's justice and perfection, and He did so perfectly. Now, He's the benchmark. He's the way! He's the truth! He is the life!

"Even the righteousness of God which is by faith of Jesus Christ unto all and upon all them that believe: for there is no difference" Faith is the victory, but it's the object of your faith that's important. Your faith won't save you. Jesus will. What you believe just won't get you where you want to go. Jesus has to take you there. Why? Faith cannot replace unrighteousness. It's the righteousness of God that replaces your unrighteousness. It's Jesus that makes the difference, not your faith. You can have faith in who and what Jesus is and never be changed. You must be changed. Our unrighteousness must be replaced with righteousness. Why? Because God requires righteousness before His presence, and you and I, and every person who has ever been born, just don't have any. In fact, we have just the opposite, unrighteousness. And all our righteous acts are

like filthy rags to God because all our righteous acts are nothing more than unrighteousness from God's perspective. Why? Keep reading.

"For all have sinned, and come short of the glory of God" Doesn't get any clearer than this, friends. Every person ever born or those who will be born have sinned or will sin, and just one sin causes us to be unrighteous. Doesn't really matter what the sin is. Sin is sin. Sin is missing the righteous mark God has established (His glory!). Anything short of the mark is unrighteousness. Therefore, sin is unrighteousness. And God says we're all sinners.

Chapter 3 Verse 24-26

"Being justified freely by his grace through the redemption that is in Christ Jesus" We are now introduced to justification. Justification is God's act of removing the guilt and penalty of sin while at the same time making a sinner righteous through Christ's atoning sacrifice. Notice this is freely given to those who would know they are in sin, repent of it, and call upon Jesus to be their Lord and Savior. By paying the wages of our sin, Jesus has "redeemed" us thereby making us now justified before God. This is a hallelujah moment, folks. If you have been reading these commentaries up till now, and you are unsaved, what are you waiting for? You will never be given a better offer than this. If you are saved and you have been reading these commentaries up to now, you should be in a state of spiritual euphoria as you recall what Jesus has done to and for you.

"Whom God hath set forth to be a propitiation through faith in his blood, to declare his righteousness for the remission of sins that are past, through the forbearance of God" If you're not on a spiritual high from our last verse, hang on. Here, we are told that God proposed to send forth Jesus to be the sacrifice needed to allow us to experience verse 24. Notice a very key fact though: It is not His teachings, power, example, life, miracles, or kindness that make Christ our propitiation. It is His blood, His sacrifice, His death, that makes the way. Why blood? The Bible says the life of the body is in the blood. Jesus gave His righteous life's blood

to give us a new, righteous life before a righteous God. Do you see this clearer now? If you are saved, how in the world can you be content to be complacent in your walk knowing Jesus suffered so for you? How can mediocrity be sufficient to the person saved eternally by the blood of Jesus? Was He a mediocre God? Was He a mediocre sacrifice? Was His blood mediocre? No! All of these were the epitome of excellence. Our daily walk with Him should be no less. No, seriously!

"To declare, I say, at this time his righteousness: that he might be just, and the justifier of him which believeth in Jesus." Righteousness has one great purpose: to declare God's justice and perfection. If you've been made righteous by Jesus, it wasn't to just get you out of hell. If you think that was the only reason, then you're being pretty egocentric. No, it was to make you a living, breathing spokesperson for the justice and perfection of a just and perfect God. It was to get you out of living a life of mundane mediocrity into one of blessed assurance that others would be attracted to the bright and glorious hope that is in you. It was to allow others to see the righteousness of Jesus living within you that dispels the darkness of apathetic, worldly living. Oh what a Savior He is! Oh what a life you have been given! Oh what a glorious future you have because of Jesus. Tell mediocrity to bother someone else. You have a life to live and a story to tell.

Chapter 3 Verse 28-31

"Therefore we conclude that a man is justified by faith apart from the deeds of the law."

Faith justifies a person; not the law, or good works, or anything else for that matter. We need to ask ourselves who is to be praised and set up as the subject of glory. Is it us? Well, if we created us and saved ourselves from ourselves with our own works and deeds, then we should glorify ourselves. (This is exactly what humanism tries to teach). But we didn't, and we can't. If we could, we would have done so by now. And we didn't create ourselves either. We can procreate, but we can't create. The first one of us had to come from somewhere.

"Or is He the God of the Jews only? Is He not also the God of the Gentiles? Yes, of the Gentiles also, since there is one God who will justify the circumcised by faith and the uncircumcised through faith." Faith reveals only one God who deals with us all equally. Man has conjured up all kinds of "little g" gods and idols, but the Bible tells of only one true God, and He's a creator God. Since there is only one true God, then all are justified in the same way; by faith in the one true God! God does not play favorites; He deals with every person in the same manner, which is biblical truth. Now, if we want to remain ignorant or unconcerned about His truth, we have that option, but we would then need to go back and reread all of the commentaries on Romans chapter one to determine where we really are with God. Hopefully you remember and don't need to go back!

"Do we then make void the law through faith? Certainly not! On the contrary, we establish the law." Faith upholds and establishes God's Word. Jesus, through His faithful life, established the law. The true believer, when he admits he's a lawbreaker or a sinner, establishes the Word by faith. To therefore be driven to draw closer to God through a real relationship with Jesus, the true believer establishes God's Word as real and legitimate (not that it needs that) and falls under the authority of God and His Word. It's all connected when it's connected! There should never be mediocre living when a true believer's faith is strengthened by a real relationship with Jesus, and God's Word is honored and respected to the point where a believer's faith is strengthened. The logic of God's Word is brilliant!

Chapter 4 Verse 1-3

"What then shall we say that Abraham our father has found according to the flesh? For if Abraham was justified by works, he has something to boast about, but not before God. For what does the Scripture say? "Abraham believed God, and it was accounted to him for righteousness."

Abraham held a unique position in Jewish history. He was the man God would use to establish the Jewish nation and to be His witness to all nations of the world. God appeared to Abraham and challenged him to leave his home, his friends, his job, and his country (to radically change), and to do so without knowing the place he was going or the outcome of his obedience (This was a walk of faith, friends). God made two great promises to Abraham if he would follow God unquestionably. First, God would make him the father of a new nation, and second, all other nations would be blessed by his seed. The Bible records that Abraham did as God requested. But note something of great importance. It was not Abraham's keeping of any law that got him blessed, for the law of God had not even been written at this time. What pleased God was Abraham's willingness to trust God and be obedient to doing what God had said. Abraham simply believed in what God had promised. What's the big deal? Read on.

Many people think they become acceptable to God by doing the best they can. If they are reasonably good, they gain God's approval and acceptance.

But as we have seen, mankind is not justified by works, even great works. Mankind is justified by faith. Mankind is justified by believing in the promises of God and simply trusting Him. God uses Romans 4:1-8 to demonstrate the logic of these facts. In verses one through three, a person can logically see that one is not justified by works but by faith. No one, even Abraham, could be justified by works, or he or she could glory in himself or herself. But when you read the story of Abraham, you'll soon see how Abraham was a failure in many regards. Yet God still justified him because of his faith in God, in spite of his failures! It's not your good works that will get you to heaven; it is God's righteousness that will. It's not your failures that will keep you out of heaven. It isn't believing God's righteousness will cover your failures. You and I are failures because of sin, and sin will never be allowed in His presence. But our faith in His righteousness is all that He requires, and His righteousness is Jesus! Faith in Jesus will make a way. Now, it is true that true faith will generate good works, but good works will never generate righteousness; otherwise we could enter heaven bragging on how we got ourselves there. That's just never going to happen, friends. No matter what we may think. Why? Because God had laid it all out truthfully in a book we call Romans, and we know a little better now, don't we? And all of this is about to become very clear, and things are going to get very, very real as we continue on in our study of this great book.

Chapter 4 Verse 4-8

We need to take a moment and praise God. God will never turn from a person who realizes and confesses his or her ungodliness and wants to recognize God for who He is and what He has done. God will always welcome the truly repentant sinner. But before we finish praising God for the good stuff, let's also praise Him for the converse teaching of Scripture. Look, the person who refuses to confess and repent from his or her ungodliness is pronounced unjustifiable not because God has rejected him or her, but because he or she has rejected God. We can praise God for this because He has been truthful to us from the beginning. If we want to fight against Him, we need to realize our arms are far too short.

"Now to him who works, the wages are not counted as grace but as debt." The logic here is that work means debt. When a person works, someone owes him or her something. If a person could work his or her way into righteousness, then God would owe that person something; God would be in debt to that person. But God is completely self-sufficient and can never owe anyone anything. Therefore, people working their way to righteousness and God owing them a free ride is impossible.

"But to him who does not work but believes on Him who justifies the ungodly, his faith is accounted for righteousness." But for the person who believes in and on God by faith, God does the work! Or more accurately, He has done the work. The ungodly, the failures, the sinners, the outcast, all are justified because they understand the diagnosis, which is death due to sin, and the prognosis, separated from God for all eternity, but they also believe in God's promise of the cure: Jesus!

"Just as David also describes the blessedness of the man to whom God imputes righteousness apart from works: Blessed are those whose lawless deeds are forgiven, and whose sins are covered;Blessed is the man to whom the Lord shall not impute sin." Now the logic turns to the "blessed man." This person is clearly justified not by works but by faith. By his or her faith, God imputes or counts the person as now being made righteous. So the question is faith in what? Mankind's machinery? Humanity's technology? People's theories? How about humanism? Pluralism? Modernism? What about gravity? Physics? Politics? No! It is faith in the righteousness of Jesus! Jesus' righteousness is the only righteousness God recognizes and accepts. Our lawless deeds, the deeds that bar us from God now and forever, are forgiven if we, by faith, admit we are as God says we are, sinners, we repent from our sins, and we accept Jesus' sacrifice, death, burial, and resurrection and come to God with His righteousness.

Chapter 4 Verse 9-12

Let's continue with our study, but let's change the word "circumcision" to "covenant" because, well, that's what it represents, and it's a little easier to work with. I am sure you'll appreciate it.

"Does this blessedness then come upon the covenanted only, or upon the uncovenanted also? For we say that faith was accounted to Abraham for righteousness." God is telling us that Abraham was made righteous when he believed in God's promise, not when he was given the sign of the covenant. It was faith, not function that God honored. It still is. A person's baptism is meaningless to a person's salvation. It is the person's faith that matters. And it is the object of one's faith that matters. External or internal "signs" are meaningless. It's faith, plain and simple.

"How then was it accounted? While he was covenanted, or uncovenanted? Not while covenanted, but while uncovenanted." Here's the smoking gun: Abraham decided to follow God fourteen years before he decided to be circumcised. Therefore, Abraham is counted righteous years before he observed any ritual. It was his faith that God honored, not his religious observances. Faith moved Abraham out of spiritual mediocrity and placed him directly in the center of God's will. Faith will do the same thing for us. But don't be surprised if God asks us to do something or go somewhere.

"And he received the sign of covenant, a seal of the righteousness of the faith which he had while still uncovenanted, that he might be the father of all those who believe, though they are uncovenanted, that righteousness might be imputed to them also," Abraham received the sign of the covenant, but it was his faith in God's promises that God honored with His promises. In the New Testament age, the covenant is now baptism. But, just like in the Old Testament, the external sign of baptism means nothing concerning your salvation. You and I are saved by faith, not by outward acts or signs. Baptism is merely a sign that you have publicly identified with Jesus and have asked Him to be your Lord and Savior, not that you are just saved.

"and the father of covenant to those who not only are of the covenant, but who also walk in the steps of the faith which our father Abraham had while still uncovenanted." Abraham was chosen by God for two purposes. First, that he might be the "father" or originator of all believers regardless of rituals, and second, to help show all of us the steps to faith. It is important to be baptized, friends. It is biblical, and it is Christ honoring.

But the thief on the cross next to Jesus was never baptized, and yet Jesus promised Him eternal life. Why? Because of his new found faith in a soon to be crucified Jesus. It's faith, not functionality, which will get you home, as we will see in more detail in the next verses. And true faith always leads to good works. It leads to change and service. It leads to doing something for Jesus. It leads to conforming to His image.

Chapter 4 Verse 13-16

"For the promise that he would be the heir of the world was not to Abraham or to his seed through the law, but through the righteousness of faith." The promise is the world and all that is in it (more specifically salvation and heaven). The recipients are Abraham and his "seed" of believers that come after him. But the Old Testament Law had nothing to do with making one acceptable to inherit the promise. No, that came from the finished work at the Cross.

"For if those who are of the law are heirs, faith is made void and the promise made of no effect," The law demands perfection, and it can never be satisfied, because there are none righteous, no not one. Man is a lawbreaker as we have discussed. If the promise is dependent upon the law, we will never inherit the promise. If we can't inherit the promise, then what good is the promise? Is God that hateful to offer us a carrot we can never reach? Of course not. He offers us His truth upon which we can have faith.

"because the law brings about wrath; for where there is no law there is no transgression. The purpose of the law was threefold. First, the law points out our guilt, and we're all guilty of something. Second, the law puts us in bondage in trying to keep it. It's impossible to keep it though, so it's frustrating and causes anger and wrath. Third, the law makes us focus on the law and not on God. The problem with the law is it can only accuse; it cannot deliver. It can only point out our sin, but it can't do anything about it. It can show us where we failed, but it cannot show us how to keep from failing. It can condemn; it has no power to free. For that, we're going to need someone who can fulfill the law and show us the way. His name is Jesus.

"Therefore it is of faith that it might be according to grace, so that the promise might be a sure to all the seed, not only to those who are of the law, but also to those who are of the faith of Abraham, who is the father of us all." Now God gives us the argument for faith. Three facts are given. First, faith brings grace. When a person really believes in God and His promise, his or her faith in God brings forth His grace. God's grace is His acceptance of us in spite of our failings. The second point is faith makes the promise sure. When God is really honored and made the center of focus in one's life, that person can rest assured God will accept him and give him the promise of eternal life. Third, faith assures that the promise is for everyone. The promise is given to all, and faith activates it. Every person can believe and trust God and His Son Jesus by confessing their sins, turning from them, and having faith in what God says is true. Friends, mediocre living is not faith living; it is flesh living. And flesh living is deadly, it will never conform you into His image!

CHAPTER 4 VERSE 17-22

"(as it is written, "I have made you a father of many nations") in the presence of Him whom he believed—God, who gives life to the dead and calls those things which do not exist as though they did;" We are continuing to see truth in God's Word, as Scripture tells us God can and does give eternal life to the eternally separated from Him. Abraham believed in the living and true God, and his faith was in God. Look, there wasn't anything particularly special about Abraham. He just chose to not live a mediocre life. He chose to let his walk speak for itself in spite of the issues it might have brought him. And God honored him and his faith. God honors meaningful faith. God does not honor mediocre faith.

"who, contrary to hope, in hope believed, so that he became the father of many nations, according to what was spoken, So shall your descendants be." Notice Abraham's faith was based on what God said, not what he saw. God promised Abraham that if he would be faithful, God would bless him as the father of a mighty nation. Abraham did not even have a child at this point, and having one was going to be a real stretch because he and his

wife were way past child bearing years. The phrase "*contrary to hope, in hope believed*" means he knew his situation as being childless was hopeless, yet he believed God. That's faith, friends. Believing in what God has said in spite of the hopelessness of the situation from our perspective. It is believing that God's Word supersedes yours. You say you can't be forgiven? That's not what God says. You say you can't be saved because your sins are too grievous? That's not what God says. You say God could never love you because of what you've done? That's not what God says. You say mediocre Christian living is good enough? That's not what God says! And what God says supersedes everything else ever said.

"And not being weak in faith, he did not consider his own body, already dead (since he was about a hundred years old), and the deadness of Sarah's womb." They were too old to procreate, folks.

"He did not waver at the promise of God through unbelief, but was strengthened in faith, giving glory to God, 21 and being fully convinced that what He had promised He was also able to perform." But that didn't deter him from believing God's promise, no matter how absurd it might have seemed to him and his wife.

"And therefore "it was accounted to him for righteousness." It's not what you or I think, no matter what we base our thoughts upon. It's what God says that matters. It's all that matters. In spite of the absurdity of this elderly couple having a baby to start a nation, Abraham counted God as faithful and put his faith in Him. Because of that, God counted Abraham's faith in Him as righteousness. Who cares? No one if this is just a story about some old dude roaming the desert. But if it is a precursor to the Messiah, we better understand it. And it is, friends; it is.

Chapter 4 Verse 23-25

"Now it was not written for his sake alone that it was imputed to him, But also for us." Do you know why these true stories are recorded in Scripture for all eternity? Do you know why the Bible was written in the first place? It wasn't for profit or to satisfy idle curiosity. It wasn't to entertain us. It was

to lead us all to Jesus. All of the Bible, from Genesis to Revelation, has been given to us to answer our questions about who we are, why we exist, what went wrong, and how it can be made right again. The part that's wrong we own. The part that's right belongs to Jesus. There is no grey area here, friends. The story of Abraham's faith, while exhilarating as it is, is meaningless to me if that's all it's about. So what are the bigger issues here?

"It shall be imputed to us who believe in Him who raised up Jesus our Lord from the dead," God has just told us why. Four thousand years after the timeline in Abraham's story, a very special person was brought before man's law in a mock trial and sentenced to death. He was innocent, but willingly went to the cross to fulfill God's righteous requirement for justice against sin. Man declared Him guilty, but upon His death, God declared Him innocent, and like I said, God's Word supersedes man's word. He died for our sins, but had no sins of His own. He went to His death based on God's requirements for man's death, but upon His death, God said wait a minute. This Man was not guilty of sin. If the wages of sin are death, and this Man was innocent of sin, then He should be alive. God righted this wrong and resurrected this Man from the grave to prove once and for all this Man fulfilled the requirements of the law. In dying without sin, He has just made a way for a sinner like me to live. I just have to have faith in Jesus and what He has done. That's the bigger issue here. No offense to our friend Abraham, but it's not about him. It never has been about him or his life on this earth as incredible as it may have been. It's always been about the life, death, and resurrection of Jesus. It always will be. And no matter what we think or say, it's what God says that matters. And God says there's no other way to Him except Jesus.

"who was delivered up because of our offenses, and was raised because of our justification." I want you to provide the commentary for yourself here based on what you have been taught so far. This is one of the most powerful verses in all of Scripture. Do you see it? It will change mediocre living into a burning lifetime mobilization. Do you see it? It will change apathy into a holy applause. Do you see it? It will turn complacency into a lifelong commitment. Do you see it? Look at each powerful word and pray to see it.

Chapter 5 Verse 1-5

"Therefore, having been justified by faith, we have peace with God through our Lord Jesus Christ," We are now blessed beyond all imagination. We are now blessed beyond all recognition. Because of what God has done through His Word, His patriarchs, and far more importantly His Son, we now have the opportunity to return to Him in peace. We can now be justified, or looked upon as righteous. The enmity that existed at our birth as sinners and that continues to exist at our point of living because of sin has been dealt with at the Cross. But faith is the key, friends. And it boils down to this: Can we really trust Him and believe Him? If we can and do, we should ditch the mediocre living once and for all and devote our lives to serving Him as a true follower. We should happily and willfully allow the Spirit to conform us in His image. If we can't trust Him or believe Him, there's no hope. And friends, with Jesus there's hope. There's peace. There's abundant living, not mediocre living. God loves His Son so much that He honors any person who honors His Son by believing in Him. At some point, the person will start living a Christ-honoring life. And that is not mediocre. Believe in Him, repent, and be discipled so you may grow more like Him and watch what happens to your life!

"through whom also we have access by faith into this grace in which we stand, and rejoice in hope of the glory of God." Faith leads to grace. Grace is God's

method of bringing forth justification. But please understand that grace *is not unlimited leniency* when we have sinned. Grace is the enabling gift of God not to sin. Grace is power not to sin; not just pardon when we do. Understanding this is the difference between mediocrity and magnificence. It's the difference between believing you're just merely a sinner who still sins habitually but saved by grace compared to believing you're a true saint of God rescued not just from the penalty of sin but from the power of sin too. This is a concept we must learn if we're going to be conformed to His image. You and I must understand and believe this concept or the enemy will play us like a puppet.

"And not only that, but we also glory in tribulations, knowing that tribulation produces perseverance;" The world is a hard place, even for those saved for heaven. Your salvation will not insulate you from the hardness of this world, but it will deliver you from it at the appropriate time. Until then, there will be tribulations, or oppression, that we all must face. But we can receive and give glory in the face of the distress. In fact, if we handle ourselves biblically in the tribulations, we can learn to persevere. We learn to endure in Christ when we experience tribulations. It's one reason why God allows the tribulations in the first place.

"and perseverance, character; and character, hope" Perseverance builds character, or integrity and strength. When a believer endures the trials of life, the believer's character is made stronger. When a believer's character is made strong, hope endures forever. Do you see mediocrity here? No, you don't. Mediocrity happens when a person fails the perseverance test. I'm afraid there's a lot of mediocrity in Christian circles today because there's so much lack of integrity.

"Now hope does not disappoint, because the love of God has been poured out in our hearts by the Holy Spirit who was given to us." Note that the Holy Spirit has been given to us. Is He a mediocre being? Of course not. Has God given us an average Holy Spirit? Of course not.

The love of God is a gift too. There's a connection to both God's love and God's Spirit. God's Spirit dwells within the believer, so we could experience the continuous and unbroken experience of God's love during tribulation. This should make us strong, but if we're weak or mediocre, maybe there's an issue between us and the Holy Spirit. Intimacy with God is based on justification. Intimacy with God is never mediocre. If your "intimacy" with God is mediocre, something is wrong.

Chapter 5 Verse 6-8

"For when we were still without strength, in due time Christ died for the ungodly." These verses are simply phenomenal. This particular verse defines God's love for all people. As we have seen, there are no godly people according to God. We are all ungodly. You. Me. Us. Them. Everybody. God says here we were without strength, meaning we were worthless, helpless, destitute, and couldn't undo it. This is the situation we are all in outside of the blood of Jesus, and we can't help ourselves get better as we have studied. But it gets worse. We are also described as ungodly too, meaning profane and not like God. It boils down to God is perfect, and He can't let any imperfection into His presence. We are imperfect and can't make a way to Him. We're hopeless. And yet, in His amazing love, God would make the necessary sacrifice for anyone who would just know and accept truth and come to Him as He has instructed. God says in due time (during Jesus' life on earth) He (Jesus) would die for us even though we are ungodly. I want you to think about that for a minute. Let that sink in. Amazing doesn't describe it.

"For scarcely for a righteous man will one die; yet perhaps for a good man someone would even dare to die." God is using pure logic here. He's saying there may be someone, somewhere, at some time, that might die for someone who is worthy. But it's extremely rare. But Jesus, being godly, died for every person the world has ever known; and every one of them is ungodly. He died for murderers and ministers; for prostitutes and priests; for drug addicts and doctors; for the brilliant and criminally insane. It's something so unbelievable it has to be true because no one could make this stuff up. Why would they? This is true, friends. He died

for me; he died for you. That's love. I can't honestly say I understand the whys of it, but it's true nonetheless. I wouldn't die for you, and you wouldn't die for me. He died for both of us. He's worth learning about and following. He's worth drawing closer to and serving. He's just worth it, friends. And mediocrity isn't befitting a Savior like Jesus, and you and I know it. We might be fooled with all the lies thinking it is ok. But deep down, we know better. The only logical outcome for true followers is to be conformed to His image.

"But God demonstrates His own love toward us, in that while we were still sinners, Christ died for us." I'm not sure it can be explained any clearer, folks. The word "*demonstrates*" means "*to show; to prove; to exhibit.*" It is a present tense verb meaning God is always showing and proving His love to us. While we're all sinning, while we're all sinners, God constantly shows He loves us. Maybe we're not paying attention. Maybe we're too hardened to appreciate it. Maybe we're too brainwashed with the latest carnal ideas. But truth is still truth, and the truth is Jesus died for you and me. And He died before we were all clean and pretty. He died while we were nasty and filthy and worthless. And His death makes a way for us to be cleansed so we may be with Him and His Father forever. And I'm going to stop the mediocre, worldly living and begin to be the person He calls me to be. I'm going to praise Him all the days of my life. What about you?

Chapter 5 Verse 9-11

"Much more then, having now been justified by His blood, we shall be saved from wrath through Him." God sent Jesus to die for us. He gave up His only Son for you and me. Why would He do that? We did not deserve it. No, we deserve death because the wages or payment of sin is death, and we're all guilty, aren't we? The whole point to all of this is God will demonstrate wrath because of sin, ultimately letting us become eternally separated from Him if that is what we choose. But who in their right mind, knowing what we know now from these studies, would make a foolish decision like that? You can be saved from God's wrath and

eternal separation from Him by simply repenting from sin, believing God's Word, and accepting His offer. A person would have to be fooled or distracted to the point of mediocrity to not see the great opportunity he or she has to be reconciled to God and protected from His coming wrath. I mean, seriously.

"For if when we were enemies we were reconciled to God through the death of His Son, much more, having been reconciled, we shall be saved by His life." Some have tried to make this mean that we are enemies of God, but He is not our enemy. We are opposing Him, but He is not opposing us. We have enmity toward Him, but He has no enmity toward us, unless we say "no" to Jesus. Then He has no choice but to judge us under His wrath. The dividing line is the line between life and death, and from God's perspective, eternal life and death. To be with God and His love is described as paradise and speaks of eternal living. To be separated from God and His love is described as hell and speaks of eternal dying. We have a choice between the two, but we have to make the choice while alive in this realm. If the enemy can keep us in complacency and mediocrity, we won't be as motivated to choose conforming (or live it after we choose). Sometimes, it's too late, as death comes unexpectedly to many people. Please don't make that mistake. And if you choose life, why live like you're dead? If you are truly saved, why not live like it now and not wait until after you die? Look, our salvation is every bit as important here as it will be there. Why not practice it here too?

"And not only that, but we also rejoice in God through our Lord Jesus Christ, through whom we have now received the reconciliation." True, eternal joy is only found with Jesus, according to God's Word. It could be that it's found with money, but it's not. It could be that it's found with self-pleasures, but it's not. It could be that it's found with others, but it's not. And honestly, everyone knows that too, whether we admit it or not. Eternal joy can only be found in eternal life. Eternal life can only be found in the One who is alive forevermore. His name is Jesus. And He is absolutely amazing when you get to really know Him and live for Him now, not after you die. (And the way a person is reconciled to God is by the death of His Son.)

Chapter 5 Verse 12-14

Here we are at a crossroads. The next several verses will deal with how sin and death entered into the world, and how Jesus destroyed both. When you read these, make sure you're not distracted or tired. The enemy will love to get you off focused right about now.

"Therefore, just as through one man sin entered the world, and death through sin, and thus death spread to all men, because all sinned" Sin entered this world through one man, Adam. Eve was instrumental in getting Adam to sin, but God clearly holds Adam accountable. Men, you are held accountable to God for your walk, your discipleship, your spiritual growth, and teaching others the right things about God. You are accountable to God for your family and leading them to a closer walk with Jesus. Putting that responsibility on your wife or any other female is mediocre living at best and diabolic at worse. I'm just keeping it real, men. You are the one who will stand before God for you, your spouse, and your children.

Notice the Scripture says, *"death spread to all men, because all sinned."* We won't be held accountable for Adam's sin; Adam will be. We will be held accountable for our sin, because we have sinned. We have inherited Adam's infectious sinful bloodline and his sinful nature, like all children do with their parents. We are all personally responsible to God for what we have done, what we are doing, and what we will do. Adam started the whole dying process in the first place. So, since we're all dying from the moment we're born, what do we need more than anything else? A career? A new car? A bigger house? A European vacation? No, dying people need, more than anything else, a "life."

"(For until the law sin was in the world, but sin is not imputed when there is no law.)" This is a parenthetical insert from verse 13 to verse 17. The proof that we inherit Adam's nature is that sin and death existed even before God's law was given. God told Adam if he was disobedient (sinned) that he would surely die, yet he lived another 700 years afterwards. Was God confused? No. God was referring to Adam being separated from God, which is exactly what happened and is the best definition of death.

Since we inherited Adam's sin nature at our conception, when we are born, we are born alive physically but dead (separated) spiritually. And we are in the process of dying physically the minute we are born. But physical life isn't the issue. The spiritual life is.

"Nevertheless death reigned from Adam to Moses, even over those who had not sinned according to the likeness of the transgression of Adam, who is a type of Him who was to come." Notice sin is the cause of death, and Adam was the cause of sin, and every person who has ever lived or ever will live is under that curse. But the good news here is Christ is the cause of righteousness. Jesus is the cure to the curse. Adam was a failure; Jesus is the victor. It's just that clear and simple.

Chapter 5 Verse 15-17

"But the free gift is not like the offense. For if by the one man's offense many died, much more the grace of God and the gift by the grace of the one Man, Jesus Christ, abounded to many." The "free gift" may be free to us, but it was and is very costly to Jesus. Look, free doesn't mean worthless, friends; the value of this free gift cannot be measured. By Adam's failure (offense) many (all) die. Therefore, so much more the need for God's free gift of grace through the death, burial, and resurrection of Jesus. Jesus has reversed what Adam did. Jesus has made a way for all of us to live righteously and conquer death. Jesus was able to do much more "good" than Adam was to do "bad". And it's free to all who would simply surrender to it. Look, every other "religion" in the world requires its followers to do something to get to heaven. Christianity is the only religion where God says "It is done." He's done what needs to be done. There's nothing you can do to work your way to Him except accept what He has done.

"And the gift is not like that which came through the one who sinned. For the judgment which came from one offense resulted in condemnation, but the free gift which came from many offenses resulted in justification." Adam's sin (and yours and mine) bring condemnation. It's just the way it is, folks. But Jesus' gift brings justification. The person who truly has placed their eternity

in the hands of Jesus by faith in Him has been given the greatest gift imaginable. *And the person who has truly done this will become obedient to God and His Word.* The person will conform to the image of His Son. That person will want to live a just and sanctified life for the One who died for him and gives him eternal life. So, where does all this mediocre Christian living we see all around us come from? It comes from our old Adamic nature, which we allow to take over and rule us even though Jesus died to set us free from it. Now, does that make any sense to you? Me either. So here's the deal. If we're living a mediocre Christian life, either our old nature hasn't been crucified with Christ (we're still unsaved) or we're living so far from Him we're allowing the old way of living to take precedence (we're backslidden). That makes sense. But it's so far off what God requires and wants, it's sad to even think about it, much less write about it.

"For if by the one man's offense death reigned through the one, much more those who receive abundance of grace and of the gift of righteousness will reign in life through the One, Jesus Christ.)" Adam's sin brought the reign of death; Jesus' gift brought the reign of life. Living under the influence of sin is deadly living, and it manifests itself at first with mediocrity. Living under the influence of Jesus is lively living, and it manifests itself with victory. Do you see this in the lives of Christians today? Do you see it in your life?

Chapter 5 Verse 19-21

Chapter 5 is full of hallelujah moments. But living in sin has a way of dulling our senses to all of it. When our senses are dulled to God's truths due to our sinful living, the best we have to offer is mediocrity. It's a shame too because God is worthy of so much more! When will we all say no to mediocrity and yes to excellence? By now, we all know a truly saved person will be filled with excellence, not mediocrity. How can mediocrity live in the palace of excellence? It can't.

"For as by one man's disobedience many were made sinners, so also by one Man's obedience many will be made righteous." The conclusion to this

chapter is one of the most instructive and striking passages in the entire Bible. It includes three points. First, Adam's disobedience made many (all men, vs.12&18) sinners, but Christ's obedience made many (all who would repent and believe) righteous. He was and is the Ideal Righteousness, and as such, His righteousness overcomes sin. Only Jesus' righteousness can withstand God's wrath and scrutiny. Anyone who will so honor God's Son by believing and trusting in Him, God will honor by counting his or her faith as the righteousness of Christ. But note: a person must really believe; he must truly believe; he must have the kind of faith that trusts Jesus fully, even to the point of being changed dramatically and living a new life because of this change. If there's no change in a person's life, mediocrity will set in and stay (or worse). If mediocrity is present in a Christian's life, is it possible there's been no change? And if there's been no change, is it possible there's really no Jesus in the person's life? I think it is very possible. By now, you should too. And if someone claims to be a true follower, yet they don't follow, what is their explanation? It just doesn't work, does it?

"Moreover the law entered that the offense might abound. But where sin abounded, grace abounded much more," Second, the law was given to point out and magnify sin, so we could all see the need for Jesus. The law is a good thing in that it points us to the truth about ourselves that we need a Savior. In seeing Jesus, we see God's answer to His own law and us lawbreakers; His magnificent free gift of grace. God's grace is far more powerful and effective than any sin or sins, no matter how magnified the sins are. God's grace can forgive any sin and any sinner. And when one understands grace better, one begins to understand the hurtfulness of mediocrity and living a life of apathy towards God, His church, and His people. Knowing this now, has anyone been fooled into thinking being an "average" Christian is good enough? Do we now see how the devil has fooled us? I certainly hope so.

"so that as sin reigned in death, even so grace might reign through righteousness to eternal life through Jesus Christ our Lord." Third, sin reigned to death, but God's grace reigned to eternal life. And the source of that is Jesus. But notice it says Jesus Christ *our Lord*. If He's your Lord, you'll follow

Him and obey Him daily. If He's your Lord, you will serve Him gladly. If He's your Lord, you will worship Him corporately with other believers in spirit and in truth. Imagine a church worship service full of truly born again people worshipping the Lord magnificently instead of mediocrely. It would be awesome, wouldn't it? But if He's just your "get out of hell free card," you've missed the entire point of it all, and mediocre worship and living will be your destiny.

Chapter 6 Verse 1

We are about to study theological truths in this chapter that, if we can fully understand and surrender to them, they will radically change our lives. I mean *radically.* These truths will penetrate the darkest mediocrity and free us from the shackles of spiritual apathy. They will allow complacency to fall off of us like the joy robbing weight it is. But be warned: if you master these truths, you will be changed forever. Yes, forever. Proceed at your own risk.

"*What shall we say then? Shall we continue in sin that grace may abound?*" The believer who is justified (whose faith is counted as righteousness) is to let his or her righteousness work holiness, not naughtiness. The believer is to live a holy life and become a servant of righteousness. In other words, a genuinely saved person cannot and will not abuse the mercy of God. He cannot habitually walk in sin. And all the excuses in the world won't cut it, including the excuse as described in this verse. People were thinking if God gets glory for His grace forgiving sin, then the more sin they committed, the greater glory God would receive. This is insanity, but the people actually thought this, and Paul was teaching them how insane this was. Today, we hear things like "well, God loves me, so I'm okay or "Well, sin is sin, so my sin is no different than your sin, and God is love and He will always forgive me" or "You should only speak love to people" and the excuses go on and on. Look, if you are a true, born-again believer in Jesus, you must know the truth and your position and responsibility in Christ. Positionally, you and I are in Christ Jesus and He is in us. Can Jesus sin? No. Can Jesus in you sin? No. Can you sin if Jesus is in you? Yes, but why would you? Your responsibility is to grow up and not sin. Look, this truth will absolutely revolutionize your life. You and I, as true believers, must not walk in habitual sin, or should we make excuses when we do. Jesus didn't. This isn't my opinion; this is biblical fact based on theological truth. If a person thinks he can live any way he wants, he's either not truly saved, or he's making carnal excuses, and his or her theology is weak, superficial, and egocentric. Please hear my heart on this. I struggle too. But I know enough of God's Word now that I know it's not how I feel or think, but it's what He says that's important. And God says you and I cannot, must not, should not sin and make excuses that it's okay to do so while assuming His grace will continue to cover us. This is not biblical. Grace does not give a person free reign to sin. It just doesn't, friends. Grace is not our green light to live how we please.

Look, grace isn't supposed to be the means by which we get around the rules; it is actually the means by which we can now, from the heart, strive to obey God with increasing success. Paul's desire was to make it crystal clear that in no way could anyone, anywhere, at any time, ever be justified by "keeping the rules." We are utterly unable to obey God perfectly and attain the righteousness we need. We can only be made right with God by faith in the redemptive work of Christ. That's it. However, Paul also makes it crystal clear that God's moral commands are not something we are "free" from or can toss to the side because we are now under grace. The moral commands are still there. The Holy Spirit has been unleashed from Heaven and poured into the hearts of all who are justified by Jesus. He creates desire in us and therefore enables us to walk in the commands of God and sin no more.

Stop the madness with all the excuses which lead to a mediocre walk with Jesus. Mature in your walk with Jesus by deepening your knowledge of His truth. Make the commitment to know the truth; then live it. It will radically change your life and the life of many other people. And we all need some change in our lives.

Chapter 6 Verse 2

"What shall we say then? Shall we continue in sin that grace may abound? 2 God Forbid! How shall we who died to sin live any longer in it?" Paul is saying, in today's vernacular, "If you think you can sin and call on God to simply forgive you over and over, *you have lost your mind!"* For heaven's sake no. Here's the question you and I must answer once and for all, and if we understand the answer, we will be changed forever. The question is: how can we live in sin if we're dead to it? If we're dead to something, how can that something control our life? What does death have to do with life? What does deadness have to do with living? What does sin have to do with a born-again believer? Nothing. So, the question is: if a person is dead to sin, how can that person sin? And it is the most important question of our lives. You must think about this. Yes, as long as you're alive in this world you can sin, but why would you want to if you're dead to it?

Can we, as true believers, as mature followers of Christ, finally understand that our union with Jesus Christ is completely opposed to a life of continuing sin? Look, our identification with Christ in His death and resurrection frees us from slavery to sin and allows us to walk in newness of life. God knows that we're prone to forget our new position in Christ (which is why we need to be in His Word and in His Church learning as much as possible) which is the foundation for holy living. And so he hammers it home in these verses. Living in light of our union with Christ is the key to overcoming sin, and overcoming sin is why Jesus came and lives in you in the first place. Not to let you sin and get away with it, but to live holy, as He is holy. This concept is life changing and world altering, friends.

Is this too good to be true? I admit it is both good and true. Still struggling? Ok, let's look at it this way: if you have truly been saved, you shouldn't live in sin as you used to live because you aren't the same person that you used to be. Before, you were in Adam. Now, you are in Christ. In Adam, you were dead *in* sin. In Christ, you are dead *to* sin and alive to God (I'm going to prove this in the coming verses). So the key to breaking mediocre living is to believe and act on the basis of your new identity, not your old identity. This is strong, biblical theology, folks, and it explains why so many are living mediocre lives and not conforming to His image. We don't really know or fully understand the truth. The truth is what the Bible says is true. And this is what the Bible says about the believer. But the believer must know truth; he must understand truth, and he must surrender to truth, or life will be boring and mediocre and not much different than those who aren't saved. Then why accept Jesus' offer of salvation in the first place? So you can go to heaven? What about today? What good does having Jesus do for you today? He keeps you from sinning if you let Him. And if more Christians lived like this, we'd have more heaven on earth! More heaven on earth, and more people wanting some of it.

Chapter 6:3-4

"Or do you not know that as many of us as were baptized into Christ Jesus were baptized into His death?" After God lowered the boom on us in the last couple of verses, he asks a very pertinent question that uncovers the reason why so many of us live mediocre lives. We truly don't know. Know what? We don't know or understand that if we have accepted Jesus as our Lord and Savior, we are, from God's perspective, dead! Dead? Yep, Dead. Dead to sin. How? Well, if Christ died for our sins, and if we have been baptized into Christ's death, then we have died to sin. It should now be impossible for a true believer to sin. But I still sin, you say? Well, why? Either we haven't truly accepted Jesus as our Lord and Savior, or we don't fully understand what has happened to us, or we just don't care. Any of those options will lead us to live mediocre spiritual lives and very carnal or fleshly physical lives. I've just described the average Christian in America, in my opinion. Can we never sin? Can we live perfectly now? We will all struggle with sin until our glorification, but we can purposely live a sinless life as we conform to His image and seek repentance and forgiveness when we occasionally do sin. Is that truly us?

"Therefore we were buried with Him through baptism into death, that just as Christ was raised from the dead by the glory of the Father, even so we also should walk in newness of life." Could it be any clearer? If you truly have been saved, you should be walking in the newness of life. What does walking in the newness of life look like? It looks like a new person. It looks like less sin and more holiness. It looks like honoring Christ with who we are and what we do rather than honoring this world and our old habits. Does that describe you? I hope it does because if it doesn't, you may be in trouble. How can you walk in the newness of life? Read on.

You must experience the death of Christ if you endeavor to walk in the newness of life. If you have made a true profession of faith in Jesus, from God's perspective you were the one buried into death. The new you who has been resurrected to walk in the newness of life is not the original you, (the one who was buried in Christ), it is now Christ in you.

We Christians are too simple as we try to make things too complicated. Our thinking and our understanding are so basic and mediocre. We even understand the Bible according to our natural mentality because we are still governed by our natural concepts, all of which lead to mediocre living.

I'm going to leave you with this thought: Walking in the newness of life is not possible if we have not been buried with Christ (salvation) and if we do not remain in death (daily surrender to Christ). If we come out of death (start sinning again), how can we walk in the newness of life? It is impossible. It's a very simple concept, but we're going to have to think about it.

Chapter 6 Verse 5-6

"For if we have been united together in the likeness of His death, certainly we also shall be in the likeness of His resurrection," The key word in this verse is "if". Here's the logic of my previous statement: If we have been united together in the likeness of His death (if we've truly been saved), we will walk in the newness of life (we shall be in the likeness of His newness

of life, His resurrection). Do you see this incredible truth? If a person is really saved, the person will live a resurrected life. A resurrected life is not a mediocre life. It is a righteous life. It is a holy life. It is a changed life. It is a conformed to His image life. A life not of excuses, but of empowerment. When a Christian lives in habitual sin and says it's okay because God loves them, they are not living biblically. When a Christian lives in habitual sin and says it's none of your business, they are fooled. If a Christian lives in habitual sin and proclaims they are alright with God, they are deceived. I pray you see this with me, because it is biblical as the next verse points out.

"knowing this, that our old man was crucified with Him, that the body of sin might be done away with, that we should no longer be slaves of sin." Our "*old man*" is who we used to be before we were saved. The Bible is crystal clear that who we use to be has been crucified with Christ upon our legitimate profession of faith. If our profession of faith was legitimate, then the sin we used to do in our "old self" must not be able to be done. Why? So we could be servants of Jesus and not slaves of sin. Friend, you can't serve two masters. You can't legitimately claim you're a follower of Jesus and not follow Him. You can't legitimately claim you're a doer of the Word and not do it. You can't claim you're a born again believer if you never live as a born again believer. You cannot sin habitually and say God is okay with it. God clearly says He is not okay with it, and He tells us up front that kind of living *does not* impress Him, and He has issues with it. Look, we must learn the truth and stop the madness.

Chapter 6 Verse 7-8

"*For he who has died has been freed from sin.*" Buckle up, friends. Here's where truth meets mediocrity, and we're going to have to make a decision and take a stand because doing nothing is in actuality, doing both. If you are a true believer in Jesus Christ, you have died with Him at Calvary from God's perspective. God places you "in Christ" and here "in His death." The old you was crucified with Christ. Your sin nature, the old you, was placed on the cross when your faith in Jesus was legitimate and your confession and profession was real. If it wasn't real or just emotional, it may have never happened. It didn't happen to me the first time I said I was saved. I was lost, but I'd argue the horns off a goat that I was saved because I went down the aisle at church, spoke up, and got baptized. Had I died during the years following, I would have gone to hell, maybe kicking and screaming, but I would have gone. My profession was verbal and intellectual. But Jesus was not my Lord nor had I changed. I was not free from anything, but I thought I was saved. My life was mediocre at best. Sound familiar?

Look, in the physical world, we are born, and then we die. In the spiritual world, we must die, then we are born (here in this world we call it "born-again"). How is this possible? We must die protected by someone who has defeated death. (There's only one person who died and lives and never will die again. That's Jesus. There's only one person who has been born, died, and lives again, and that is Jesus and now the one who is born again *in* Jesus.) If you are truly saved, you don't just get to heaven one day as you keep sinning while here on earth. You are given a new nature immediately for this world, not the next. You are free from sin now, not when you get to heaven. This concept is a game changer, friends.

"Now if we died with Christ, we believe that we shall also live with Him," Here's the Christian theology in a nutshell. If we are saved, we are dead to sin and alive *in* Christ. Period. End of report. Excuses are just words and actions we use to mask the lies. Mediocrity is just a by-product of sin and death. It's honestly just that simple. But I will never be perfect, you say? God addresses that too in the coming chapters. But for now, remember this: God doesn't require perfection, but He does require obedience. Mediocrity undermines obedience and settles for second or third best, or worse. You and I are called to be obedient to God and His Word. We are called to conform to His image. When we do that, perfection starts to creep in, and mediocrity starts to diminish.

If you are alive in Jesus Christ, can you habitually sin and be okay with it? Well, would Jesus habitually sin and be okay with it? No. Then how can you or I be in Him and be okay with it?

He died a horrible death to put an end to sin and its effect on people. Why would He live in mediocrity then? He wouldn't. And neither should we. The question we must be asking ourselves is: Am I truly saved? We need to be deadly serious about it too. Does your life reflect the life of Jesus, or your sins? Are you being conformed to His image, or are you just reflecting the world?

CHAPTER 6 VERSE 9-10

"*knowing that Christ, having been raised from the dead, dies no more. Death no longer has dominion over Him.*" We as Christians believe we shall live with Jesus because we know and trust the truth of God's Word. The key to breaking through the mediocre life is to believe, know, and trust that Jesus was resurrected. The resurrection of Jesus Christ is the apex of Christian theology and thought. If Jesus is still dead, be happy you've reached mediocrity. But if He's alive, you and I are in trouble if we're content with mediocrity.

If Jesus, who had no sin, died for sin, (because the penalty of sin is death), then at some point God must have concluded He didn't deserve to die. Yet He did die. Something glorious was happening! At His death, Jesus was separated from God the Father (which is the definition of death, remember?) Why would Jesus do this? So you and I wouldn't have to be separated. So, Jesus paid a penalty He didn't owe, and His payment was so incredibly valuable there's enough payment for everyone who will simply trust and obey. This is amazingly the opposite of mediocrity. Anyways, God realized the payment was made, but the One doing the payment was not in debt. So He offers the payment to those who are in debt while raising the One who paid the debt to everlasting life as the first of many. There's no god like God and nobody like Jesus, my friend. And to live a life of sin outside of the incredible life He offers is ridiculous. I am sure you agree.

"For the death that He died, He died to sin once for all; but the life that He lives, He lives to God." We're faced with another decision at this point. When Jesus died, He rose to new life by the power of God. God's holy justice

had been met. God was satisfied with what Jesus offered. It was done. Now, at this point, Jesus could have done anything. He could have relaxed and gone on vacation. He could have gotten with some friends and gone partying. He could have turned His back on "believers" and the church. He could have gone off in solitude and led a hermit's life. But He chose to live for God. And He did it openly, publicly, and unashamedly. Why? Because the eternal life God gives is worth putting everything else off at the curb. Jesus knew the truth. He was and is the truth. And Jesus lived His life to God.

If a person is truly saved, and they want to be in the closest relationship they can be in with God, and they want to be biblical, then they must live their life to God. The person must understand who they are in Christ, what has happened to them (they have died to sin), and what the future holds for them (they are alive in Christ right now, not just when they get to heaven).

Because of what God has done to, for, and through a believer, a believer should and could live their life as excellent, exceptional, distinctive, distinguished, extraordinary, incomparable, superb, superior, unexcelled, unrivaled, unsurpassed, different, great, outstanding, peculiar, remarkable and/or unusual, but never mediocre.

Chapter 6 Verse 11-12

"Likewise you also, reckon yourselves to be dead indeed to sin, but alive to God in Christ Jesus our Lord." If it happened to Jesus, and you are now in Jesus, then it happened to you too. God says "*reckon yourselves*" to be dead to sin and alive to God. The word "*reckon*" means "*to calculate.*: It means "*to add it all up logically and come up with an answer.*" God is calling us out, friends. He is saying stop the madness and "do" the math. If two plus two equal blue elephants in your world, you've got issues. If two plus two equal twenty-two, you're just as bad off. The truth is two plus two must always equal four, or all of us are in trouble. If you and Jesus are together, then God is saying the only possible logical outcome is you are dead to sin and alive to God. If that is so, then your life will eventually

start to show this logic in how you live and behave, and at some point mediocrity will be replaced with zeal. Conversely, if our lives do not demonstrate these changes and zeal, then maybe the equation is one minus one is zero.

Look, if a person is in daily sin, in spite of any profession of faith, they are separated from the daily activity of God in their life. If they are in Jesus and not willfully and habitually sinning, and repenting when they do, they are in a daily relationship with God. Here's the bottom line: true believers are in principle dead to sin and alive to Christ, therefore this must become the abiding conviction of their hearts and minds, the take-off point for all their thinking, planning, rejoicing, speaking, and doing. They must constantly bear in mind that they are no longer what they used to be. Their lives from day to day must show that they have not forgotten this. This must be done, for a true Christian must walk in truth daily, as Jesus did (and does). The concept that you can live and act in any manner whatsoever and God is okay with it has never been biblical nor ever will be. What happens when a person makes a profession of faith and remains in sin for a period of time? Mediocre living, and that is neither biblical nor Christ honoring. And God will not bless that.

"Therefore do not let sin reign in your mortal body, that you should obey it in its lusts." Because of all that has been spoken by God in His Word, God is telling us what's up. Need a reason to stop sinning? How about this verse? Because of the earlier verses, this verse sums it all up and says because of what Jesus has done and is doing, we should never allow sin to take hold of us. The word "*reign*" means "*to influence or control.*" God is saying, for the true born again believer, sin (to violate God's Word) must never control or influence them. We should be Spirit led, not sin led. We *must* be Spirit led and not sin led. Otherwise, what good is having the Holy Spirit in the first place? Who in their right mind, when faced with the truth, would continue to live in sin knowing God's position on it? Seemingly most of America, (and the world), that's who. It's sad, isn't it?

If the believer is to fully live out his or her new life in Christ, he or she must begin by knowing he or she is not what he or she used to be. Once the believer knows the foundational truths about his or her death, burial, and resurrection with Christ, and his or her victory over the penalty and power of sin, he is well on his or her way to victory in the Christian life. The true believer has been resurrected to new life, and therefore, has the confidence to strip away his or her grave clothes and live victoriously, not mediocrely. But the key words are "true believer."

Chapter 6 Verse 13-14

"And do not present your members as instruments of unrighteousness to sin." Your "*members*" mean "*your body parts.*" Your ears, lips, eyes, hands, mind, and so forth. The idea is very practical: You have eyes, but don't look at sinful things. You have ears, but don't listen to sinful things. The teaching is do not use your body to sin, and do not sin as it will affect your body. The crucial challenge and expectation for Christians is to live righteously. We are called to new life and to live that new life righteously, not sinfully. At our true conversion, God gives us His Holy Spirit to lead us to righteousness. If we're "saved" but we are still okay or complacent with living un-righteously, something is wrong. Something is bad wrong. Something is biblically wrong. There is no way we as Christians can justify unrighteousness or sin. If we're doing so, we are wrong, plain and simple. And if we're wrong, we're not following Jesus. And if we're not following Jesus, who are we following?

Friends, what good does having a relationship with Jesus do if it does no good? Look, righteous living is the key to victorious living. Unrighteous living leads to mediocre living. Do you see this? This is the reason our country is deteriorating from the inside out. It's the reason why, as a country, we are showing signs of spiritual decay. It's the reason why the majority of churches are dying. As Christians, we should live, act, and think differently from the world. It is not always easy, but it is possible. In Romans 6, we see the call to godly living.

"but present yourselves to God as being alive from the dead" If you are truly saved, you are alive to God and dead to sin. If so, present yourself to God as alive. Not half-dead (mediocre) or mostly dead (apathetic). If you're saved, you're alive. Why seem dead? That's just crazy, right?

Look, no one wants to be controlled. We want to be our own person and in full control of our own destiny. But stop and think about a person controlled by sin. He may live in fear of being discovered. He may surrender his or her health, wealth, and even his or her family for one more sin. He may literally gamble his or her life away committing sins. Once in place, sin is a slavish master and does not easily release those caught in its grip. As Paul says, sin will "make you obey its passions." For all of the harm and in spite of all of the pain we just keep going back again and again. Why? Because we can't possibly know the truth of who we are in Christ and what we have.

It would be nice if we could just blame the devil and walk away without any responsibility for our sin. That is not possible. The apostle says we have a choice. We may offer ourselves to sin or to God, but one way or another we choose.

"For sin shall not have dominion over you, for you are not under law but under grace," A true follower of Jesus will be free from sin. He will have supernatural power to break free from sinful living patterns. Sin will not have "dominion" or power over him. Yes, he may be tempted; he may succumb occasionally out of fleshly weakness, but ongoing, habitual sin will be a thing of the past with the true believer. Praise Jesus! That's not you, you say? It wasn't me either, until I started getting serious about knowing God and His Word and the truth therein. If faith is the victory, truth is the key, friends.

Chapter 6 Verse 15-16

"What then? shall we sin, because we are not under the law, but under grace? God forbid." Look, if we truly love our Lord and Savior then it will be our heart's desire to obey and glorify Him, not our flesh. Surely that makes sense.

This then is the path, the means, by which we can live in this freedom. It will never happen in a legalistic, performance-oriented Christian life. It will happen as we live not under law but under grace. This is another way to describe the radical change in the life of someone who is born again. For the Jewish person of Paul's day, living life under the law was everything. The law was the way to God's approval and eternal life. Now, Paul shows that in light of the New Covenant, we are not under law but under grace. His work in our life has changed everything, including us. Paul has answered his question from Romans 6:1. Why don't we just continue in habitual sin so grace may abound? Because when we are saved, when our sins are forgiven, and God's grace is extended to us, we are radically changed. The old man is dead, and the new man lives. This is the exact opposite of mediocrity. Do you see it? Look, in light of these remarkable changes, it is utterly incompatible for a new creation in Jesus to be comfortable in habitual sin. A state of sin can only be temporary for the Christian. I heard it said that, "The grace that does not change my life will not save my soul." You must think seriously about this.

"Know ye not, that to whom ye yield yourselves servants to obey, his servants ye are to whom ye obey; whether of sin unto death, or of obedience unto righteousness?" Whatever you present yourself to obey, you become its slave. For example, if I obey my appetite constantly, I am a slave to it. If I obey the school bully constantly, I become his slave. If I obey a political party constantly, I become its slave. If I obey the world constantly, I become its slave. If I obey my flesh constantly, I become its slave. So we have a choice in our slavery: sin leading to death or obedience leading to righteousness. We can choose sin leading to mediocrity and eventually death, or righteousness leading to victory over sin and magnificence. But we must choose. And we must choose daily.

God has brilliantly freed us from our slavery to sin, and because of that the point is clear: You put your faith in God and His Word, and you are set free. Now live every day consistent with that freedom. As was seen earlier in Romans 6, we can be legally free and still choose to live like a prisoner. Paul has a simple command and encouragement for the Christian: be what you are.

Hypocrisy is the contrivance of a false appearance of virtue or goodness, while concealing real character or inclinations. A hypocrite is someone who says one thing but does another. It is trying to be something you're not. Well, trying not to be something you are is just as bad. If you truly are a Christian, but you don't live and act like one, this is the height of hypocrisy. Is God okay with this? Will He bless this? Is He overlooking this? Will He invest time and resources in a person like this? What do you think?

Chapter 6 Verse 17-18

"But God be thanked, that ye were the servants of sin, but ye have obeyed from the heart that form of doctrine which was delivered you." A very crucial point for us to understand and cope with is this: one either yields to sin or one yields to God. This does not mean a person becomes sinless and perfect. It means the person does not plan to sin. It means the person fights against the flesh in a daily effort to please God by not sinning. It means the person diligently seeks to make the Lord the Master of his or her life. It means the person stops using excuses to live mediocre lives and starts allowing his or her life to be conformed to the image of His Son.

This verse reminds us of a great and deep theological truth. As a believer, you have chosen righteousness. Note the stated fact: we used to be the servants of sin. Before our salvation, we used to yield to sin, but now believers have obeyed the doctrine of God from the heart. What this is saying is that the true born again believer has heard the truth from God's Word, and they have become spiritually alive in this truth to the point where it has changed their lives from sinner to saint. This is the epitome of conforming to His image.

Do you remember the phrase, "I'm just a sinner saved by grace?" It's a wonderful and truthful phrase, and I am so very thankful it's true. But it only tells half of the story. If a person clings to only this, they now have the excuse they need to live an ordinary and mediocre life. I may try hard to not sin, but if I do, well, I'm just a sinner saved by grace. Do you see how easy it is to compromise and brush off sin and make a mockery out of God's grace? Instead of being broken over sin, repenting from it, asking God for His forgiveness, and changing our ways, we just throw out the old I'm just a sinner, so what do you really expect; but because of God's grace. I'm okay. As we have seen, we are not okay. The better phrase for Christians is "I used to be a sinner, but by God's grace I am now a saint of almighty God. I will live according to who and what I truly am now." Isn't that a much better mindset? And it's gloriously true. How? Well, continue reading.

"Being then made free from sin, ye became the servants of righteousness." God now sees the true believer as being "re-born" and righteous. He sees the true believer as not just a former sinner who has gone through some multi-step program to get their act together. He sees the true believer as righteous and not sinful. He sees the true believer as saints and not sinners. I have to stop to praise Jesus for a few moments right now.

I'm back. Let me share with you something very significant. The true believer will become the servant of righteousness now. There is no way a true believer could ever serve habitual sin again, not if he has been justified, not if he has really come to know God's love revealed in the Lord Jesus Christ. Once he knows God's deep truths, he is driven to serve God in appreciation for what God has done for him in Christ. He will be spirit driven to be the servant of God by living righteously and godly in this world. The degree in which a believer grasps the truth of God in justification is the degree to which he is driven to serve God and live righteously. This is just factual, biblical truth, friends.

You're not living very righteously? Is your life worldlier than it is biblical? Has sin become the norm because, after all, everyone is doing it, including mediocre "Christians"? You say you're just a sinner saved by grace as you continue on in sin? I did too. I was just a sinner saved by grace until I got serious about understanding God's rescue for me. I still struggle with sin. But Jesus has a firm grip on me, and I have a firm grip on His Word. Sin is not my master. And I wouldn't go back to my earlier life for all the gold in Ft. Knox. Look, it's okay to repent and be set free right now. Turn to Jesus and start living like a saint of God.

Chapter 6 Verse 19

"I speak in human terms because of the weakness of your flesh. For just as you presented your members as slaves of uncleanness, and of lawlessness leading to more lawlessness, so now present your members as slaves of righteousness for holiness." Oh boy, here we go, friends. We are being called out. God is calling all believers out. And this is what He is saying: Get out of spiritual mediocrity and apathy and conform to the image of my Son! What are we to do? Conform to the image of His Son and serve God with the same fervor that we served sin. Hang on; this is going to get bumpy.

When we were lost, our sins resulted in more and more sin. As unbelievers, we quickly found out that sin just increased and increased. It is unstoppable and uncontrollable. Sin led to more sin, no matter what the sin was. Smoking a few cigarettes led to multiple packs a day. Drinking a beer or two led to blacking out. Eating a burger and fries led to supersizing the portions. Looking at a few pictures of bikini clad women led to hard core pornography. Being somewhat critical led to criticizing everything imaginable. A few "colorful" words led to talking profanity like a pro. A few little white lies led to lying like a rug. A few little secrets shared with a close friend led to being the biggest gossip in town. You get the picture. Fill in whatever sin you want. The point is we all know this is true, and there's nothing we can do to control it. It controls us. We can't break the chains of sin. But Jesus can, and He will. If you are a true born-again believer, your chains have been broken. If you want to live mediocre by carrying the broken chains with you now, that's up to you. But wouldn't letting them go be so much better? God is saying in this verse: let the chains go Christian. Live for Jesus the same way you lived for sin. Be passionate for God the same way you became passionate for sin. Start with a little Jesus if you must, but at some point get all you can get. True followers of Jesus will serve Him with the same fervor they served sin.

"For when you were slaves of sin, you were free in regard to righteousness." I'd rather be a slave to Jesus than a slave to sin. I'd rather be "intoxicated"

with His Spirit than drunk on man's spirits. I'd rather be hearing His truth in my life than spreading half-truths all over town. I'd rather speak His Word than profane words. I'd rather see Jesus in all His glory as recorded in Scripture than see nakedness as recorded in pornography. I bet you would too. When I was lost, I was a slave to sin and shouldn't expect much more than that life of slavery. But when I became truly saved, I hated those things because for the first time in my life I was truly set free from those things, and I saw them for what they really were. Well. It's time to praise Jesus again. I'll be right back.

"What fruit did you have then in the things of which you are now ashamed? For the end of those things is death. In the earlier verse, we needed to do something. Here, we need to question something. And the question is what fruit is there in our sin? The only true fruit, if we are brutally honest with ourselves, is shame. We can say we're just sinners saved by grace and put a Band-Aid on a mortal wound, but the truth is we should be ashamed. Unfortunately, the world glorifies sin so much now that few people feel shame anymore. Sad, huh?

The Bible declares that the on-going result of sin is shame, but the end-result is death, or separation from God. If one is separated from God, there's really no hope. The choice is ours: follow the world and sin to shame and death, or follow the Lord and His Word to truth and life.

Chapter 6 Verse 22-23

"But now having been set free from sin" Remember, Paul is talking to believers in Rome. These verses are for true believers. "*But now*" means since you are saved now, you are set free from sin. God's love for us, through the death of Jesus, has set us free from that which controlled us and brought us shame. We were prisoners in sin's prison, yet the Governor has given us a pardon and a stay of execution. The iron bars are opened, and we are free to leave and live. Who in their right mind would stay incarcerated? Who in their right mind would grab the iron bars and shut them back? No one. We would get out of there and never

go back. So why would we accept mediocrity in our walk with the One who has set us free? We wouldn't if we truly knew the truth.

"and having become slaves of God," Unless you're a king or a queen somewhere, you've got to serve someone. Might as well be the One who has paid your penalty and set you free. Sin sure hasn't set you free and won't. The flesh and the world haven't set you free and won't. The devil hasn't and won't. If you're going to serve someone, why not serve Jesus who loves you enough to die for you and has? The devil hasn't and won't. No need to serve him or his kingdom anymore.

"you have your fruit to holiness," The person who has made the decision to trust Jesus and follow Him is the person who will begin to have the fruit of holiness. Their lives will change. Their conversations will change. Their attitudes will change. Their outlook will change. Their convictions will change. Their life will change. Mediocrity is not a fruit of holiness. Their normal life will be replaced with above normal living. Their natural self will be replaced with the supernatural Jesus. And Jesus is not mediocre, friends. He is the first-fruit of holiness. Without Jesus, you're in sin's prison and may not even know it.

"and the end, everlasting life." A spiritually fruitful life is a great indicator that a person will live an everlasting life with Jesus in eternity. A spiritually unfruitful life is a great indicator that a person will live eternally in sin's prison. We call it Hell. It is the one place where God will not be. And that's the true definition of Hell; where God is not.

"For the wages of sin is death, but the gift of God is eternal life in Christ Jesus our Lord," The payment (notice the word wages is plural, it keeps costing us) of sin (notice the word is singular; one sin is all it takes) is eternal separation from God. Why? Because sin is acting against God; it strikes against Him and His Word. It is rebellion to God. Because this is true, sin deserves to die as God has said. All workers receive their wages. Workers of righteousness and holiness will receive just rewards, as will workers of sin. It would be unjust to pay some workers and not all of them. And God is a just employer. But He's also a gracious gift-giver

to those who will look up and tell themselves there's a better way and a much better Master. He offers all who would trust and obey the opportunity to have eternal life with Him (which is the very definition of heaven) rather than eternal separation from Him (which is the very definition of hell). But, again, one must choose, and the choice must be daily. What is your choice? Has it made a difference?

Chapter 7 Verse 1

"Or do you not know, brethren (for I speak to those who know the law), that the law has dominion over a man as long as he lives?" Paul is speaking to believers. I know what you're probably thinking. What does this have to do with anything? Well, it has everything to do with anything.

By now, you've probably come to the conclusion that we are all faced with choices, and those choices basically break down to just two: life or death; freedom or incarceration; truth or lies; vibrancy or mediocrity. This verse is no different in the fact that we must choose between law and grace. Here, the Law of God stands before mankind. It stands in two positions that must be understood if we wish to secure peace in this life. The first position is found in 7:4, and the second is found in 7:5, which we will get to. But for now, the teaching is that the law dominates mankind only as long as he or she lives. This is brilliant, friends, and must be thoroughly understood. If a person is dead, the law no longer binds him or her. He or she is free from its effect upon him or her.

But the Law will never be destroyed; it cannot be destroyed. God has promised it never will be destroyed. It's not bad or evil; it is from the mind of God, so it is powerful and convicting. The only way out from its convicting purpose is to die from it. The law applies to the living; it has no bearing whatsoever upon the dead. A dead man is free from the law; it has no jurisdiction or power over a dead man. Do you see where God is going with this? If you are a true believer and you're not seeing the point, you've missed something. Do you see what's being taught here? Again, when death enters the picture, a person is no longer under the law and can no longer be condemned by the law. Death forever frees a person from the law, from its demands, guilt, and condemnation. Do you see it? Paul is not saying when you physically die you are free from the law. What good would that do? He is saying when you have been placed in the death of Jesus, and also the resurrected life of Jesus, you are now under no condemnation from the law. You are dead to it. You are free from it. You now operate under a higher law, which is grace. It's okay to praise Jesus right now if you want. I am.

Let me offer you an illustration. I am a pilot, and I had to study various things to become one. Part of the study included aerodynamics and physics. We all know about the physical law of gravity. You release an object from your hands, and, unless it is manipulated by some other force, it will fall one hundred percent of the time, and you can't do anything to change it. It is an immutable law of physics in this world. You and I don't float around because of gravity. Cars operate on highways because of gravity. What goes up must come down because of gravity. It is fixed and cannot be altered, period. It is a law that has no remedy, unless a higher law can be found to overcome it.

Man has wanted to fly for centuries, but gravity kept him earthbound most of that time. That is, until a higher law was discovered. That higher law is the law of "lift" and this is exactly how airplanes overcome gravity. A car has no lift hence it is earthbound. You and I have no lift, hence we're earthbound. But a plane with operational wings has lift, hence it can overcome gravity. Lift is the higher law. Lift overcomes gravity. In the same way, the higher law of grace has overcome the law. God's grace is the lift you need to overcome the pull of sin. But you have to die first. Jesus has made the way for that too, friends. This is absolutely incredible. He is the wings of our body. The Holy Spirit is the air flowing. This grace produces lift. It might sound unbelievable, but it's just as true as gravity.

To me, there's not anything sadder than an airplane tied down at an airport, just sitting there in mediocrity waiting for something to happen. No, the airplane was designed to fly, and it finds its purpose in doing just that. A plane, in the hands of a good pilot, becoming airborne is a beautiful sight. As a true believer, you're not designed to be tied-down and earth-bound due to sin's gravitational pull. You are designed for flight. You are designed for purpose. And the Pilot is ready to take you up to show you new things. But you first must allow yourself to conform to His image. An airplane is just a gaggle of wires, cables, and aluminum until it is fashioned into a workable model, put together from a plan by someone who knows what they are doing. You and I are no different. In order for us to soar, we must be conformed to the image He has for us. Pretty amazing stuff.

CHAPTER 7 VERSES 2-4

"For a married woman is bound by law to her husband while he lives, but if her husband dies she is released from the law of marriage." It is amazing that these verses should be thought of as a statement of New Testament doctrine on the matter of divorce and remarriage. They're not. Don't read into Scripture what isn't there. Look, twice in verse 1 Paul states that his reference is to a circumstance of law. In verse 2, it is stated twice more that the reference is to the law. In verse 3, it is stated yet again, a total of 5 times in the space of 3 verses! This is about the law, not divorce. (By the way, the "Law" is typically a reference to the first five books of the Old Testament, or the "Torah").

So what is it about? I'm glad you asked. These verses are here to help substantiate verse 1. Again, the subject is not about a divorce and remarriage transition, but rather a spiritual analogy to help the Jew (or any reader) understand their transition from Moses (the Law) to Christ (Grace). They would have to see it from a woman's perspective as Jesus is the Groom, and the believer is part of the church, or the Bride of Christ. There wasn't a remedy for women in biblical times for divorce. Paul is saying the only way a woman was free from her marriage was for his or her spouse to be dead, but that's not the issue. The issue is the only way a believer becomes free from the law is for the believer to be dead to the law.

"Accordingly, she will be called an adulteress if she lives with another man while her husband is alive. But if her husband dies, she is free from that law, and if she marries another man she is not an adulteress." The life of fruitful obedience to God, Paul explains, comes as we die to our old "husband, the law, which was a threatening master over us, and we marry a new husband, the Lord Jesus Christ. Again, this is just an illustration Paul is using to help us understand the concept better. The concept is if a person is dead in Christ, the person is not under the legal requirements of Old Testament Law. The person is free to become a new person under the leadership of a new "husband" or "head of household." This new leadership is the resurrected life of Jesus. This is exactly what the next verse states.

"Likewise, my brothers, you also have died to the law through the body of Christ, so that you may belong to another, to him who has been raised from the dead, in order that we may bear fruit for God." When Paul speaks of "brothers" he's talking about true believers. So you must be truly saved to be under this teaching. He states because of salvation, they have died to the law through the body of Christ (which had died), and now they belong to another. This other is Jesus. They don't belong to the law (or the effects of it), but they now belong to the living, resurrected Jesus. Has all of this happened so a person can do anything they want to do in this life? Has this been done so a person can have a special "pass" with God, so they can sin like everyone else yet still get to heaven? Does that seem right or fair to you? Of course not. Notice what is supposed to happen. First, as the believer has died to the law, he is now united to Christ in a relationship analogous to marriage. He is now under His rule and authority, not the law's. But the believer is also now required to bear fruit for Jesus. He is to bear righteousness, holiness, other converts, Christian character, fruit of the Spirit, etc. Is that me? Is that you? If not, we're just sitting on the tarmac of the airport of life, tied down, watching the activities of others. Not much of a life, is it?

Chapter 7 Verses 5-6

"For when we were in the flesh, the sinful passions which were aroused by the law were at work in our members to bear fruit to death." If the first position of the law is that it is dead to those in Christ (7:1-4), the second position is that those not in Christ are still alive to the law. This is what Paul means when he says "when we were in the flesh." When we are alive to sin, we are still passionate about it. But the problem is, at least from God's perspective, that sin bears its own fruit. But it's not good fruit, it is the type of fruit that bears death. You and I are going to die from something. It's either going to be from our sin life, or it's going to be from our decision to be placed in the death of Jesus before we die physically. We must make a decision, before we die physically, to either stay dead spiritually or come alive spiritually. If we stay dead spiritually, we will always sin and die from our sins at some point. If we come alive spiritually, we should no longer be passionate about sinning. In fact, we should be as passionate about holiness as we originally were about sinning. If that's not part of our testimony after we've made a profession of faith, the profession is useless. Verse 6 helps to clarify this statement.

"But now we have been delivered from the law, having died to what we were held by, so that we should serve in the newness of the Spirit and not in the oldness of the letter." As true believers, we are now delivered from death, the law, the old us, our propensity to sin, etc. We have died to what we were held by. This is another fantastic hallelujah moment, friends. All of that has been inactivated by our true conversion. True believers have been delivered or discharged from all of that. Why? So we might live better? No, so that we may serve Jesus "in newness of Spirit."

God has not saved you just so you can be in paradise as some form of an "Atta boy" later on after your life. No, He has saved you from yourself and the death that followed you, so that in the newness of His life through Jesus you may have a daily relationship with Him now. You now have the opportunity to experience heaven on earth, even in spite of the death and sin and degrading of the world around us. And friends, a true biblical, experiential relationship with God is never mediocre. Look, He has saved us so we may be used by the Holy Spirit as the human element in His program of saving others. If your life is average and no different from the life of lost and unsaved people, how are you going to be influential and used by God to attract others to Him? Well, guess what? You're not. If you have a new spirit, you will automatically be focused not on your old life and sins, but on Jesus and your relationship with Him.

Chapter 7 Verses 7-8

"What shall we say then? Is the law sin? Certainly not! On the contrary, I would not have known sin except through the law. For I would not have known covetousness unless the law had said, "You shall not covet." "What shall we say then?" is a great question. There's nothing really to say except the truth. And the truth is the law of God is morally, ethically, socially, culturally, and seriously good. There's nothing bad about it at all, except it can't do anything about your sin. It can only show you that you are sinning. So, it's designed purpose is exceptional, and the law does an exceptional job of showing us our need for help. Paul states it well as he says he would not have known sin if it were not for the law. Why is it so important? If we do not know we are sinners, we will not believe we need a Savior. The law lets us know we're lawbreakers. That is a good thing, friends. Our self-righteousness is so entrenched that until the law strips us of it and convicts us of our sin, we will not cast ourselves totally upon Christ. Our culture adds to this by telling us that we're not sinners. We're pretty good folks. We may want to bring Jesus into our lives as a useful coach or helper in our self-improvement program. But to trust Him as our Savior, we have to see the depth of our sin as God's law exposes it for what it is. That's what Paul is describing here. It's one of the biggest reasons why the Bible exists.

Here, Paul argues that the law functions to reveal our sin to us. He uses as a personal example the tenth commandment against coveting. This shows that, by "the law," Paul mainly had in mind the Ten Commandments as the embodiment of God's requirements for holy living. Probably he picked the tenth commandment because it is the only command that explicitly condemns evil on the heart level.

Most people think that they are basically good. Sure, they know they have their faults. Who doesn't? They're not perfect, but they are good. They excuse even their bad sins, just as Paul excused his violent persecution of the church. After all, it was justified because it was for a good cause. So guys (and gals) excuse a little pornography because, "After all, everyone looks at that stuff, and I'm not hurting anyone. Besides, I've never cheated on my wife." And many excuse their violent temper because that person had it coming, and, "Hey, I didn't hurt him; I just told him off!" Some people sleep with anyone and say, "It's my body, and nobody's business." Other people will lie like a rug and think, "well, if they're willing to believe me, then shame on them." People excuse all manner of sin and still think of themselves as basically good people because they have not come to know God's law, especially the law as it confronts our evil desires. At the heart of coveting is the enthronement of self as lord.

"But sin, taking opportunity by the commandment, produced in me all manner of evil desire. For apart from the law sin was dead." Can you identify with Paul's experience? Has God's holy law hit home to your conscience so that you died to all self-righteousness? Has the law killed all your hopes that your good works will get you into heaven? If so, that's a good thing, because Jesus didn't come to call the righteous, but sinners to repentance. When you see God's holy standard and how miserably you have violated it over and over, you then see your need for a Savior. And the best news ever is that Jesus Christ came into this world to save sinners.

Chapter 7 Verses 9-10

"For I was alive without the law once: but when the commandment came, sin revived, and I died." These verses may seem confusing, but they're not. Paul is telling us the law reveals the fact of condemnation and death. This is the major purpose of the law. There are three points I want to share with you concerning this.

First, a person who does not know or care about God's law will feel alive because they don't pay attention to sin. They say ignorance is bliss, and to be knowingly or unknowingly ignorant of God's law may feel blissful, but it typically leads to blistering. Paul says there was a time in his life when he felt "alive" because he didn't pay attention to God's Word. He could sin and feel no guilt because he had no desire to focus on God's Word which would have led him to understand he was sinning. In other words, he was living a lie and did not know the truth or did not care to acknowledge the truth. I know many people like that. I bet you do too.

Second, a person who does know God's Word or law and pays attention to it sees sin come alive. By knowing and acknowledging God's Word, the person becomes acutely aware of sin and recognizes when he or she is guilty of it. The purpose of the law contained in God's Word is to make the reality of sin come alive to a person, so the person guilty of the sin can do something about it. Why is that important? Because unrepentant sin is the only thing that will keep a person away from God and God away from them, which is a biblical definition of death. So why wouldn't we just deal with it biblically and move on to live?

"And the commandment, which was ordained to life, I found to be unto death." Third, the law is ordained to bring life, but not in the way people think. People think that God's commandments were given to be kept, and by keeping the commandments they can earn the acceptance of God and work their way into heaven. But this has never been the case. God's commandments bring life to mankind only because they destroy mankind's self-centeredness and self-righteousness. The commandments reveal truth by showing humanity he or she truly is a corrupt and sinful being and he or she needs deliverance from God's clear decree that He will judge and condemn sin.

God has given us His Word to show us our need for Him. He has been honest and truthful with us since the very beginning. Shouldn't we study His Word and know it? Shouldn't we be as honest with Him as He's been with us? Shouldn't we regularly go to a place where His Word is being taught in its entirety? Shouldn't we understand our spiritual world better? Shouldn't we know better, think better, and do better? I think we all should.

Chapter 7 Verses 11-12

"For sin, taking occasion by the commandment, deceived me, and by it killed me." There are two primary ways sin takes God's Word and deceives us. First, sin uses the law and makes us feel safe and secure in thinking that we're not that bad. Have you noticed that it is our habit to compare ourselves with others who are worse than us? "I may be overweight, but I'm not as overweight as so-and-so is." "I may steal occasionally, but I'm not a thief like you-know-who is." "Yeah, I may have had a few affairs, but I'm not as bad as what's her name." "Well, it's true I may have told a few lies before, but you can't believe a word that comes out of some people's mouths." Don't we all do that? It (sin) makes us feel better about ourselves when we compare ourselves to a bigger sinner than us. But all it takes is one sin to break our relationship with God, and the only benchmark we must contend with is Jesus, and, folks, we all fail. Sin will try to make you believe you're not that bad, but you really are that bad. So am I. We both need Jesus.

Second, sin will use the law and make us feel helpless and hopeless. But the law can never drive a person to despair. That's what sin does. Have you ever felt God couldn't possibly forgive you? He couldn't possibly love you? He couldn't possibly want you? That's sin lying again because as we have seen, that's a bunch of baloney. God wants to forgive you, and He loves you enough to make a sure way. God wants you so badly He willingly died in order to offer you and me and everyone else life. Sin wants to distort all of that. Sin wants to keep you incarcerated in discouragement's prison. Why in the world we glorify sin so much, make excuses for sin, and play with it as if it were something nice and fun is beyond me. It really is!

Sin will try to make you happy or miserable living in it, but either way it is not God's desire for you or me to sin. It is God's desire for you and me to get out of sin and into life. God wants you and me to shed the mediocrity and replace it with marvelous. His name is Jesus.

"Therefore the law is holy, and the commandment holy and just and good." The law is holy and set apart from God and to God. It is full of glory, majesty, and splendor. It is designed to work, and it works its design, if we will let it. The law is just, righteous, fair, equitable, and impartial. It is for everyone. Everyone finds equality under God's law. Everyone is an equal sinner. The law is good. It shows man how to live and tells him when he fails to live that way. We should all be well studied in God's law because it's that important. But the greatest thing the law does is it points us to the Lawgiver. If I haven't told you before, His name is Jesus, and He will rescue you if you will just surrender to His truth; then through the power of His truth and Spirit, live the Christian life you are supposed to live.

Chapter 7 Verses 7:13-14

"Has then what is good become death to me? Certainly not! But sin, that it might appear sin, was producing death in me through what is good, so that sin through the commandment might become exceedingly sinful." An illustration here will probably explain this better than an explanation. If you were to take "murder" and stand it beside the commandment "Thou Shalt Not Kill (Murder) you will see a great contrast.

The commandment protected man's life, but "sin" takes man's life away.

The commandment protected man's presence, but "sin" takes man's presence away.

The commandment protected man's existence, but "sin" takes man's existence away.

The commandment protected man's contribution, but "sin" takes man's contribution away.

The commandment said man could live, but "sin" says man must die.

So it is with every sin, whether adultery, stealing, or taking God's name in vain. God gives; sin takes away. Get it? Again, why we coddle and protect sin so much is beyond me, if we really know what God's Word says.

"*For we know that the law is spiritual, but I am carnal, sold under sin.*" God deals with us in the spiritual realm, and the law is spiritual in nature. There are three ways this is seen. First, the law was given to man by the Spirit of God. Second, the law describes the spiritual nature of God. Third, the law is spiritual because of the purpose for it; namely, getting us to see our need for spiritual life and a Savior.

Paul starts to make confessions now. His first confession is he is carnal, not spiritual. Non-conforming living stems from our carnality. Paul says there was a time when he lived a carnal life because he was a carnal being. But God helped him to see his need for him to focus on his spiritual life, not his fleshly life. He was a slave to sin being sold under sin, but there came a time when he was set free from that slavery. Friends, he wasn't set free from the slavery of sin just so he could dabble in it when he felt the need. No, he was set free so he could live for Jesus. And boy did he! He changed dramatically after his meeting with the resurrected Christ. He changed dramatically. You can read about it in the Book of Acts. He wrote, under the influence of the Holy Spirit, most of the New Testament. He stopped persecuting the church and started planting churches. He stopped killing Christians and started leading people to be one; thousands of people. He stopped slandering Jesus and started serving Him. In fact, he literally lost his head over Jesus.

If we were to meet Paul today and ask him if he'd like to go sinning with us, I believe he'd teach us a better way. Paul thought about his Lord and His sacrifice. Paul thought about his salvation and what it really meant. Paul thought about his conversion and his life's change because of it. Paul also taught and preached tirelessly against willful, habitually sinning. I believe Paul would laugh, or maybe cry, at the way most Christians live their lives today. Truth will set you free. Paul spent the remainder of his converted life in conforming to the image of Jesus. We must also. Where are the Paul's of our generation?

CHAPTER 7 VERSES 15-16

"*For what I am doing, I do not understand. For what I will to do, that I do not practice; but what I hate, that I do.*" Paul, like everyone else, struggled with the process, though. Paul makes three points about being carnal and sold under sin. We need to pay attention; this applies to all of us too. As a side note, many scholars differ in their opinion as to why Paul wrote these verses. Some say he was saying as a believer he still struggled with sin. Others say he is referring to a time in his past when, although he was saved, he hadn't truly discovered God's truth about sin and freedom from it. I take the latter stance. Why? Because it's the only stance that makes sense to me with his earlier teachings as we have been learning. Anyways, let's look at the three points.

"*For what I am doing, I do not understand.*" The first point he makes is that he recognized and perceived he was doing the things he shouldn't have been doing, but he can't understand why he is doing them. He fights and struggles not to sin, but sooner or later he succumbs to sin. Sound familiar? There's hope!

"*For what I will to do, that I do not practice,*" Second, he says he wanted to do right; he had the desire to please God, but the more he tried, the more he failed. Paul wanted to be conformed to the image of Christ and to become all that God wanted him to be. But despite his desire and expectations, he found himself coming up short time and time again. This is a cycle most Christians find themselves in. Why? Well, what Paul was trying to do was to succeed in his own power rather than be surrendered to God allowing Him to live His life through Paul via His power. Paul couldn't do right; God living in Paul couldn't do wrong. Paul was complaining his life was always suffering because he couldn't, or wouldn't do right. There has to be something wrong. Do you see where I'm going with this?

"*but what I hate, that I do.* Paul hated sin and hated coming short of the glory of God. He struggled and wrestled with the sin in his life. But no matter how much he hated and struggled, he always came up short and found himself failing. Again, Paul did not have the spiritual resources to be successful in his daily walk on his own. You and I don't either. But God, through Jesus and His Spirit, has abundance for everyone. It's a matter of surrender, or more correctly, conforming. Nowadays, the world wants you and I to believe sin isn't bad, you can't help yourself, and you and I are just sinners with a little grace sprinkled on us to get us to heaven. The Bible says differently, as you have seen if you have read all of the comments so far. Let's not believe the world's lies or our flesh's ability to fool us.

"If, then, I do what I will not to do, I agree with the law that it is good." A carnal life demonstrates that human nature and knowledge are inadequate. Always has been; always will be. Trying to live a Christian (Christ-like) life is impossible for any of us. Only Christ can live a Christ-like life. You and I will fail before we even get started if success is left up to us and our carnality. Unless we surrender to God daily and allow Jesus to live His life through us unencumbered by our self-seeking wants, we will always live mediocrely. Sin will triumph, the cause of Christ will be deterred, and nothing will change. We can have all the excuses we want, all the cute sayings that make us feel better about ourselves, all the people who will kiss our boo-boo's and tell us we're going to be okay, but we are only fooling ourselves. God is telling us here that this type of lifestyle is a dead giveaway that something is spiritually wrong. It tells us we are living our lives apart from Jesus, and if it describes you, you are too.

CHAPTER 7 VERSES 17-19

"*But now, it is no longer I who do it, but sin that dwells in me."* Here is where we need to stop and take a long pause; a really long pause. Paul has just identified the whole issue. We have just found the parasite living within us, and we're about to get a dose of some strong medicine.

Do you want to know why we all fall short, and why we all fail? It's because sin dwells in all of us. No matter what resources and faculties mankind uses, and no matter how diligently he or she tries, he or she is unable to control sin and keep from sinning. Sin is within the flesh, and it dwells in us like a parasite. We are all diseased with the seed of corruption. I wish God would do something about it for us so we could all be free from it. Oh wait, He has! Haven't we been studying this? We can choose to allow the parasite to consume us and everything around us, or we can take a big helping of spiritual truth and make the parasite ineffective. It's our choice.

"*For I know that in me (that is, in my flesh) nothing good dwells; for to will is present with me, but how to perform what is good I do not find.*" There's nothing good about a parasite in the body or rust on a car. Paul wants to do right, but he can't find a way. He never will find a way. You and I will never find a way. We must find The Way. Only Jesus can live a sinless life. Only Jesus living in you can help you eliminate the parasite and remove the rust so you can experience His way. And it's worth it, friends. He's worth it.

The most important question you will ever answer is: "When you die (when you are separated from this world) are you going to heaven (not be separated from God for all eternity)?" It is not a question of how good you are, whether you go to church, or how much money you give to charity. God says, in order to go to heaven, you must be born again (John 3:3). He means the parasite of sin must be eliminated. God gives us His clear plan for being "born again."

First, we must acknowledge God as the Creator of everything, and accept our humble position in God's creation. "You are worthy, O Lord, To receive glory and honor and power; For You created all things, And by Your will they exist and were created" (Revelation 4:11).

Next, we must realize that we are sinners: "*For all have sinned, and fall short of the glory of God*" (Romans 3:23). Because we are sinners, we are condemned to death: "*For the wages of sin is death*" (Romans 6:23). This includes eternal separation from God (not going to heaven). God cannot allow parasitic hosts into His perfection.

But God loved each of us so much that He gave His only begotten Son, Jesus, to bear our sin and die in our place: "*God demonstrates His love toward us, in that, while we were still sinners, Christ died for us*" (Romans 5:8). Although we often struggle with understanding how, God said our sins were laid upon Jesus, and He died in our place. Jesus became our substitute.

It's very clear in the Bible: believe in Jesus as the one who bore your sins, died in your place, was buried, and whom God resurrected. It's Christ's blood and resurrection that assures us of everlasting life when we call on Him as our Lord and Savior: "*For whoever calls on the name of the LORD shall be saved.*" (Romans 10:13). "Whosoever" includes each and every one of us.

Therefore, if you understand that you are a sinner, and you believe that Jesus Christ came as the one and only Redeemer of sin, then you understand the plan of salvation. The question is are you ready to implement the plan, by receiving God's gift of His Son, Jesus Christ? If so, believe in Christ, repent of your sins, and commit the rest of your life to Him as Lord, and allow Him to live through you to defeat sin. This is conforming to the image of His Son.

Chapter 7 Verses 19-20

"*For the good that I will to do, I do not do; but the evil I will not to do, that I practice.*" I can relate to Paul, and I bet you can too. Paul knows the good he's supposed to do. He knows what is and isn't appropriate. He knows doing good is good doing, yet he says he doesn't do it. He wills and resolves to not sin, but it is all to no avail. No matter how much he resolves to "do better" he fails. Note he says he's willing to do better, just not capable of doing better. Look, resolving to live or do better every time we fail, like some kind of perpetual resolution, just doesn't work. What's worse, Paul even says the bad stuff he knows he shouldn't do, he does. What's this all about? God is using Paul to illustrate the fact that we can all want to live better and do right, we can all have the will to do so, but we fail. Desire and will is not enough. Why? Because there is something inside of all of us, which is much stronger than our desire and will. Paul tells us what that is in the next verse.

"Now if I do what I will not to do, it is no longer I who do it, but sin that dwells in me." Paul's conclusion to the dilemma of doing what he shouldn't and not doing what he should is the fact that he has a very different true nature. His true nature is sinful. Sin is everyone's true nature. We all suffer from a corrupt and depraved nature. It's who we are. It's how we're born. We are born fallen creatures in a fallen world. All the desire and willpower in the world can't overcome it. Sin is too powerful. That's why we fail no matter how hard we try not to.

Paul wants to, but doesn't. Paul doesn't want to, but does. Sound familiar? Paul knows that there must be something overriding his will and desires. That something is his sin nature. What is the sin nature? I'm glad you asked!

The sin nature is that aspect in man that makes him rebellious against God. When we speak of the sin nature, we refer to the fact that we have a natural inclination to sin; given the choice to do God's will or our own, we will naturally choose to do our own thing. Proof of the sin nature abounds. No one has to teach a child to lie or be selfish; rather, we go to great lengths to teach children to tell the truth and put others first. Sinful behavior comes naturally. The news is filled with tragic examples of mankind acting badly. Wherever people are, there is trouble.

From generation to generation, the sin nature was passed down to all of humanity. Remember Romans 5:12? *"Sin entered the world through one man, and death through sin, and in this way death came to all people, because all sinned."* This verse also presents the unsettling truth that the sin nature leads inexorably to death (Remember Romans 6:23?). Other consequences of the sin nature are hostility toward God and ignorance of His truth, and we're going to deal with this in Romans 8. We don't lose our sin nature once we receive Christ. The Bible says that sin remains in us, and a struggle with that old nature will continue as long as we are in this world. Paul bemoaned his own personal struggle here in these verses. But we do have help in the battle. The Spirit of God takes up residence in each believer and supplies the power we need to overcome the pull of the sin nature within us. Through His finished work on the cross, Jesus satisfied God's wrath against sin and provided believers with victory over their sin nature. Those who are born again now have this command: *"Count yourselves dead to sin but alive to God in Christ Jesus"* (Romans 6:11). The key to victory over sin is knowing who we are in Christ and then surrendering to that truth, not making a resolution to do better and trying in our own strength.

Chapter 7 Verses 21–25

"I find then a law, that evil is present with me, the one who wills to do good." Sin is every much a law as is gravity. There is a battle going on between right and wrong, and to win this battle you must have stronger "good" than evil. You're going to have to have outside help because evil is present in all of us, and what little bit of good we might muster up on our own is not going to counteract the evil we have. The law of sin is the rule, disposition, urge, tendency, pull, and or corruption within man's nature to please ourselves and do our own will. But I'm not that bad, you say? I'm confident you're not as bad as me, but the benchmark is Jesus, and from God's perspective we're all losing the battle. And His perspective is the only one that is important.

"For I delight in the law of God according to the inward man." As a believer in Christ, I delight in it too. The law of the inward man is the law, rule disposition, urge, tendency, pull, and or conviction of the Holy Spirit of God in a person's life to please God and do His will. Do you see the two opposing forces at work in every believer? Surely you do.

"But I see another law in my members, warring against the law of my mind, and bringing me into captivity to the law of sin which is in my members."

Well, when the Holy Spirit convicts us of sin, and the natural "us" wants to sin, there's going to be some warfare; there's going to be some friction. Where there is friction, there's heat. Where there is heat, there's discomfort. Paul was miserable, as seen in the next verse.

"O wretched man that I am! Who will deliver me from this body of death?" When we finally know the reason why we're the way we are, and we finally decide that the misery isn't worth it, we have a tendency to cry out to God. As a believer, I should be doing what I should be doing, and I shouldn't be doing what I shouldn't be doing. At some point, this internal battle should bring us to the same conclusion Paul came to. If I am habitually sinning, I can't possibly be following the leadership of the Holy Spirit. If that's so, and I am a true believer, God's going to bring the heat. Why? Because He hates sin and will not allow sin in His presence. He has to do something about it if He truly loves us and has made a way to allow us to be with Him.

"I thank God—through Jesus Christ our Lord! So then, with the mind I myself serve the law of God, but with the flesh the law of sin." I thank God too! I thank Jesus! This is an exclamation. The Great Deliver from all this battling and warfare is Jesus. Jesus can, will, and has delivered the true believer from sin. His cross dealt with our sin, or what we are; His blood deals with our sins, or what we do. Jesus has made a way in spite of our old nature by giving us a new nature. This new nature should at some point take over the old nature, and mediocrity with all of its excuses with sinning should be eradicated. And when you really, I mean really study it and meditate upon it, you are free from the warzone, and mediocrity fades away. Your life will be totally different. Forever. And that's worth thinking about. In fact, you and I must think about This if we are ever to be conformed to His image.

Chapter 8 Verses 1-3

"*There is therefore now no condemnation to them which are in Christ Jesus, who walk not after the flesh, but after the Spirit.*" Have there ever been sweeter words written? Since Christ has come, a most wonderful thing has happened: the people who truly believe in Christ are not condemned. "*No condemnation*" means the true believer is not doomed and damned, but is free from the penalty and condemnation of sin; he is not judged as a sinner, but delivered from the condemnation of death (separation from God) and hell (separated forever); he is not judged to be unrighteous, but is counted as righteous. Why? Because the person has accepted the truth of who they are without Christ and who they are with Christ, and there should be a big difference. Why? Well, shouldn't Christ make a difference in a person's life? If He doesn't make a difference, why bother? No offense to Jesus, but if He can't change a person's lifestyle, who needs Him? I know that sounds harsh, but is it not true? If Jesus can't or won't get you to change your sinful living habits, what good is He here to you in this world? If getting you to heaven is all Jesus can do, then let's all wait until we're dead to follow Him. That's just what the devil wants true believers to think. After all, we're all just sinners, saved by Jesus. But to what end has Jesus saved us? To get us to heaven? What if I'm going to live here on this earth another fifty years?

Look at the passage again: "*There is therefore now no condemnation to them which are* in *Christ Jesus.*" This passage ties in everything we've been studying. A person must be *in* Christ Jesus to experience no condemnation. Are you starting to see the big picture here? If you are only 99% sure you're saved, you're 100% lost. If you think you're saved, but you're living as if you're not, you probably aren't saved. If you're not saved, you're still in 100% condemnation because Jesus can and does change the true believer's heart and lifestyle.

Look, this is one of the greatest passages in all of Scripture, but it is also one of the most misquoted and misunderstood passages too. Notice exactly what it says. If you are in Christ Jesus, you are no longer in condemnation. Praise God. But if you are not in Jesus, you are in condemnation. How can one tell? How will you know? Glad you asked. Look at what Scripture says.

"*There is therefore now no condemnation to them which are in Christ Jesus, who walk not after the flesh, but after the Spirit.*" Pretty plain to me! If you are in Christ, you would be in Christ day after day right? If that's so, your daily walk, or lifestyle, should match that of Jesus'. If we were truly in Christ, we wouldn't be flippant about sin, because Jesus sure wasn't. If we were truly in Christ, we wouldn't be living in sin because Jesus sure didn't. If we were truly in Christ, we wouldn't make excuses about our sins because Jesus wouldn't allow us to. If we were truly in Christ, we wouldn't be content with just being a sinner saved by grace. No, we would live exceptional lives of sainthood, not mediocre lives of sinners bound for heaven someday. We would be spiritually minded, not fleshly minded. We would develop a biblical worldview like Jesus, not a carnal or man-centered worldview like most people.

Chapter 8 Verse 2-3

Hopefully, we have learned that it's not our talk that matters; it's our walk. It's not what we say, it's what we do that's important. You can say you're a starting quarterback for the New Orleans Saints, and honestly believe it in your heart, but unless we see you on Sunday afternoons playing in a game, we're all going to think you're insane. Why? Because the reality is (unless you're Drew Brees) you're not an NFL quarterback no matter how badly you wish you were. I'm not either. My point? A person can talk the Christian lingo, but if we see that person living in the flesh, we're going to think there's something amiss here, right? I go to church on Sunday (if I go at all), and I act all pious and religious like Bobby the Believer, but when you see me out in the world I act like Harry the Hypocrite, so people are going to believe Harry is the real me. Said another way, if your walk isn't *meaningful*, your talk is *meaningless.*

The person who is truly in Christ Jesus will walk after the Spirit. He will walk after God. He will strive to be more like Jesus each day. Sin will not successfully compete with what Jesus is doing with the believer. On the other hand, the person who constantly walks after the flesh or after their own desires and wants cannot possibly be walking in the Spirit. It's just the way it is, friends. Why? Well, please read on.

"For the law of the Spirit of life in Christ Jesus hath made me free from the law of sin and death." "The law of the Spirit of life" is an immutable law just like the law of gravity. The law of the Spirit of life refers to the spiritual life that is only found in Jesus Christ, the Author of Life. Whatever life is (energy, being, spirit, love, joy, peace, etc.), it is all found perfectly in Jesus and nowhere else. This resource or law of life is found in Jesus. To find it, to have access to it, one must be in Jesus.

God requires all true believers to daily walk with Him (and He's not going to participate in our sins), and He's given us the provisions we need. If we leave home without the provisions and try to provide for ourselves through the flesh, we might as well try to walk on the Saints training camp and take over. That's just not going to happen no matter how much we want it to.

"For what the law could not do, in that it was weak through the flesh, God sending his or her own Son in the likeness of sinful flesh, and for sin, condemned sin in the flesh:" Still don't think sin is that bad for the believer? Still

think being a mere sinner saved by grace is all that's required? Look at this verse. God sent Jesus to condemn sin. Think about that. What we excuse, what we do with little regard to why, is what Jesus was sent to condemn. The word "*condemned*" means "*to judge worthy of being punished.*" Think sin isn't a big deal? Think sin is just what we do because we just can't help it? God says Jesus judges it to be worthy of punishment. So if you're in sin, you're worthy to be punished. But if you're in Christ, there's no more condemnation. Where would you really rather be? But remember, if you're going to talk the talk, you need to walk the walk. If you talk the talk, but you don't walk the walk, your walk and talk isn't worth talking about.

Chapter 8 Verse 4-5

"*that the righteous requirement of the law might be fulfilled in us who do not walk according to the flesh but according to the Spirit,*" Ready for this verse? God is saying here that, in the full sense, only Christ has fulfilled all the law's requirements, but when we are in Christ we in our measure begin to live the kind of life that God would have us live. This is known as progressive sanctification. What does this mean? It means if you are truly in Christ you will truly begin to live like Christ which is the only example of true living God gives us. A mediocre spiritual life should therefore be impossible, friends, if you are truly saved. That's what it says. That's what it means.

Now, notice that Paul does not say, "*we fulfill the law's righteous requirement,*" but that "*the righteous requirement of the law is fulfilled in us*" surely pointing to the work of the Holy Spirit in the believer. We are in Christ; Christ is in us. When this is a true reality, habitual sin is out of the picture in a person's life. In other words, we are confronted with the fact that God won't accept any more excuses concerning our mediocre sin life. Wow is right. Would you like to know why we make excuses when we really know better? The next verse gives us the answer.

"*For those who live according to the flesh set their minds on the things of the flesh, but those who live according to the Spirit, the things of the Spirit.*" God's Spirit living in the true believer will draw the true believer to spiritual things. If a person is making excuses for physical sins, the person is physically minded. If the person is making excuses for committing fleshly sins, the person is fleshly minded. Since Jesus said a person can't serve two masters, we have to decide, daily, who we're going to serve. Will we serve sin or the Savior? Will we serve flesh or the Father? Will we serve carnality or Christ?

Believer, don't be fooled. You can make all the excuses you want, but they won't hold water with God. He has plainly told you in His Word what He expects and requires. How much more do we need? The battle for your spirit begins in your mind, as we shall soon see. Isn't it strange how the world glorifies the flesh and carnality but not truth? Isn't it outlandish that the enemy wants us to believe we can all just sin and be okay? Isn't it peculiar that when we think of sinful things we want to do sinful things? And when we do sinful things we think about doing more sinful things? Isn't it inexplicable how believers can be so easily fooled? Does any of this make you wonder what in the world is going on?

Before we came to know Christ, we were continually defeated by sin. When we came to know Him and to receive the indwelling Holy Spirit, we were able to attain a standard we could never reach in our own strength. In interpreting these words the emphasis is clearly on the way the Christian life is lived. The true believer will live the Christian life daily because Jesus lives in him, and that's what Jesus does; it starts by being conformed to His image.

Chapter 8 Verse 6-8

"For to be carnally minded is death, but to be spiritually minded is life and peace." It doesn't get any clearer than this. To be carnally minded means to walk in the flesh. It refers to those of us who make the excuses and validate our sins because after all, we're just sinners. I can't help it; surely God understands, and after all, He loves me just the way I am. Do you still believe these excuses are acceptable? It is true He loves you just as you are, but once He has saved you, He expects you to change. You and

I were once carnally minded when we were lost, but now we should be spiritually minded if we truly are born-again new spirits. In fact, life and peace can only be found when we are in Jesus and start developing a mind like Christ. No wonder the world and the enemy puts so much time, effort, and money in keeping you carnally minded. But you may ask, what's the big deal? Can't I just be left alone and live my life the way I want? Well, yes, but how is that working out for you? Besides, the next verse tells us what the big deal is.

"Because the carnal mind is enmity against God; for it is not subject to the law of God, nor indeed can be." If we have a carnal mind, or our thinking is worldly and fleshly, we will be at enmity with God. The word "*enmity*" means "*hatred*", and the verse is saying the carnal way of thinking is hatred towards God. Explains a lot, doesn't it? Want to know why there's so much hatred for God in the world now? Because there's so many people in the world with carnal minds. Why is Jesus often ridiculed in music, movies, and theaters? Well, because there are so many carnal minds in the arts. Why is God often mocked in our schools? Well, because there are so many carnal minds in our education system. Why is Jesus often persona non grata in our government? Well, because there are so many carnal minds in our political system on both sides. Why is God not honored in many of our homes anymore? Well, because there are so many carnal-minded families. Why do our churches seem to struggle when God is revered and His Word is preached with authority and zeal? Well, because the pews are full of carnal-minded people. The proof? Well, schools, government programs and promises, homes, churches, neighborhoods, etc. are all deteriorating before our very eyes. The stench of death is all around us. Don't think it's a big deal? Neither does the devil.

"*So then, those who are in the flesh cannot please God.*" Anyone in Christ should want to please God just like Jesus did, right? But if you or I allow ourselves to walk in the flesh, the Bible says we cannot please God. The word "*please*" is defined as "*to accommodate one's self to the opinions, desires, and interests of others,*" in this case God. As we walk in the flesh, it is impossible to accommodate ourselves to God's opinions and desires. In other words, when we walk the way we want to, it is increasingly harder to live for Jesus. At some point, we start making excuses for our walk in an attempt to make ourselves feel better about our walk. That's when mediocrity sets in, and if it's not dealt with, apathy will soon follow. The person will be like a spiritual zombie, going through the motions, but there's no life there. Does that describe anyone you know?

Chapter 8 Verse 9

"*But you are not in the flesh but in the Spirit, if indeed the Spirit of God dwells in you. Now if anyone does not have the Spirit of Christ, he is not His.*" Read this again, slowly, especially the first sentence. As plainly and simply as possible, the Bible says if a person is in Christ, the Spirit of God lives in him. *God lives in you.* Amazing huh? So if God lives in you, shouldn't God be seen in you? Shouldn't your life reflect His life? Shouldn't there be a change in a person's attitudes, actions, and demeanor if the person has God living in them? Any honest person would have to say yes to these questions. So, now, let's look deeper at this verse. Put your thinking caps on.

God is saying if His Spirit lives in you, you are not in the flesh but in the Spirit, right? This is exactly what God is saying in this verse. He is saying that He is mighty enough to overcome the power of sin in your life. He has destroyed sin (who you are) at the Cross, and He has made provisions for breakthrough from sin daily (what you do) with His blood. Now, His Spirit, which lives in every true believer, provides the daily guidance to allow the true believer to walk not in the flesh (the flesh has been crucified) but in the Spirit. This is an incredible theological truth. But if we look at it in reverse, we see where the enemy has made us blind to truth. Let's develop this a little further.

If no one can see God in us, in other words we show no signs of the Spirit of God in our lives, then the Spirit may not indeed dwell in us. Or at least the Spirit does not control us. If the Spirit is not there, or He is not in control of us, then the only other thing that can and will control us is sin. Do you see this?

Look, if A+B = C, then C-B=A, right? If 5+10=15, then 15-10=5. This is an immutable truth as long as we all agree in the truth of simple math. But if I convince you otherwise, if I can cause you to lose sight of mathematical truth, I can ruin your life with mediocrity and apathy and an "I just don't care" attitude. If 15-10= Scooby Doo to you and 15-10= Popsicles to someone else, it's just a matter of time before chaos sets in. Friends, God's Word is truth, and it is immutable. What He says must always equal the sum, and it always does, no matter how you do the math. But the enemy has fooled millions of us into thinking mediocrity is the norm, that "average" Christianity is the norm, but it cannot be! The "norm" for Christianity is Jesus, and if we are living our lives in any other manner than how He would live His, perhaps the Spirit of God is not really in us. Perhaps we have been fooled into thinking we're saved, but we're really not, and we fight at the thought some preacher would write a commentary to tell us otherwise. But a preacher did write a commentary. His name is Jesus, and His commentary is His Word, the Bible. In its pages are wonderful, encouraging, convicting, hard truths we all need to deal with. And in spite of what so many people wish, His Word is not going away.

Chapter 8 Verse 10-11

"*And if Christ be in you, the body is dead because of sin; but the Spirit is life because of righteousness.* If the Spirit of God is in you, then Christ is in you, for they are of the same essence. And if Christ is in you, then who you are (sin) is dead because Christ died for all the sins of the world; past, present, and future. If He died for all the sins of the world, He must have taken the source of sin to the grave too, otherwise, all this is a lie. That source of sin is your sin nature, the nature you and I were born with. How would Christ, who is alive, live in a dead vessel, or someone who still has a sin nature? He won't. He couldn't. So, He makes you alive to Him and dead to the entity that causes you death, which is sin. Jesus has eradicated the sin nature you and I have been born with, and through the process of our "re-birth" we are born again to a new nature, His nature. Now, A+B=C!

So, if Christ is in you, and He is in all true believers, then the body of sin you used to be has been changed to a body of righteousness because of His life in you and His Spirit guiding you. If Christ is in you, you have the guarantee of His Spirit being in you too. If the Spirit is in you, then righteousness should be in you too. If righteousness is in you, shouldn't people start noticing it at some point? "I'm just a sinner saved by grace" just doesn't seem to measure up anymore, does it? What if we started to say (and truly believe) this: "I was once a sinner, but by the power of God in Jesus I have been made a righteous saint, and I'm going to live my life in His power and stop all the nonsense!" Do you like that better? It's theologically truer that what we're weakly saying now.

"*But if the Spirit of him that raised up Jesus from the dead dwell in you, he that raised up Christ from the dead shall also quicken your mortal bodies by his Spirit that dwelleth in you,*" We can't hide from this verse either. If Jesus has been resurrected, and He lives in you, you have been resurrected too. Spiritually at this point, physically at some point, but resurrected nonetheless. Jesus was resurrected into new life; we are too. The word "*quicken*" means "*to make alive.*" True believers, according to the Bible, are made alive in Christ.

So, if we are resurrected into new life, then why are we living so dead? Why are we so mundane in our walk? Why are we so average? Why are we living such mediocre lives? There are only two logical answers. First, we're really not saved; Jesus does not live in us, the Spirit is not guiding us, and we are going to Hell, but we are content in believing the lie that we're not going. Second, we have quenched the Spirit so much from our insistent attitudes of self and we are just sinners saved by grace that He has allowed us to go our own way. We might get to heaven some-day, but it'll be hell on earth until that day. Does that sound Christ honoring to you? Does it sound acceptable? It doesn't to me either. I want you to really think about this.

Chapter 8 Verse 12-13

"*Therefore, brethren, we are debtors, not to the flesh, to live according to the flesh.*" God has not done all He has done for us to let us live like we want to live. The notion that we can habitually sin and God is okay with it is not biblical, as we have seen. We are indebted to God for His Spirit who lives in us, not to the flesh that once controlled us. There is no good thing in the flesh, but there are all good things in the Spirit. The word "*debtors*" means "*obligated or duty bound.*" For a person to reach out to Jesus to ask for forgiveness of sin and to keep them from going to hell makes that person duty bound to Jesus and His desires, not theirs. And His yoke is not burdensome, but sin's yoke truly is. Honestly, a person is a fool to focus his or her life upon a weak thing such as the flesh. A person is a fool to live as though he is in debt and obligated to something that gets sick and diseased so often and will soon perish from this world. Doesn't make sense, does it?

"*For if you live according to the flesh you will die; but if by the Spirit you put to death the deeds of the body, you will live.*" Anyone foolish enough to obligate themselves to the flesh, to live a fleshly life, to glorify self in the flesh, will die. Those aren't my words; they're God's. God says if you live your life daily in the flesh, you will surely be separated from Him, daily. This explains a lot, relating to how people live, doesn't it? God goes on to say that, if you allow the Spirit to take control, you have the power to put to death the deeds of sin, and if you do that, you will enjoy His presence in your life. So, the person who says, "God can't expect me to live obediently to Him every day" is biblically wrong because that's exactly what He expects and what He has equipped you to do. The person who says, "Nobody is perfect" is simply making excuses to keep God's Spirit (perfection) from controlling his or her decisions (of imperfection). The person who says "I live under grace so I don't have to worry about all of this" better get a new attitude and worldview.

Bottom line: The Holy Spirit of God gives the true believer the power to mortify or put to death evil deeds. So if you or I are content to live in sin, something is drastically wrong. I prayerfully hope you see this clearer now. Our flesh, while attractive as it may be to us, has never done anything for us. It only brings misery, sickness, and eventually death. God's Spirit, on the other hand, has given us everything including life and freedom from sin and death, and it fulfills righteousness in us, pulls our minds towards spiritual things, gives us peace, dwells within us, and leads us closer to Jesus. We should be indebted to Him, not trying to quench His work. Quenching leads to mediocrity; mediocrity leads to dullness; dullness leads to death. One last thing; putting to death the deeds of the body is a continuous struggle as long as we live on this earth. It is a daily effort. Don't give in or give up and don't rest on yesterday's victory for yesterday's victory is meaningless. It's today that we need to focus on.

Chapter 8 Verse 14-15

"*For as many as are led by the Spirit of God, these are sons of God.*" How does the Spirit lead? He does so by carrying us through the trials and temptations of life. He guides us through the way of righteousness and truth. He directs us on where to go and how to get there. He actually becomes actively involved in the life of the believer. We need to learn how to follow Him perhaps, but He never, ever, leads us to or agrees with us in sin. So once again, for a person to make light of and make excuses for sin while claiming to be spiritual or Spirit led, the person is wrong. And I've been there. I bet you have too. So let's develop a correct biblical worldview and stop the mediocrity!

As a son of God, however, I should represent my family with dignity and honor, and my Father with reverential awe and respect, shouldn't I? I could be a prodigal son. I could come to my senses at some point and come back to Him after I've learned life's hard lessons, but since I now know better, why would I go through the pain and suffering? Besides, wouldn't the Spirit lead me away from all of that? Wouldn't He try to keep me from making those poor decisions? Of course He would.

"*For you did not receive the spirit of bondage again to fear, but you received the Spirit of adoption by whom we cry out, "Abba, Father.*" Do not miss this verse. This is one of Scripture's most beautiful verses about our relationship with God through faith in Christ. It once again describes how God has changed every Christian's relationship with Him through the power of the Holy Spirit.

In the previous verse, Paul wrote that all who are led by the Spirit of God are His children. Now he gets more specific. Earlier in this letter to the Romans, Paul wrote that through faith in Christ we are freed from slavery to sin and become "slaves to righteousness," and Paul is not backing away from that in this verse. Here, though, Paul assures us that God does not view us as His slaves or even just good servants. He did not free us from slavery to sin simply to add us to His team. He rescued us from sin to make us His children. That involves the Holy Spirit. And that's incredible, friends!

God did not give us the spirit of slavery by giving us the Holy Spirit. Abused slaves often live in fear of their masters, and that is not the relationship God wants from us. No, Paul insists God gave us the Spirit of adoption as His children. In other words, God legally changed the status of those who come to Him by faith in Christ as adopted sons and daughters.

This is not a distant or strained parent/child relationship, either. This Spirit of adoption, another name for the Holy Spirit, allows us to cry out to God as little children call out to a loving daddy. The word Abba is a Greek and English adaptation of the Aramaic word for father. It was often the word used by young children for "papa" or "daddy." That's the relationship God wants with us, and He has made it possible through the Spirit. Now, who would want to sin now or make excuses for it when we do? It really is absurd, right? Of course it is. Being conformed to His image is by far a better option.

Chapter 8 Verse 16-17

"*The Spirit Himself beareth witness with our spirit, that we are the children of God:*" We have just two main methods by which we gain knowledge of our world. Either we learn information from someone else, or we use our senses to discover a fact. All this knowledge enters our mind, but our mind does not always use it in the same way. For example, we can learn something as a fact although we still do not believe it.

It is very hard for our natural minds to understand God and heaven. There are some things that we simply cannot understand. So God has provided another method by which His people may know such things. He has given them His Holy Spirit, who lives in them. The Holy Spirit shows these things, not firstly to their minds, but to their own spirits.

New Christians often worry whether they are truly born again as children of God. They cannot yet see, from their senses that God has made this wonderful change in their lives. The problem is that they are depending upon their own feelings. Their feelings change constantly, and so does their confidence. Even in matters of this world, our feelings are a very poor way to discover anything.

The true test of whether someone is a Christian is the work of the Holy Spirit in his or her life. For example, the Holy Spirit teaches God's people those things that Christ taught. So, the Holy Spirit shows them that God's promises truly are for them. Such knowledge may not satisfy a person's natural mind, but, by it, God can bring life and peace to a person's spirit. But we must remember that the Spirit is holy and since He indwells all true believers, there is always some evidence of a supernatural change in a genuine believer's behavior. There has to be. While they will never manifest perfection in this life, there is always a change in the "direction" of their life. If not, then one seriously needs to examine the state of their soul, which is part of the process of working out one's salvation and being conformed to His image!

"And if children, then heirs; heirs of God, and joint-heirs with Christ; if so be that we suffer with him, that we may be also glorified together." What an astounding truth and promise. True believers are adopted children of God, and as such, they are legally qualified to be heirs to what God has. In fact, the reason God adopts us as His children is to share with us what He has. And He has Jesus, and eternity, and peace, and wellness, and holiness, and power, and authority, and grace, and love, and mercy, and well, you get the picture.

Being a fellow heir with Christ means at least three glorious things: we will share in the nature, position, and responsibility of Christ. First, we will share in the inheritance of His nature by being blameless and eternal in a glorified body. Second, we will share in the inheritance of His nature positionally by being legal citizens of the Kingdom of God with the right to surround the throne of God. Third, we will share in the inheritance of His nature responsibly by having the right to rule and have authority in His millennial reign. There might be (will be) some suffering here in this world because of sin (more reason to stop sinning, right?). But when we are in His presence in heaven and we have been glorified, this will all be made right for those who truly believe and follow Jesus and His Word faithfully. Is that what you really want? It should be. It is what God has provided.

Chapter 8 Verse 18-22

"*For I consider that the sufferings of this present time are not worthy to be compared with the glory which shall be revealed in us.* The effects of sin (disease, pain, corruption, abuse, persecution, urges, desires, aging, loss, deterioration, decay, etc.) will all be a distant memory for the true believer in the presence of God, and this truth should be revealed in all true believers. You know, it's kind of hard to have anything revealed from something that's not here or alive. So, if a person is here, physically alive, and spiritually alive, there should be some glory revealed in us and through us. If there's not, I wonder why?

"*For the earnest expectation of the creation eagerly waits for the revealing of the sons of God.* The Fall of Man was so destructive, even the creation itself suffered. The word "creation" means "everything under man": animal, plant, mineral. All of creation struggles for life and to stay alive, but death is everywhere for all living things. Lions, tigers, bears, oh my. Trees, shrubs, grass. Fish, birds, orangutans. Why? By now we should all know why.

"*For the creation was subjected to futility, not willingly, but because of Him who subjected it in hope:*" God's creation is subject to man's fall because man was given authority over it. The creation didn't do anything to deserve deterioration and decay, but its ownership did, and now it suffers too. Our sins absolutely do affect others, and they affect creation.

"*because the creation itself also will be delivered from the bondage of corruption into the glorious liberty of the children of God.* The good news is that creation will receive deliverance too! Whatever happens to man, happens to this world. So when man is delivered from eternal bondage, so will the creation, I would think, therefore, those who are so concerned with bettering our environment would be true born-again Christians worshipping God the Father and not earth the mother.

"*For we know that the whole creation groans and labors with birth pangs together until now.*" The entire creation awaits the arrival of a renovated world. Creation resents evil and struggles against decay and death, and rightfully so. It fights for survival. It fights against the bondage of being slaughtered or changed.

The "groaning" we experience together with creation is not futile or despairing but looks with hope toward the new world being birthed, brought upon us by Jesus and His Word and Resurrection. Our hope is in Jesus. Not Greenpeace or the Green New Deal.

Chapter 8 Verse 23-27

"*Not only that, but we also who have the first fruits of the Spirit, even we ourselves groan within ourselves, eagerly waiting for the adoption, the redemption of our body.*" The believer suffers and struggles for deliverance from corruption. But true believers have the first fruits of the Spirit. What are they? First, there is His presence because of our salvation. Second, there is hope as we continuously seek more of God. Third, there is the great resource of prayer and access to the Father. Fourth, we are redeemed and adopted children of God. If we are a true believer, our lives will reflect it. It would be impossible for our lives not to.

"*For we were saved in this hope, but hope that is seen is not hope; for why does one still hope for what he sees?*" The believer's hope is entirely different from the world's hope. The world hopes for what it can see, use, and often abuse. The believer's hope is based on what God has promised, even though it may be unseen at this point. The believer's hope is spiritual; the world's hope is typically material.

"*But if we hope for what we do not see, we eagerly wait for it with perseverance.*" God has saved us based on the hope, or faith, we have in His promises to us contained in His Word. We don't need to see anything if we have a proper understanding of God. In fact, understanding God with a biblical worldview allows us to wait eagerly with perseverance without the need to see anything. Do you remember the illustration I wrote about lift overcoming gravity? I rarely ever "see" the wind flowing over the wings of an airplane, but I don't need to see it. I have hope (faith) that it is there. That's how I can get in an airplane and fly without worrying about watching the wings the whole way.

"*Likewise the Spirit also helps in our weaknesses. For we do not know what we should pray for as we ought, but the Spirit Himself makes intercession for us with groanings which cannot be uttered.*" As we have seen, the work of the Spirit is a prominent theme in Romans 8. Romans 8:26 and 27 are the final explicit installment in Paul's discussion of the ministry of the Spirit, and the main focus of these two verses is prayer. No passage of Scripture provides greater encouragement for prayer. The Spirit comes to the aid of believers who are overwhelmed by the perplexity of prayer and takes their concerns to God with an intensity far greater than we could ever imagine or do ourselves. This is so encouraging.

The work of the Spirit described in these two verses is the second in a string of three truth statements designed to help sustain believers. Because of depravity, believers are often not capable of knowing what to pray unless God's will is explicitly stated. However, in these two verses Paul encourages believers because the Spirit is interceding as only He and the Father understand, and it is through this ministry that intercession is made according to God's will on behalf of the believer.

"*Now He who searches the hearts knows what the mind of the Spirit is, because He makes intercession for the saints according to the will of God.*" God searches our hearts as we pray, but He incorporates the mind of the Spirit living in us. Between the Spirit's intellect and our desires, God moves. But notice He moves only as it satisfies His will. Not ours.

Chapter 8 Verse 28-30

"And we know that all things work together for good to those who love God, to those who are the called according to His purpose." Here's one of the most misquoted verses in the Bible. Let's look at this theologically:

All "things" are not good. It would be mockery to say that they are. The death of a child is not good. Cancer is not good. Drug addiction is not good. War is not good. Blasphemy is not good. Committing sin and saying God can use it for good is not good. Spiritual mediocrity is not good.

But God can help us through life's challenges if we're repentant. Here's an illustration to help us see how He does it. Many of us have some salt with our meals. Table salt is made up of both sodium and chloride. By itself, sodium is a deadly poison, and so is chloride. Take either of them separately and you will die. Put them together, and you have table salt. Salt flavors food, and a certain amount of salt is necessary for health and life. We cannot live without some salt in our bodies. Salt is good for our body. Sodium and chloride, taken separately, are deadly. So it is true God can take things that are bad and put them in the crucible of His wisdom and love and make them good. But some things are not and they're going to stay that way.

Now, God can work all things together for good if we're repentant and turn from sin and start living for Him, and He gives us the glorious, wonderful promise that He will do so. We know that we have victory over sin and over Satan, but this verse in Romans teaches us that we also have victory over our circumstances and sins if we repent. His purpose is for us to repent and trust Jesus. God says that all things work together for good then. But we can't use this verse as an excuse to justify habitual "bad". That goes against the clear teaching of Scripture. Surely we can all agree to this.

"For whom He foreknew, He also predestined to be conformed to the image of His Son, that He might be the firstborn among many brethren. 30 Moreover whom He predestined, these He also called; whom He called, these He also justified; and whom He justified, these He also glorified." Note the progression of the verbs in verses 29-30. They start at the beginning of time (foreknew) and extend to the end of time (glorified): Foreknew. Predestined. Called. Justified. Glorified. Wow.

God's ultimate goal is our justification and glorification, which entails being *"conformed to the image of His Son,"* so that we might become part of God's large family. From the beginning, we were created in God's image. But that image was distorted and broken in the Fall. God foreknew that we would fall, but predestined us to be restored in our original image by becoming like the Son. God intends us to become Christ-like, to bear the image of Christ, not the sin nature we're so fond of defending. It's just that simple.

Chapter 8 Verse 31-33

"What then shall we say to these things? If God is for us, who can be against us?" This verse is proof God has acted for us, not against us. He didn't have to, but He did, and I'm grateful. True believers can rest assured that God will deliver them to their destination. The true believer can rest assured that God will ultimately work out all things for His or her good; namely, deliver the believer to His or her eternal presence as promised. The point is God Himself is the true believer's assurance. He has done everything necessary for the believer, and therefore, who (or what) can be against us to the point God can't deliver us? There's no one. What can we say about that except thank you? What should we do with that except live for Him now?

"He who did not spare His or Son, but delivered Him up for us all, how shall He not with Him also freely give us all things?" Someone had to pay the penalty for sin that we couldn't pay, but we certainly owed. We needed help; we needed rescue. We needed someone who had the power, authority, and desire to pay our debt off. The only person holy enough would be Jesus. God did not spare Him; He did not ask to be spared. He did this all for

us which means all for me and all for you. What a glorious, marvelous, wonderful love. How could I just willfully live a life of habitual sin and be okay with it knowing what it cost someone else for my indifference? It gets better though. If God is willing to give us the very best (Jesus), what else would He hold back from us? Nothing. He will give us all good things. But sin won't.

"*Who shall bring a charge against God's elect? It is God who justifies.*" Only God can bring a charge against us, and through His justification, He will not do so. This great truth is absolutely amazing. If we truly have trusted Jesus Christ as our Savior, if we are one of God's elect, He does not charge us with the penalty of sin. But we must not take advantage of Him by thinking we can sin habitually and be ok, or that He will be okay with it. We have clearly seen that this is wrong, and that He won't. But if we do, especially after being taught it is wrong, we have to deal with the discipline.

Chapter 8 Verse 34-35

"*34 Who is he that condemneth? It is Christ that died, yea rather, that is risen again, who is even at the right hand of God, who also maketh intercession for us.*" Who condemns us? Who has the right to condemn us? The devil? No, he has no true claim on our lives. He can condemn you, and if you want to believe his claim go ahead, but what could be more mediocre than believing a liar lying about lies? Can we condemn ourselves? Not really, but we can sure feel the guilt of self-condemnation. No, the only entity in the universe that can condemn us is Jesus. And His condemnation is right, thorough, and damning. And it will cost us everything, if we allow it to happen. But who in their right mind, knowing the truth would allow it?

While you're thinking about that, think about this: Scripture says here that Christ has died, risen again, and is at the right hand of the Father discussing your forgiveness. He has died for your sins; He has risen for your new life; He is at the power side of God; He is relinquishing condemnation by making intercession for us. Don't miss this hallelujah moment.

"Who shall separate us from the love of Christ? Shall tribulation, or distress, or persecution, or famine, or nakedness, or peril, or sword?" Great question! Who (or what) has the ability to separate us from God's love for us? Since God has no equal, what can separate us from Him if He says we are in a relationship? There is no circumstance, no situation, and no event that can cause Christ's love to turn away from us. Even God's discipline towards us for our rebellious sins can't keep God from loving us.

No matter how terrible a situation may be, no matter how severe the circumstance may be, it cannot separate the true believer from the love of Christ. The Bible records the most severe of all worldly circumstances and proclaims they are powerless. Tribulation, with all of its suffering and affliction, can't. Distress, with all of its anguish and agony, can't. Persecution, with all of its abuse and attacks can't. Famine, with all of its poverty and starvation, can't. Nakedness, with all of its worldly comforts taken away, can't. Peril, with all of its dangers and risks, can't. The sword, with its killing and martyrdom, can't.

What can then? How do you feel about it? Can your sense of unworthiness keep you from God's love? No. Low self-esteem? No. A defeated life? No. Self-accusations? Nope. Why? Because we're not in charge of what God wants to do. And if He wants to love us in spite of everything else, who are we to say He won't or can't?

Want to know something? Christ loves you right now, right where you're at, even if you are in mediocrity. He just doesn't want you to stay right where you're at. He wants you to experience Him deeper and truer. You say you've messed up? Who hasn't? Look, His love is not a memory. It is a moment-by-moment action by the omnipotent, living Son of God, to bring us to everlasting joy out of the bonds of mediocre living. And nothing can change that.

Chapter 8 Verse 36-39

"As it is written: "For Your sake we are killed all day long;" We are accounted as sheep for the slaughter." Unfortunately, the world in its spiritually dark

condition could care less about Jesus or your faith and identity in Him. True believers are going to suffer in this world just as everyone else will. In fact, the world has a tendency to single out true believers for persecution. If a person truly lives for Christ, it's going to upset those who don't. Isn't that strange? Statistics show on an annual basis that around two-hundred million Christians are persecuted around the world yearly. Why? It's because an unrighteous world is at enmity with righteousness.

"*As it is written:*" This is a quotation from Psalm 44:22. Believers in the Old Testament, as well as those in the New Testament, suffered. Paul quoted Scripture in this verse to show that Christians will suffer in this life. The point of this quotation is to demonstrate that the extent of Christ's love for us does not mean Christians will never face trouble in their lives. We cannot be tempted to think that because Christ loves us there will be no trouble for us in this life. The reason believers face persecution and trouble is for the sake of the Lord, who loves us so. There should be nothing strange or unexpected about suffering for the Lord. This world has been cursed by The Fall of Man, and the world curses God. One of the reasons I believe in Christ is because of how the world responds to Him even to this day, and the response is out of sheer ignorance of who He really is.

Why is this so? It's because the world is content with mediocrity, especially in spiritual matters. The world wants to conform to its patterns, not God's. But the world knows that Jesus is far beyond mediocre, and that challenges the world to deal with Jesus. Unfortunately, the usual way is slaughtering His followers through various persecutions. But the sheep will be vindicated.

"*Yet in all these things we are more than conquerors through Him who loved us.*" With Jesus, there is always good news. In spite of any circumstance, we conquer through Jesus' love for us. Christ has and will carry His true believer through any and all situations, including martyrdom and death. To live is Christ, and to die is gain. How can you gain more than living in Christ spiritually? Living in His presence physically. Nothing can separate us; it can only move us closer to Jesus. Here's the proof:

"For I am persuaded that neither death nor life, nor angels nor principalities nor powers, nor things present nor things to come, nor height nor depth, nor any other created thing, shall be able to separate us from the love of God which is in Christ Jesus our Lord."

9

Chapter 9 Verse 1-5

The instructional change from chapter eight to chapter nine is abrupt and striking. The next three chapters deal with the nation of Israel in world history. The church faces the same problem as addressed in these chapters because the church is often seen as the spiritual Israel. When Jesus was sent to this world, the Jews rejected Him because they had settled for spiritual mediocrity and deadness. Oftentimes the church does the exact same thing by accepting mediocrity in its membership.

"I tell the truth in Christ, I am not lying, my conscience also bearing me witness in the Holy Spirit, that I have great sorrow and continual grief in my heart," Paul is demonstrating great love and concern for people. Paul pleads for people to trust him. He had a deep sense of urgency for people to grasp the spiritual truth that he was trying to teach them. There was a time when I would not have understood this; I understand clearly now.

"*For I could wish that I myself were accursed from Christ for my brethren, my countrymen according to the flesh,"* Paul had an unbelievable willingness to sacrifice for people. He says he wished he was lost if it meant people could be saved. There was a time when I would not have understood this too; I still don't. I'm not willing to give up my salvation for anyone, although I have surrendered my life and work daily to reach those people who might want to join me in salvation. The point isn't giving up our salvation; as we've seen in earlier verses, that's impossible. What is possible and expected is for every true believer to be willing to work and suffer whatever in order to bring people to Jesus.

"*who are Israelites, to whom pertain the adoption, the glory, the covenants, the giving of the law, the service of God, and the promises;* Paul recorded his love for people; now he shows the great respect he has for people. In spite of her failings, the nation still would be used by God for His will to be done. Paul is giving the reader of his letter the wake-up call that the nation of Israel was called to a covenantal relationship with God, just as true believers have been called too. The point is the great love of God. He did not reach out to man only once and leave man to his doom. No, God reached out to man time and time again. The Jews had God's law, or the will of God in written form. But they chose to ignore it. I'm afraid many "Christians" are guilty of this too, and it causes great mediocrity because that's the best ignorance of God and His Word can do. One of the great tragedies of human life is for a person to know that something is right and not do it.

"*of whom are the fathers and from whom, according to the flesh, Christ came, who is over all, the eternally blessed God. Amen.*" The Jews had the privilege of the Messiah coming from their roots. Christians have the privilege of us coming from His roots. My position is we ought to honor our Father and understand our roots, so we may live extraordinary lives. I am sure you're starting to agree. If you have been reading and paying attention, by now you must surely see it and agree too.

Chapter 9 Verse 6-9

"*But it is not that the word of God has taken no effect. For they are not all Israel who are of Israel,*" The next several verses are startling and should awaken many people to their true and actual relationship with God. The next eight verses explain exactly who the children of God are.

First, they are not from a certain race or institution. God's promise has not failed. Christianity is open to all people from all nations, all races, all cultures, and all backgrounds. God loves all people, and to be biased or prejudice against anyone for the above reasons is to be going against God's will, which is sin. It may be culturally acceptable to hate people's genealogies, but it is not biblically acceptable. The only thing we are to hate is sin according to the Bible.

"*nor are they all children because they are the seed of Abraham; but, "In Isaac your seed shall be called."* Next, the true children of God are not from any particular parentage or heritage. Many Jews felt they were God's children because of the promise God made to Abraham. They felt they had a godly heritage because they were born in a Jewish family. This just isn't true. The modern day equivalent is for a person to think they are okay with God because "My daddy was a preacher," or "my great-aunt was a missionary," or "I was baptized when I was twelve." I hear these things all the time. All of that is absolutely meaningless as we have discussed in earlier verses. I have met people who live as if they are unregenerate, yet when confronted with this they quickly proclaim they are (or were) married to a preacher, a deacon, or a Sunday school teacher. It is meaningless. One's salvation is personal. You don't marry into it; you're not born into it; and you don't inherit it from anyone. It must be a personal decision based on personal faith and a willingness to be personally responsible and obedient.

"*8 That is, those who are the children of the flesh, these are not the children of God; but the children of the promise are counted as the seed.'* It couldn't be any clearer here. If one is living in sin, the Bible proclaims again and again they are not saved. People who live a life outside of the will and guidance of God and His Word are not the children of God. The person cannot please God because he or she lives for the desires of the flesh, and those who live according to the flesh live for self rather than for their Creator. They live for sin, not righteousness. And if a person lives for something they're allegedly dead to, something is vastly wrong.

"*9 For this is the word of promise: "At this time I will come and Sarah shall have a son."* A person becomes a child of God through faith in the promises of God. Since God cannot lie, whatever He says He will do. Here, we have the reminder that God promised Abraham a son in his very old age, and at the right time He fulfilled His promise. His promise to you, at whatever age you are, is that you can have a true relationship with Him, but you must do it His way, and then He expects you to live as if you've actually done it. And if you have actually been saved, living that way should be your heart's desire. If it's not, is it possible something is wrong?

Chapter 9 Verse 10-13

"10 And not only this, but when Rebecca also had conceived by one man, even by our father Isaac (for the children not yet being born, nor having done any good or evil, that the purpose of God according to election might stand, not of works but of Him who calls) it was said to her, "The older shall serve the younger."

Here is a good example of the concept of election, which is the doctrine that salvation is wholly God's work. In the above verses, the promise given to Rebecca for a child was reiterated. But note the promise was given before Esau and Jacob were born. God chose Jacob to be the child of promise, not Esau. God elected Jacob over Esau. Not a big deal really as you'll read in the next verse. However, this would have been very strange to the people of this day because the oldest sibling (Esau was born first) was always the one who received the lion's share of any blessing the family would give to their children. The promise was by election, not because of any "good or bad" of the children as they hadn't even been born by the time God said He was going to do what He was going to do. We need to realize that "election" is not of works but of promise. God's promise. It is God's promise that calls men to salvation. Here's the point: a true child of God is not a person who belongs to God because of his or her pedigree or family tree. He or she belongs to God because God has called him or her for salvation, or has elected him or her. It is my opinion that God has elected everyone; but each of us must decide for ourselves if we're going to trust Him for our salvation. In other words, we shouldn't take the doctrine of election and misuse it because the concept that everyone in the end will be saved is not biblical, friends. If that concept was true, Jesus died such a horrendous death for nothing.

"As it is written, "Jacob I have loved, but Esau I have hated." God didn't hate Esau, in the sense we usually employ that word. In fact, He blessed him. He made of him a great nation. He gave him promises which He fulfilled to the letter. What these verses imply is that God set His heart on Jacob, to bring him to redemption, and all Jacob's followers would reflect the possibilities of that. As Paul has already argued they were not all necessarily saved by that, by any means, but Jacob would forever stand for what God wants men to be, and Esau would forever stand as a symbol of what He does not like.

Do you know the final confrontation of Jacob and Esau that is recorded in the Scriptures? It was when Jesus stood before Herod the king. Herod was an Idumean, an Edomite, a descendant of Esau. Jesus was, through David, a descendant of Jacob. There, standing face-to-face, were Jacob and Esau. Herod has nothing but contempt for the King of the Jews, and Jesus will not open His mouth in the presence of Herod. This is God's strange and mysterious way of dealing with humanity. In this last meeting between "Esau" and "Jacob" I can see God saying the same thing: Jacob I love. Esau I hate. Jesus I love. Sin I hate. Obedience I love; disobedience I hate. Surrender I love; rebellion I hate.

CHAPTER 9 VERSE 14-16

"What shall we say then? Is there unrighteousness with God? God forbid." Since God was doing things as described in the earlier verses that went against many of the laws of mankind in the ancient world, primarily the laws pertaining to the inheritance left to children, Paul asks the next logical question. Is God unjust? Can God allow "undesirables," who accept His call to be in a relationship with Him, while not allowing "desirables" and still be found righteous? Is this fair? Is it fair for God to offer salvation to everyone, yet accept only those who accept Him and deny those who deny Him? Is this unrighteous? Well, maybe from

the mind of fallen mankind, but from a biblical perspective it is not unrighteous. Why? Does it really need an explanation?

"*For he saith to Moses, I will have mercy on whom I will have mercy, and I will have compassion on whom I will have compassion.*" Look, God has the right to do anything He wants to do. But He chooses to be merciful and just, and it's perfect mercy and perfect justice because He is perfectly holy above everything else. God can and does show mercy as He wills. But it's not because He's impressed with our ability to analyze deep theological questions as above. It's because He simply chooses to do so. He has the right to do so; He chooses to do so, and He elects to offer it to everyone. You and I need to desperately seek God for His mercy. We would be foolish not to. The enemy of your soul will tell you to not believe this because it's too good to be true. But here it is, friends. God is offering you and me mercy and compassion, but the offer won't last forever. What will we do with it?

"*16 So then it is not of him that willeth, nor of him that runneth, but of God that sheweth mercy.*" God also has the right to do as He wills. This is His creation. He called it into existence. He establishes the laws of physics with which we must all operate under. His spiritual laws are just as immutable. It is His will that will be done. And God has a right to have His will in your life if you are a true believer. Humanity has no right to accuse God of unrighteousness. Why does God allow suffering? Because people sin, and if He didn't allow sin to take its course, people would not seek Him for mercy. Bad things happen because we allow it to happen, not because God does. God uses it to get our attention on how broken we are, so we will return to His righteousness. Here's a shocker: God has the right to use both honorable and dishonorable people to work all things out for good. He uses honorable and dishonorable events to work all things out for good. He has the same right over all people and events in the lives of people as a potter has over all clay, which we will see in our next verses. But for now, let's take some time to pray over this.

God "*has mercy on whomever he wants to have mercy, and he hardens whomever he wants to harden.*" I would simply add that the "*whomever*" he has mercy on refers to "*all who choose to believe*" while the "*whomever*" he hardens refers to "*all who refuse to believe.*" The passage demonstrates the wisdom of God's loving flexibility, not the sheer determinism of God's power.

I am grateful for Jesus, hearing about Him, learning about Him, believing and accepting Him, and receiving God's mercy through Him. Mediocrity has left because of who I am in Christ now. Sometimes I allow it to take back over, but that's on me, not Him.

Chapter 9 Verse 17-21

"*For the Scripture says to the Pharaoh, "For this very purpose I have raised you up, that I may show My power in you, and that My name may be declared in all the earth.*" God will allow the hearts of those who refuse Him to harden, which is exactly what happened to Pharaoh in the story of the Exodus found in the Bible. It wasn't God's choice for Pharaoh's heart to harden; it was Pharaoh's choice. It is important to understand that in this whole process, Pharaoh had ample opportunities to repent and let God's people go. He saw the countless displays of God's power, and instead of softening his heart towards God, he hardened it. He had free will in the matter, but he chose not to respond to God. After a certain point, he was past the point where he could even respond to God, and therefore, God allowed his heart to harden against God so maximum power could be displayed in what He did. It is important to understand it all started with Pharaoh's choice to disregard God and not God's choice to harden Pharaoh's heart. It's the same way with us today.

"*Therefore He has mercy on whom He wills, and whom He wills He hardens.*" As we have seen, Chapter 9 deals with the sovereignty of God. If we truly enter into the meaning of this passage, we will praise and thank God that He is willing to show mercy unto some, and we will see that God is perfectly justified in allowing others to harden their own hearts towards God. Remember, the background involves God's dealings with Israel and Pharaoh as recorded in the book of Exodus, and it's important to realize that both parties were sinners who deserved to be judged for their sins. Yet God was willing to show mercy to one (Hebrews) and to allow the other (Pharaoh) to grow harder and harder to the plainly visible actions of God. One escaped the punishment they deserved, and the other received the punishment he deserved. The point? Those who do escape judgment have God alone to thank; those who are judged have no one to blame but themselves. It's still true today. If you constantly and consistently refuse what God wants to do with you, you will eventually be allowed to grow hard towards God and suffer the consequences. I am sure Pharaoh thought he was justified and right, but he wasn't. Once again, I just described a large percentage of people who think they're ok, but from God's perspective they are not.

Can I ask you a question? As you have read this book, have you come to see that you are a sinner that deserves God's judgment? Have you ever cried out as the man in Luke 18:13, *"God be merciful to me a sinner"?* The moment you take your place before God as a lost, hell-deserving sinner, God will indeed "have mercy on you." Listen to Paul's words to the believers in Ephesus when he reminds them of God's mercy towards them in Ephesians 2:4-5: *"But God, Who is rich in mercy, for His great love wherewith He loved us, Even when we were dead in sins, hath quickened us together with Christ, (by grace ye are saved)."* Paul echoes this same truth in Titus 3:5: *"Not by works of righteousness which we have done, but according to His mercy He saved us."* Christ's death on the cross has made God's mercy to you possible and made it possible for you to believe the good news of God's mercy through Christ, and, therefore, repent of your sins. If you reject God's offer of mercy to you, your heart will become hardened to the gospel, and thus the Spirit would plead with you through the words of Hebrews 3:7-8: *"Wherefore as the Holy Ghost saith, Today if ye will hear His voice, Harden not your hearts."* Do not "*harden your heart*" as Pharaoh did, but accept God's gracious offer of salvation before it's forever too late. Have you done that? Does your life show that you've done it? Or is your life mediocre, and you think that's ok? It's not. Anything short of conforming to His image just isn't.

Chapter 9 Verse 19-21

"*19 You will say to me then, "Why does He still find fault? For who has resisted His will?"* The idea here is if God shows favoritism, isn't mankind just a puppet? That's what people usually think after skimming through the previous couple of verses. But that would go completely against the full teaching of Scripture. No, mankind is held accountable and he or she is responsible to God. Depending on where a person stands with God will depend on God's mercy towards them. Isn't that fair?

:20 But indeed, O man, who are you to reply against God? Will the thing formed say to him who formed it, "Why have you made me like this?" We are living in a day when people have made salvation so much humanity's doing they have forgotten the fact that salvation is all God's doing. Israel did the same thing in the Old Testament. We have been privileged. We think we have done something. We think we deserve something. But we are clay, and the clay never, ever has a right to say anything back to the potter. The potter is the one who has all the rights over the clay, or in this case the humanity He has made. He may not exercise His rights, but He certainly has the right to do and say and work in any manner He wants.

Do you realize that God could kill you in the next minute and be absolutely righteous in doing it? Do you believe that? You need to because it is quite true. The next time you sin and quickly say, "Well, I will ask God to forgive me after I enjoy this a little bit longer," just remember something. God has a right to take you out of here. But we don't believe that. We think, "God is a loving God and just wouldn't do that!" Most of the time you would be right. Thank God He is long-suffering. But when you understand that one sin condemned the whole human race, one sin, and one sin brought sin into the human race, then you understand how serious that is with God. He has the right. He may not exercise it, but He has the right at any time to take you and me out of here. But He shows you and me mercy. One day His mercy will be unavailable as we lay in a grave. We shouldn't ever get there without making a decision for Jesus. Am I right? Of course I am. Don't allow mediocrity to cloud your thinking.

"Does not the potter have power over the clay, from the same lump to make one vessel for honor and another for dishonor?" Ask yourself this: how far do you think you can push God? God has the right over what He has made. Don't ever think

for a second that He has to answer for what He does. We are the creation, the clay. He is the potter. That is the idea Paul is trying to get across. What does God have a right to do? Paul goes on to say, *"To make from the same lump one vessel for honorable use, and another for common use."* We have a choice to make on a daily basis, after our conversion. We must decide daily if we're going to be vessels which can be used to bring respect and honor to God daily. It is very possible to do, but sin wants to birth mediocrity. And mediocrity cannot and does not bring honor to a magnificent God.

Chapter 9 Verse 22-24

"*What if God, willing to shew his wrath, and to make his power known, endured with much longsuffering the vessels of wrath fitted to destruction:"* I will be the first to admit Romans Chapter 9 is a very deep and difficult chapter in a very deep and somewhat difficult book. But it's not impossible. Look, mankind has free will, and God will not override our choices in life. Throughout our entire life time we are presented with the opportunity to accept the gospel message, which has the power to save us, or we can reject it. The outcome of this choice is based solely upon us. God does not choose for us, nor does he predestine some to be saved and some to be damned.

Paul writes to us that God endured with exceeding patience the objects of his wrath. These are the individuals who have rejected his salvation message and the payment for their sin. These individuals are destined for destruction of their own volition because they have chosen this path for their life and have rejected Jesus. It is common and easy to struggle over a statement such as this and focus on the wrath of God towards them, but what about his enduring patience concerning them? Why don't we focus on that? They are clearly enemies of the cross, and yet God is patient with them. He tolerates and endures those who have rejected his salvation and forgiveness of sins. Why do so many struggle with this? Why are so many living in mediocrity and seemingly apathetic to it? Heads up. They're about to get challenged.

"And that he might make known the riches of his glory on the vessels of mercy, which he had afore prepared unto glory," The Book of Hebrews says, *"If we deliberately*

keep on sinning after we have received the knowledge of the truth, no sacrifice for sins is left, but only a fearful expectation of judgment and of raging fire that will consume the enemies of God" (Hebrews 10:26-27). I am afraid that all our excuses to sin and belief that God is okay with it have just been made obsolete. Are you "saved" but think sin is just normal and natural? Well, let me ask you a very serious and sober question. How much more severely do you think a man or woman deserves to be punished who has trampled the Son of God under foot, who has treated as an unholy thing the blood of the covenant that sanctified him or her, and who has insulted the Spirit of grace? For we know Him who said, *"It is mine to avenge; I will repay," and again, "The Lord will judge his people." It is a dreadful thing to fall into the hands of the living God"* (Hebrews 10:28-31). Friend, it is severe to reject Jesus and his incredible gift of salvation. But it's more severe to live in sin once you have accepted Him.

"Even us, whom he hath called, not of the Jews only, but also of the Gentiles." The amazing thing about a passage such as this, is that it shows an incredible facet of God's nature when you fully understand it. God is not dealing unfairly with mankind; the opposite is actually true. He is showing incredible mercy and grace in tolerating people's rejection of Jesus. He does this to demonstrate to believers His incredible wealth of mercy. It shows us the depth of His love and grace that has no bounds. It is important to get revelation of this truth because this will change the way we look at life. If we can understand how patient and loving God is towards even those who reject Him, we will know how accepted and loved we are in Christ Jesus. God even uses His enemies to show his incredible love towards us. When we stand before Christ and see His majesty and splendor, we will fully understand how offensive and awful it is to reject such a gift. We will understand the severity of it and the depths of the mercy displayed in patiently enduring His enemies.

Chapter 9 Verse 25-33

I know this is a long set of verses, but they must go together so this may be a bit lengthy. You might want to put your seat belt on because the ride is going to get a little bumpy.

Since life is short and eternity is forever, nothing is more important than understanding the right way to be right with God. And since both fallen human nature and every religion in the world teach the wrong way to come to God, we especially need to understand God's way of righteousness. Paul addresses this crucial issue in our text.

"What shall we say then?" serves both to draw a conclusion from the preceding arguments and to introduce a new section. The question that Paul has been focused on in Romans 9 is this: "If God is faithful to His covenant promises to His chosen people, then why are most of the Jews rejecting Jesus as their Messiah and Lord?" (This is the exact issue we face today with most Christians, in my opinion. I ask myself these questions about Christianity in this country continuously). Look, Paul has shown that it was never God's purpose to save all Israel (because they refused Him), but rather only a remnant (those who truly had faith in Him). God always accomplishes His purpose through a chosen remnant, according to His grace. Since all deserve God's wrath and judgment, it would not be unfair of Him to choose some as objects of mercy (for His glory), but to leave the rest in their sin to glorify His justice in judgment. In other words, He will not accept mediocrity forever. There will be a payday someday.

There is an inexplicable mystery here, but the Bible is clear that if we're saved, it's totally due to God's sovereign grace and mercy; if we're lost, it's totally due to our sin and unbelief. No one can blame God for being lost by complaining, "You didn't choose me!" No, the truth is we rejected Him.

In our text, Paul lays out the right and wrong ways to come to God. To state the wrong way first: To approach God through our works will cause us to stumble over Christ and be lost; to approach God through faith in Christ results in righteousness and salvation. The contrast is plain and stark. If we pursue the righteousness that we need to stand before God by our works, we will fail. If we come to God by faith in Christ, we attain righteousness, even if we were not previously pursuing it.

This leads to the questions, "Why would God deliberately place a stone of stumbling and rock of offense in Zion (Israel)? Why would He give the world a lowly, crucified Savior and a way of salvation that causes many to be offended?" In my secular career, I was involved in marketing with a very well-known international corporation, and from that perspective this is not the way a modern marketing executive would devise a campaign to "sell" the gospel. No, what I would do would be to show people how Jesus will help them succeed at work and have happy families. I would show them how Jesus will understand and approve of mediocrity and apathy. I would absolutely minimize all that negative stuff about sin and judgment. I understand to effectively sell is to give people what they perceive they need: a positive, uplifting message to build their own self-esteem because I know people, and people want what builds them up.

But the reason the true gospel inherently offends is that it confronts our sinful pride. If God sovereignly shows mercy to whom He desires and hardens whom He desires, then I can't boast in why I was shown mercy. In fact, the very idea that I need mercy is offensive. Sure, I'm not perfect, but why can't God just give me a little boost? How about a few helpful hints for happy living? Mercy implies that I'm a spiritual basket case, unable to do anything to gain God's favor. I can't boast in my intellect, because it actually would keep me from trusting in Christ. I can't boast in my morality, because if you could see my heart, you would see that it is not morally pure, but putrid. I can't boast in my good works, because I just do them to make myself look good to others. And they are puny in comparison to how I look out for myself above all else. So God deliberately put Christ and Him crucified at the center of salvation to humble our pride, which is the root of all of our sins.

Marketing aside, any plan of salvation which gives no offense to self-righteous men, is certainly not of God. And so to approach God through marketing or our good works will cause us to stumble over Christ. To come in faith to Christ, God must humble our pride. That leads us to the right way to come to Him, and we must come to Him if we ever expect to be conformed to His image.

Chapter 10 Verse 1-3

"*Brethren, my heart's desire and prayer to God for Israel is that they may be saved.*" God is stripping His apostle down before the audience and allowing Paul to share his heart for lost people who think they are saved. I can honestly relate too. My heart's desire and burden, from the moment I realized this was an issue, was for lost people who think they are saved but show no fruit of the Spirit. There's only mediocrity at best. I know; I was once one of them. And I too was lost but wouldn't admit it. I couldn't admit it; I thought I was saved. But God, through His Word, showed me I was still lost. It wasn't pleasant. It wasn't pretty. I got mad and obstinate. But it was necessary, and thank God He called me to deal with the truth about myself, that my mediocre Christian lifestyle was death dressed up in a tuxedo. I wasn't fooling anyone but myself. But boy was I fooled. My heart's desire is for the person reading this book to be truly saved. It may be painful. You may get mad at me. But if it causes you to seriously search your heart and make absolutely sure you are saved, you can praise God for His work in your life. And you can apologize to me for being mad at me when you see me in heaven. We will both celebrate.

"*For I bear them witness that they have a zeal for God, but not according to knowledge.*" Note Israel's (and modern day Christianity's) mistake: they had a zeal for God, but it was based on information, not transformation.

The Jews knew a lot *about* God, but they did not *know* God. Jesus came to them and lived within their very midst, and they killed Him. How do we explain that? They had information about Jesus, but no real personal relationship with Jesus. Otherwise, they would have recognized Him as He walked among them.

I see this same pattern today in church. Many can recite John 3:16. Many want to keep from going to hell and I don't blame them. Many see Jesus as their free ride to prosperity. Many people attend Bible study for years. But many don't really know Him. They have the information, but they lack the transformation.

What causes all of this? Three things. First, people don't fully know God's true nature, which is holiness and perfection, not just love and forgiveness. Second, people don't comprehend mankind's true nature, which is sin and desperation and spiritual futility. Third, people don't understand God's offer of true salvation. Not fully. No, most people have some information about God, but very little, if any, transformation from God. And it's our fault. Don't believe me? Read the next verse.

"For they being ignorant of God's righteousness, and seeking to establish their own righteousness, have not submitted to the righteousness of God." Mediocrity is just ignorance in a tuxedo. Early in my walk, I was ignorant of the truth. In my self-centeredness, I felt I understood God enough to get baptized and go to heaven. I was wrong. Honestly, most of my life I've never been right. But God's Word is right. I was ignorant of God's righteousness (Jesus) as I focused on my righteousness, which was non-existent. Do you see how the enemy works? And if I have not truly submitted to God's righteousness (Jesus), then I am still as lost as a golf ball.

Chapter 10 Verse 4–6

"For Christ is the end of the law for righteousness to everyone who believes." Christ is God's final word on anything and everything. There will not be another revelation. There will not be a New Testament 2.0. No,

Jesus is the Alpha and Omega, the first and last. The buck has to stop somewhere; why not with Jesus? Man's search for righteousness, or everything right, will only be found at the feet of Jesus. Utopia rests in Him. Shangri-La rests in Him. World peace rests in Him. Perfection rests in Him. Everything else is at His feet. I am there too.

"*For Moses writes about the righteousness which is of the law, "The man who does those things shall live by them.*" A person can become righteous in only two ways. First, by keeping every law perfectly, by never sinning in act, word, or thought. You say you're now disqualified? Then your only hope is the second method, Jesus. But if one chooses Jesus, one should at the very least live by Him and conform to His image.

"*But the righteousness of faith speaks in this way, "Do not say in your heart, 'Who will ascend into heaven?' "that is, to bring Christ down from above.*" Well, who will? Who can? Nobody. Fortunately, you and I don't have to ascend to heaven to receive righteousness. Heaven came down to us.

"*'Who will descend into the abyss?' " (that is, to bring Christ up from the dead).*" Again, who can, or who will? Nobody! If you descend into the abyss, your opportunity is over. Fortunately, you and I don't have to descend into death to track Jesus down because He's not there. He was there, but the grave spit Him out (like the whale did Jonah) because the grave couldn't handle nor hold Him. The grave, for the first time ever, realized what losing felt like. And while Death was once the world's all-time, undefeated heavyweight champion, Jesus stepped into the ring, and Death forfeited because Jesus is a handful, folks. He's bad, bad news to those who stand opposed to Him.

"*But what does it say? "The word is near you, in your mouth and in your heart" (that is, the word of faith which we preach):*" But our King is great news for us who are not perishing. Grave, you got something to say to me? Death, you want to start trouble again? You're going to take another whooping because my King has your number. Listen up, Grave and Death: God's righteousness and salvation is right before a person. Jesus Christ is the Deliverer who has ascended into heaven and has brought utopia (salvation) down to man, and He is the Savior who has descended into the depths to conquer death and hell. And I am one of His, and He is my Lord. And if the grave and death don't like that, they can take it up with Him for He has the final Word.

Chapter 10 Verse 9-11

'*that if you confess with your mouth the Lord Jesus and believe in your heart that God has raised Him from the dead, you will be saved.*" Salvation is available to anyone and everyone. Here, God tells us what we must do. First, there must be a mental ascent into truth to the point where a person knows the truth and can confess truth. What is the truth? Well, Jesus is Lord. If He's not Lord of your life, I doubt He can truly be the Savior of it. The devil wants you to think He can be, and so you and I can sin and not be concerned with sin. We tend to think Jesus is a tool in our tool box, but He's not. We can't call on Him to forgive us then we forget Him afterwards. Who does that? We can't keep the Lord in the closet and drag Him out whenever we need Him to get us out of a bind. That's not going to work, friend, as we have clearly seen. And incidentally, if you were treated that way, would you tolerate it? Of course not. Why would we think Jesus would?

Second, I need to believe in my heart the spiritual truth that Jesus has been resurrected. The apex of Christianity is the resurrection of Jesus Christ. The resurrection validates everything else in the Bible. If Jesus is still in the grave, we are most miserable indeed. But if He is alive, then we better start doing things His way because that proves beyond a shadow of doubt Who He really is. The resurrection is the zenith of Christian doctrine, and again, if it is true, then you and I must deal with Jesus sooner or later. Friend, it is true. Research it for yourself. But when you have dealt with the truth of the resurrection, from an intellectual and spiritual point of view, you're going to have to deal with Jesus. Might as well do it now.

"*For with the heart one believes unto righteousness, and with the mouth confession is made unto salvation.*" Salvation is a spiritual change that shows itself true in the physical world too. When one is born again spiritually, one's confession ought to align with the truth. Repentance, confession, surrender, proclamation, all that is towards Jesus in the heart will come out through the mouth publicly at some point. I don't believe a true conversion can be without conversation about it.

For the Scripture says, *"Whoever believes on Him will not be put to shame."* As he has done in the previous chapter, Paul quotes from the book of Isaiah. Once again, he translates the verse to read that whoever believes in "*Him*" will not be put to shame. By Him, Paul means that Christ is the precious cornerstone God has laid in Zion. All who trust in this cornerstone, this sure foundation, will be vindicated. The foundation will hold. They will find themselves standing on the Rock.

In quoting this verse once more, Paul is supporting a crucial idea from verse four which began this train of thought: *"Christ is the end of the law for righteousness to everyone who believes."* God is saying that whosoever trusts upon the Lord will not be put to shame; i.e., he will not be disgraced. God is promising that whosoever trusts upon the Lord for salvation will not be disgraced, will not be disappointed, will not be let down. Jesus never fails. This is not mediocrity; it is excellence!

Chapter 10 Verse 12-13

"*12 For there is no distinction between Jew and Greek, for the same Lord over all is rich to all who call upon Him.*" This book should have gotten all of our attention way before now. Has it? Are you seeing things differently? I hope so. I sure do, every time I read Romans. What's the relevance to us in these verses?

The relevance of this text is huge for understanding how you came to be saved from God's wrath and from the guilt and dominion of sin with the hope of eternal joy in God. It is crucial for understanding how your children or parents, or brothers and sisters, or neighbors and colleagues, or the unreached peoples of the world will be saved. The process of coming to faith and salvation is laid out in the next several verses as nowhere else.

Before we go on, recall what Paul has just said. He has just stressed that Jew and Gentile have no distinction in the enjoyment of the riches of God's glory. Both, with no distinction, will enjoy the fullness of God's salvation if they call on the name of the Lord. Both, with no distinction, will suffer the consequences of unbelief too. Keep in mind that the problem Paul is dealing with in Romans 9 and 10 is mainly the unbelief of Israel, why it happened, and why this does not undermine the faithfulness and reliability of God. God's offer still stands to anyone who will simply believe and repent. God's promise is still just as binding today as it ever was. He is faithful forever. Since He is never mediocre in His performance, why should His true followers be?

Paul spells out the steps to salvation that apply to the Jews and anyone else. And he argues that they have indeed been put in place for Israel too. So, what must we do? Keep reading.

'For *"whoever calls on the name of the LORD shall be saved."* Paul quotes from the Old Testament, declaring that everyone who calls on the name of the Lord will be saved (Joel 2:32). In doing so, Paul accomplishes two things. First, he connects this truth to His statement in the previous verse that Christ, the Lord of all, gives His riches to all who call on Him, both Jews and Gentiles. This is more amazing than we probably realize and give Jesus credit for. The idea of "calling on the name of the Lord," in this context, means "those who turn to Christ in faith seeking salvation." While not literally a description of a "sinner's prayer," Paul is referring to those who express the sentiment that a "sinner's prayer" contains. This is the act of placing one's faith in Christ. This is crucially different from those Jesus described in Matthew 7:21–23, as those who *use* His name, but have no actual *faith* in Him. This is the part that we must think about until we reach clarity and the proper conclusion. Otherwise, we will make excuses and live in mediocrity all of our lives.

Paul makes a second connection, as well, showing that Christ the Lord is in fact Israel's God from the Old Testament. They are one in the same. All who call on Him in faith, both Jew and Gentile, will be saved from God's wrath against sin and will share in God's glory forever. One had to have faith in the coming Messiah in the days of the Old Testament. One has to have faith in the New Testament age that He has come as Messiah. Old or New, it's all about Jesus, friends. And He never gets old with the newness He brings.

Chapter 10 Verse 14-15

"*How then shall they call on Him in whom they have not believed? And how shall they believe in Him of whom they have not heard? And how shall they hear without a preacher*?" The world cannot be saved apart from the Gospel. Remember what God has said in Romans 10:13: *"Whosoever shall call upon the name of the Lord shall be saved."* This means the offer is open to anyone. But whoever the anyone is has to "call" on Jesus to save them and understand and treat Him as the Lord afterwards. Come on, folks. Can we really expect Jesus to be our genie who pops out of the lamp whenever we need a favor to rescue us, and then we put Him back in the lamp and on the shelf until the next emergency? How long would you and I tolerate people treating us like that? That's what I thought.

People can't call on someone they don't know or know about. They must hear about Him, and the full truth must be disclosed about Him and the person seeking Him. This is what I am attempting to do in this book. And God wants to give us preachers a little love by including our work in His Word. Notice God says people need to hear, but how will they hear without a preacher? Well, how? Here's the flow of logic: How can a person believe and call out to the Lord if they don't believe in Him? They can't. How can a person believe in Christ if they have never heard the truth about Him? They can't. How can a person hear the truth about Him unless a preacher (or anyone who knows the truth and is willing to share it) tells them? They can't.

So preachers are God's gift to humanity? No, that's Jesus. But Jesus was a preacher. Look, to receive communications, one needs a communicator. To hear a message, one needs a messenger. The epitome of all that is Jesus is found in His Word. Christians should also be willing to "preach" and bear witness about Jesus because of the true relationship they have with Him and the true knowledge they have of His Word. So why aren't more Christians doing that? They are content with mediocrity. They seem to be more content with letting someone else do it.

"And how shall they preach unless they are sent? As it is written: "How beautiful are the feet of those who preach the gospel of peace, Who bring glad tidings of good things!" When I surrendered to the ministry, I had no idea the places I would be sent, and, quite honestly, had I known what it was going to be like beforehand I probably wouldn't have gone. But I was sent; and I preached. But I never had the response to that as described here regarding how wonderful it was for me to preach.

Preaching involves basically two things. First, it is telling the truth so as the person who hears it may realize there is an offer of peace between God and themselves if they will come to Him His way. That requires truly understanding our problems and God's solutions. Next, it is glad tidings of good things which must be describing the life and ministry of Jesus and eternal life. Everything else is academic. And typically, a good, passionate, truly born-again preacher can handle it; whereas a secular professor, politician, physician, or plumber, as examples, would struggle. If you want to know about Jesus and His Word, sit under the teaching and preaching ministry of a God-called preacher. If you want to know the mathematical formula for the area of a circle, get a mathematician. But never turn to a secularist for theology. Their goal is to have you conform to their image.

CHAPTER 10 VERSE 16-17

"But they have not all obeyed the gospel. For Isaiah says, "Lord, who has believed our report?" That's the issue. So many have heard but have not obeyed, and they haven't obeyed because deep down, they really haven't believed. This is why there is so much mediocrity in the lives of "followers" of Jesus. They really don't believe. They want God to get them out of hell, but they refuse to allow God to get hell out of them. I know this sounds awfully bold, but it's true. And if you fill a church up with these types of "followers," you'll get a mediocre church too. What

does a church like that look like? Well, there will be a lot of fellowship activities inside the church, but no evangelism or outreach outside the church. There will be a lot of meetings going on, but no movement. There will be a lot of programs going on, but no real spiritual growth. There will be a lot of singing, but no salvations. There will be a lot of visiting with each other in the church and shaking of hands, but no visitation outside the church and shaking the bushes for lost people. Does that sound familiar? Is your church like that? Are you like that? Am I like that? Then we're part of the problem too.

Show me a true believing church, and I will show you a church that is obeying the entire gospel. I'll show you a church that is making a real difference in its community. I'll show you a church full of people who are not afraid to confess and repent and follow the leadership of the under shepherd instead of the prominent family, the one who tithes the most, or has been a member the longest.

Look, obedience comes from true belief. Disobedience comes from not truly believing. Disobedience is the breeding ground for mediocrity. And a lack of faith is the cause of disobedience. So, what can be done about it? I'm glad you asked.

"*So then faith comes by hearing, and hearing by the word of God.*" If a person has a faith problem, according to Scripture, the person likely has a hearing problem. You and I can attend church and never really hear the message. Why? Well, it's because we often fail at the three steps involved in growing our faith. First, a person must be willing to listen to the message of Christ (the whole message, not just the part we agree with or that speaks to us). Second, we must mentally ascend to agree with the message and do something with it. A person can know overeating is bad but then never change their eating habits. A person can know the Word of God is true and yet never allow his or her life to be changed by it. He or she is a double-minded person; he or she knows the truth and may even agree with the truth, but they never ascend to the heights of where the truth is leading them. Last, when the New Testament speaks of faith, it speaks of total commitment and a personal commitment to truth. A person hears the truth, knows it is the truth, and does something about it. Truth becomes part of the person's very being and a part of his or her life. Truth is the catalyst that begins and continues on with conforming to His image. Now, hold on to your seats.

Saving faith is not just believing in the name of Jesus Christ, repenting, and starting over. No, it is trusting Jesus Christ completely. It is trusting Jesus by putting all of one's trust in who He is and what He's done. It is fully casting one's life into His hands. Friend, the Gospel is to be obeyed. To truly believe in Christ is to obey Him and His Word, constantly and consistently. To obey Him and His Word is to truly believe in Him. Excuses for not doing this always lead to mediocrity and apathy. Obedience to Him from true faith always leads to extraordinary.

Chapter 10 Verse 18-21

"*But I say, have they not heard? Yes indeed: "Their sound has gone out to all the earth,*

And their words to the ends of the world." God is referring to Israel here. What was the issue with the Jews? They were disobedient to God and His Word. They were disobedient to Jesus and His teaching. But their disobedience was not because they had not heard the Word of God. This verse proves they did. They heard; they just didn't want to listen. Sound familiar?

Jesus taught in Matthew 13:13 that, "*This is why I speak to them in parables: "Though seeing, they do not see; though hearing, they do not hear or understand."* That was the Jew's problem; it's our problem too. We have a tendency to see what we want to see and hear what we want to hear. For example, people can read the comments I am writing and fight against them and maybe stop reading them because they don't like what they are reading. I get it because the book of Romans gets me riled up too. And yet all I have done is accurately record the meaning of each verse. But honestly, not paying attention to anything I write has no eternal consequences. If we choose not to "listen" to God's Word, we risk the chance of increased disobedience. Additionally, disobedience will cause us to not want to "listen" to God's Word. It's a vicious cycle that eventually leads to, you guessed it, mediocrity which eventually leads to death. I trust by now everyone is seeing the connection and hearing the truth.

"*But I say, did Israel not know? First Moses says: "I will provoke you to jealousy by those who are not a nation, I will move you to anger by a foolish nation."* Israel's disobedience was not because the people did not know the truth. They knew the truth. The truth was living out the Gospel right before their very eyes. Yet they chose disobedience. They chose mediocrity. We know the truth too if we're really honest with ourselves, yet we still settle for mediocrity. It's time we all get real honest with the Truth.

God provoked the Jews to jealousy to get them to see what they had and to come back to Him. Paul was ministering to the Gentiles for more than just saving them. He was using the Gentiles to cause the Jews to return to Him. Or at least He tried. But disobedience is a hard thing, and it's a personal thing. Left unchecked, it often becomes a permanent thing.

"*But Isaiah is very bold and says: "I was found by those who did not seek Me; I was made manifest to those who did not ask for Me."* Israel should have understood that God would eventually welcome non-Jews into relationship with Him. That's the case Paul is making about their rejection of Jesus as the Messiah. In the previous verse, he pointed to God's words in Deuteronomy that he would make Israel jealous of those who are not a nation, just as they had symbolically made Him "jealous" with their worship of non-gods. Now Paul quotes Isaiah, again by name. Isaiah's bold statement also quotes God's own words. Paul claims them out of the context of Isaiah 65:1 and applies them as an analogy of how God has rescued the Gentiles. He has been found by those who didn't look for Him. He has shown Himself to those who didn't ask.

"But *to Israel he says: "All day long I have stretched out My hands to a disobedient and contrary people."* So the chapter closes with this picture of

God standing with His arms open, longing to draw men to himself, admitting that the problem is a disobedient and obstinate people. I think the most amazing thing from this account is to realize that in order to perish (i.e., in order to go to hell), you must resist the pleas of a loving God. God never damns anyone to hell without a chance. Don't ever let anybody tell you the Bible teaches that. It does not teach any such thing. It teaches us that no one, *no one*, will end up separated from God who has not personally resisted the claim and appeal of a loving God who sought to reach him. The historic fulfillment of God's longing to draw men to Himself began at Bethlehem and is still going strong today. But there will be an end to the offer someday. There's always an expiration date, friends. Get yours while you can.

Chapter 11 Verse 1-4

"I say then, has God cast away His people? Certainly not! For I also am an Israelite, of the seed of Abraham, of the tribe of Benjamin." This is the glorious hope for Israel and the entire world. God's promises are always fulfilled, and there is always a remnant of true believers, whether from the Jews or the Gentiles. God has His remnant. The callousness of most people's hearts is not found in the hearts of the remnant. People everywhere can be saved if they will truly and biblically turn to Jesus. The next ten verses in this new chapter give us five proofs that there will always be a remnant of believers in spite of the culture. Are you a part of them?

The first proof is found in this verse. Paul asks, "Has God (totally and permanently) cast away His people? Well, according to Paul, He has not. The nation was rebellious and disobedient to God and His Word, just like many nations since have been. But God still wanted to keep the offer open to them. Paul's proof was he was a true Jew but also a true Christian. He had met the resurrected Jesus while he was on his way to Damascus and it radically changed his life. Paul was saying because of his conversion, he was now part of God's true remnant. It wasn't his true lineage from Abraham that was important anymore. It was his true faith and legitimate conversion in Jesus.

"God has not cast away His people whom He foreknew. Or do you not know what the Scripture says of Elijah, how he pleads with God against Israel, saying," Very simply, God knows He has a remnant because God Himself guarantees a remnant. God knows there will be some who accept Him and His Son. There will be some who truly get it and live it. God knows there will be some who are truly saved because their walk matches His talk. God saves those people. He knew what they were going to do with their decision for Jesus before they were born. The offer is for everyone, yet not everyone truly accepts the offer.

"Lord, they have killed Your prophets and torn down Your altars, and I alone am left, and they seek my life" Elijah foresaw the remnant too (1 Kings 19:9-18). He also saw the vast majority of God's alleged people in their real modus operandi. God's prophets (like Elijah) were sent to tell the people the truth. But often the message is painful, so what did the people do? They killed the messenger. They destroyed the work. They desecrated the worship. People still do this today. If you don't see it or believe me, ask your pastor to have a cup of coffee with you and see what he says. The true remnant doesn't do these things. God's true people will never have an issue with God's true message or His messenger. No, that's the devil's group who do that sort of stuff.

"But what does the divine response say to him? "I have reserved for Myself seven thousand men who have not bowed the knee to Baal." Here's a sad fact: a group is determined by the life-style of its majority. The wickedness of the majority in Israel overshadowed the godliness of the few. They must have been scared to live out their faith in front of their ungodly neighbors. How do I know? Well, even the great prophet Elijah was unaware of the seven thousand godly remnants. But they were there. Silent, ineffective, dormant, and mediocre, but they were in the nation. I wish the true remnant of the church would stand up to all of the attacks on the Lord, the faith, the church, and the under-shepherd. If more of the remnant would come out of their mediocrity, there would be a far stronger church in this fallen country.

Chapter 11 Verse 5-7

"*Even so then, at this present time there is a remnant according to the election of grace.*" Here's another proof: there is a remnant; there is no question about that fact. Even now, in this present time, there is a remnant. Why? Because of grace. The remnant may be quiet, they may be in hiding or may be combat-ineffective, but they are there. The culture may seem "remnant-less" but the remnant is there because God's grace is here. I think God is calling the remnant out; I am sure you have noticed that as you have read this book. Will they see who they are in Jesus and what they must do? I suppose that remains to be seen.

"*And if by grace, then it is no longer of works; otherwise grace is no longer grace. But if it is of works, it is no longer grace; otherwise work is no longer work.*" Again, a person can't work their way into the remnant. They must understand truth, accept it, repent from lies, and allow God to place His grace upon them for change.

"*What then? Israel has not obtained what it seeks; but the elect have obtained it, and the rest were blinded.*" Our religious pedigree is meaningless, as was that of the Jew's who claimed, because they were descendants of Abraham, they were okay with God. No, the elect is okay with God. The remnant is okay with God. The truly converted through Christ are okay with God. Nobody else is.

What Israel was seeking was God's righteousness. For the most part, the Jews did not lack sincerity. The Pharisees and Sadducees were hypocrites, but the majority of the Jews were sincere in their dedication to their religion. Nor did they lack commitment. They followed the prescribed rituals and laws with dedication that would put most of us to shame. Nor did they lack zeal. Look at Paul's zeal before he was saved. He went to great lengths to try to keep the Jewish religion pure by eliminating those whom he saw as heretics. But if your religious sincerity, commitment, and zeal are misguided, they will only move you toward judgment with greater speed. Ouch.

The problem, as Paul explained, was that their zeal was not according to knowledge; namely, the knowledge that their own good works could never be good enough to atone for their sins or to commend them to the holy God. They did not know that Christ was the final and sufficient Lamb of God, the perfect sacrifice for their sins. They didn't know that God's way of salvation is by grace through faith, not by works. And so, they did not obtain the right standing with God that they were seeking. We won't either if we live under false pretenses like they did. How can I know if I'm a remnant or a relic? Mediocre faith, service, and living are dead giveaways of a relic. Conforming to His image is common to all who are remnants.

CHAPTER 11 VERSE 8-10

"8 Just as it is written: "God has given them a spirit of stupor, Eyes that they should not see

And ears that they should not hear, to this very day." One of the great things I love about God is He says what He means, and He means what He says. And He never changes. What He said yesterday is just as valid today. And He writes it all down. He's a firm but fair God, wouldn't you say?

Paul is going back to the Old Testament and reciting God's reaction to Israel when she decided to put religion ahead of relationship. God allowed the natural progression of sin to take effect. Israel, seeking righteousness by works, not only did not obtain it, but Paul adds (11:7), "the rest [the non-elect] were hardened." Hardened is a passive verb. Who hardened them? This verse tells us it refers to God's judicial hardening of the Jews, who had heard so much truth and seen so many demonstrations of God's love and power, but refused to submit to Him. Sound familiar?

So Israel had come under this judicial hardening, as seen in their continual grumbling against God and refusal to submit to Him. Later, they followed the idolatry and evil ways of the Canaanites until God finally sent them into captivity. Even after being restored to the land, they continued to try to approach God by their works, so that they hated the Savior who came and convicted them of their self-righteousness and pride. And so in Paul's day, the nation that had crucified the Savior came under even increased hardening from God that has lasted now for 2,000 years. The frightening words of the Jewish mob that was screaming for Jesus' death have come true, "His blood shall be on us and on our children!"

There are two ways in which we need to understand this judgment where God hardens hearts so that they cannot understand the Gospel . First, from God's perspective, He is free to act according to His own counsel for His own glory and is not obligated to any creature (Romans 9:18). God is not constrained by anything outside of Himself. If He chose to condemn the entire human race without providing a Savior, He would be free and perfectly just to do so. After all, He did this with the angels that fell.

Second, God's hardening of the Jews was punishment for their sins. God did it as "retribution" to them (11:9) because of their disobedient, hard hearts (10:21) and "unbelief" (11:20). Israel had been given much light (9:4-5), but they stubbornly refused to respond to it. So God said in effect, "If you refuse to see, I'll confirm that choice: Be blind. If you refuse to hear, be deaf!" How terrifying, to have God pronounce such judgments against them. And it stems, in the case of the Jews and of many other religious people, from seeking to be righteous by their own works, which typically include disobedience, rebellion, grumbling, complaining, etc. Does any of this sound familiar to you? I suppose if anyone of any culture and time did the same thing, they'd be treated the same way by God. And the giveaway that this has truly happened would probably be mediocre and apathetic faith, followed by no faith at all. Like I said before, does any of this sound familiar?

Chapter 11 Verse 11

"I say then, Have they stumbled that they should fall? God forbid: but rather through their fall salvation is come unto the Gentiles, for to provoke them to

jealousy." A hard and callous heart can be softened and made to operate correctly again, but the person must repent, turn to Christ, and be restored to God. God offers three proofs to this statement in 11:11-16.

In verse 11, God deals with Israel's stumbling. Notice He didn't say falling. God is saying it's still not too late for the nation of Israel for they have merely stumbled at Christ. The word "*fall*" means "*to permanently fall and never return.*" The Jews had stumbled over Christ, but they had not permanently fallen to the point where they could never repent and call upon Jesus as their Messiah. God sent His messengers about Jesus to the nation of Israel first, but very few received the message. In fact, so many rejected the message that it is said the whole nation stumbled at Christ. Many people today hear the message about Jesus but few truly accept it. Why? They stumble over the message because the message is convicting, challenging, and hits people right between their eyes. And quite frankly, we don't like that. So we stumble at it as we live deeper in spiritual mediocrity. And it shows.

God, therefore, did what the Jews were not willing to do. He sent His message to the non-Jews. The Jews failed; He used others. If we fail, He'll use others. God will not accept mediocrity for long. If a church fails, He will use another church.

Two things have always fascinated me concerning churches that are growing. First, the churches that are truly concerned for the lost and actively pursue them are the churches who are always the strongest long-term. And they are always the most pleasant churches to be involved in. It's always this way. It's like an immutable spiritual law.

Furthermore, the churches that do not put a great emphasis on evangelism and soul-winning are the dying churches. When a church loses this focus, sooner or later the church starts having problems, and they eventually decline; if the trend isn't stopped, the church will eventually die. It may take fifty years, but the church will die. This too is an immutable spiritual law. Both of these concepts are fascinating and just as true as anything I've said so far.

Why? Because God is in the business of evangelism, and He's very serious about it. For the people of the church who aren't serious about it, and can accept mediocrity as the norm, the death bell rings.

Chapter 11 Verse 12-13

"*Now if the fall of them be the riches of the world, and the diminishing of them the riches of the Gentiles; how much more their fullness?*" If the Jews would have accepted Jesus and shared Him with the world, things probably would be a lot different today. But the same could be said about the Gentiles (you and me). Wouldn't our families and neighborhoods look different if we really accepted and followed Jesus and His Word? Wouldn't our churches look different if we truly followed Jesus biblically? Wouldn't God's blessings be more plentiful and obvious? Why we accept spiritual mediocrity in our lives, neighborhoods, and churches is really beyond me.

The word "*diminishing*" means "*loss or defeat.*" It means that Israel became lost and defeated spiritually. Because of the spiritual impoverishment of Israel, the Gentiles (you and me) can participate in the spiritual riches of Christ. If this is so, and it is, then how much more will the restoration of the nation of Israel cause an even greater blessing to spread throughout the world? This is exactly what God intends to do. How? When Israel is restored, and large numbers of Jews begin to accept and follow Jesus, the world will experience unprecedented blessings from the Hand of God. God will overrule Israel's stumbling and fall over Jesus. Why? Because God has promised to bless the nation of Israel. He has also promised the world to be blessed through the nation. This will be accomplished through Jesus. God is not a mediocre God, even if His people are.

"*For I speak to you Gentiles, inasmuch as I am the apostle of the Gentiles, I magnify mine office:*" The second proof that Israel has only stumbled is Paul's attempt to still stir the Jews to salvation. Paul has been writing about God's relationship with His chosen people, Israel. God's purpose was, in part, to include Gentiles and not just Jews in the promise of salvation through faith in Christ. In the previous verse, Paul introduced the idea that at some point in the future, the full inclusion of Israel to faith in Christ will result in great things for all people.

Now Paul addresses Gentiles directly, beginning a thought he will complete in the following verses. Paul describes his identity and purpose to be an apostle to the Gentiles. Christ Himself gave this role to Paul in Acts 9:15. Paul writes that he magnifies his ministry to take the good news about faith in Jesus to all Gentiles. In other words, he glorifies his ministry. He goes big. He works hard at it. He is bold and strategic and amplifies the message of God's grace for the Gentiles through faith in Christ.

Folks, is this mediocrity? No. This is a man on a mission for a God Who is magnificent. And the truth is, there's nothing particularly special about Paul that couldn't be said about anyone else who had the Holy Spirit living and guiding them. In fact, it's never been about Paul. It's about God finally living in Paul. Do you see the difference between a believer like Paul and the typical believer today? Who do you know that legitimately tries to magnify their ministry for God's honor? Who do you know that understands that as a true believer in Jesus Christ, they are by very definition an apostle sent to reach and teach others for Jesus Christ? Who do you know that goes big for Jesus constantly? No one? Only a few? Do you now know why?

Chapter 11 Verse 14-16

"*if by any means I may provoke to jealousy those who are my flesh and save some of them.*" Paul saw his own work as just a part in God's great plan, which was and is to bring all things under the perfect rule of Christ. Paul knew about the limits of the work that God had given him to do, but that didn't stop him from doing what he could do. Paul's special work for God was among people who were not Jews. The Jews are Israel's people, from the family of Abraham, Isaac and Jacob. All the first Christians, including Paul, were Jews. However, even before Paul's birth, God chose him to bring the message about Christ to people who were not Jews (see Galatians 1:15-16; Acts 26:16-18).

Although that was Paul's task, God was using his life to do something even greater. God was working, by means of Paul, to bring people who were not Jews into a right relationship with Him. However, in addition, some Jews would see that, and they would want the same kind of relationship with God. Paul was eagerly praying for that to happen. Paul was willing to go above and beyond his special calling to the Gentiles. That's way beyond mediocrity, friends!

"*For if their being cast away is the reconciling of the world, what will their acceptance be but life from the dead?*" Paul repeats the lesson he taught in 11:12, but he now adds a bold and exciting description to it. Israel's return to God will mean "life from death," he says. He seems to be describing not just the effect on Israel's people, but upon the whole world. This is the key to Jesus: experiencing life from the dead. The dead are mediocre at best. In fact, a mediocre deadness isn't that bad. But if there is true life where there once was deadness, mediocrity must be eliminated and replaced. Don't you agree?

God had promised Abraham in Genesis 12 that all nations would know God's kindness because of Him. That can only happen fully when the whole world turns to God. It will happen after the return to God of the nation that comes from Abraham's family, Israel. That is when the whole world will know the true God. They will know Him as the God who brings life to our dying world. They will know Him as the God who brings us out of mediocrity, and that should be happening to all who have received eternal life from Him now.

"*For if the first fruit is holy, the lump is also holy; and if the root is holy, so are the branches.*" It is impossible to have a tree with holy roots and unholy branches. The branches share the life that God has given to the roots. If you tried to separate the branches, you would destroy the life in the branches. If you compromise the root, the branches cannot help but be affected. Paul wrote these words for the benefit of Christians who were not Jews (11:13). He wanted to show them their connection with the Jews (Israel's people, who came from the family of Abraham, Isaac and Jacob). God first chose Israel to be His special, holy nation. Now, people from every nation can join the holy people of God. God joins them, with the Jews who trust Him, as one holy nation. It is true that, at the present time, some Jews (and Gentiles) oppose the gospel, the message about Christ. However, God's plan for His nation continues, and that plan is to get saved then live saved. The plan is conforming to the image of His Son. But the plan certainly doesn't include spiritual complacency and deadness. Do you see this?

Chapter 11 Verse 17-20

"*And if some of the branches were broken off, and you, being a wild olive tree, were grafted in among them, and with them became a partaker of the root and fatness of the olive tree,*" Paul continues using his parable of the olive tree here. The olive tree was the most useful, productive, and valuable tree in Israel. It is a good analogy to use to describe the nation of Israel in the world's garden of nations. However, some Jews did not and do not believe in Christ, therefore they are not attached to God. Some Gentiles did believe in Jesus, and they were "grafted" into the tree, or they were now attached to God; that is, they are in a right relationship with God. The glorious privilege of being nurtured and nourished by God becomes as much the right of the Gentile believer as it is of the Jewish believer. What an incredible blessing. What an amazing opportunity for those who seek real truth and then do something with it.

"*do not boast against the branches. But if you do boast, remember that you do not support the root, but the root supports you.*" Here, Paul gives the first of several warnings. The warning is for all of us to not be arrogant or prideful over the Jews, or anyone else for that matter. The true believer has no right to elevate himself over anyone else. Why? Well, we are like wild branches, very wild. We did not bear the root (Judaism) the root bore us (Christianity). If it had not been for Judaism, there would be no Christianity. We have no reason to boast. But, conversely, we have no right to be apathetic and complacent in our daily walk. Some call that mediocrity. If we are truly grafted into the Messiah, then we should be truly magnificent in our walk, even though we should not be arrogant about it. There's a big difference between walking in magnificence and walking in arrogance.

"*You will say then, "Branches were broken off that I might be grafted in."* A person can only become a Christian because of faith (trust in God). In other words, a Christian depends not on himself, but upon God. On the other hand, a proud person depends on his or her own intelligence, strength or skills. Therefore, a proud person trusts himself, and not God.

"*Well said. Because of unbelief they were broken off, and you stand by faith. Do not be haughty, but fear.'* Faith is the opposite of unbelief. Faith means our attitude when we believe and trust God. By faith, we receive the benefit of God's promises. Many of those promises are for the future, and we cannot know them fully now. That is why we must stand in faith. In other words, we must continue to trust God, even when God's promises seem impossible. So, we depend, not on ourselves, but on God.

With that attitude, we cannot be proud. It is impossible for us to save ourselves from our troubles in this world. We might hope that other people will help us, but that hope may be in vain. Instead, with faith, we wait for God to act powerfully on our behalf. We know that we are weak, but we depend upon His strength.

On the other hand, unbelief is the attitude of someone who refuses to believe God. It is not wrong to ask questions, as Nicodemus did. It is not even wrong to have sincere doubts, if we are willing for God to teach us. However, it is very wrong if we purposely refuse to accept God's message to us. Such an attitude makes it impossible for us to receive the benefit of God's promises. God cannot do what He wants in our lives because of that evil attitude.

People develop an attitude of unbelief when they do not respect God properly. They choose not to listen to His words because they do not want to accept His authority over their lives. They do not want to trust His promises because they prefer to depend on themselves. However, they forget how weak they really are. We all need God to work powerfully in our lives, but it's going to require us to walk in faith and to live our lives biblically, not in mediocrity. It takes discipline and desire.

Chapter 11 Verse 23-24

"*And they also, if they do not continue in unbelief, will be grafted in, for God is able to graft them in again.*" This is the fourth of four warnings God has given in this chapter. Israel's restoration is a probable event, but it is conditional. Notice the word "if"- "if they abide not still in unbelief." Belief is the condition for salvation. That was the Old Testament and New Testament. Here's the deal: a person has to run from his or her unbelief to belief in order to be grafted in and accepted by God. No person comes to God unless he believes in His Son Jesus. Not me, not you, not any Gentile, not any Jew. But with a true, biblically-based belief, anyone can be included. Anyone! You, me, Gentiles, Jews, anyone. What a glorious thing God has done.

"*For if you were cut out of the olive tree which is wild by nature, and were grafted contrary to nature into a cultivated olive tree, how much more will these, who are natural branches, be grafted into their own olive tree?*" God is called the God of Israel, but many of Israel's people do not believe Him. By their attitude of unbelief, they separate themselves from the close relationship that God wants with them. Paul has compared them to a branch that a gardener cuts from a tree. When a gardener does that, the effect is usually permanent. Without any connection to the roots, the branch soon dies. However, Paul insists that the same is not true about Israel's people. They will only be separate from God for as long as their unbelief continues, or, as I like to say, their mediocrity continues. If they return to God, God will again accept them fully as His people; if not, He won't. It's now the same with us, but we too must return to Him through repentance and belief.

The unbelief of many of Israel's people has given the people from other nations an opportunity to know God. It is very wonderful that God has done this for them. Paul compares them to shoots (small young branches) that a gardener joins to a tree in His garden. Those shoots then grow into strong branches because of the health and strength that they receive from the root of the host tree.

However, gardeners never actually use a shoot from a wild tree for this purpose. Normally, they select the shoot from a very good tree, in order to benefit from its good qualities. A gardener cares little about wild plants; he or she cares about the plants in his or her garden. In the same way, it is only natural that Israel's God cares deeply about Israel's people. It astonishes us to see how great His love is for the people from other nations, too. But you must be grafted in, and you must believe with a firm and unshakable belief to be grafted in.

God does not accept a mediocre faith as reason to graft you into His family. He doesn't accept mediocre faith as a reason for you to stay because mediocre faith is unacceptable to Him. It is actually proof one is not grafted in, despite the fact that there may have been an emotional profession of faith at some point. There's no such thing as mediocre faith, for true faith is never just ordinary; it is always extraordinary. Why? Because in the case of salvation, there is an extraordinary God who will lead all who truly follow to extraordinary things. Mediocrity and excellence will always struggle to coexist.

Chapter 11 Verse 25-28

"*For I do not desire, brethren, that you should be ignorant of this mystery, lest you should be wise in your own opinion, that blindness in part has happened to Israel until the fullness of the Gentiles has come in.*" Paul worried that some Christians were already starting to have wrong opinions about the Jews. People have been misunderstanding God's plan for the Jews for millennia. The same could be said about what people misunderstand about Christians. This lost and dying world seems to have a hard time understanding God's desire for His people. Look, without an accurate knowledge of God's plans, we can develop ideas that are completely wrong. And we see this fact play out throughout all history. Ignorance really isn't bliss; it's ignorance. And ignorance has caused more problems than all the enlightenment multiplied a thousand times. First century

Christians were ignorant of God's future plan for the nation of Israel. Seemingly, not much has changed; the same could be said about the unsaved versus the saved today.

"*And so all Israel will be saved, as it is written: "The Deliverer will come out of Zion, And He will turn away ungodliness from Jacob;"* The Bible has many passages about God's future plans for Israel, or the Jewish people. Those passages deal with Israel's return to its land, its return to God, and Christ's return to rule Israel and the world. There is a close link between these events, so the Bible often deals with them together. The Old and New Testament contain prophecies concerning the nation and its salvation. God does not want anyone to perish, but everyone must come to Him His way. That way is Jesus, "the Deliverer who comes out of Zion."

"*For this is My covenant with them, when I take away their sins."* The Jews are the people whom God chose as His special, holy nation. The Christians are the people from every nation who have received a right relationship with God because of Christ's death. However, God does not deal with the Jews differently from the people who belong to other nations. All people are under God's judgement because of their evil deeds, or sins. All people need to turn from those evil deeds; all people need to believe and to trust in Christ. God's message about Christ, the gospel, is for people from every nation. So the Jews, like everyone else, must turn away from sin (wrong and evil attitudes and behavior), and believe and trust in God. While God may think everyone is unique, no one is special enough to have access to Him except through Jesus. Sin will destroy kings and queens just as surely as it will destroy paupers and prisoners. The dead giveaway that sin is present is spiritual apathy which leads to spiritual mediocrity leading to a lack of desire to be conformed to His image.

Chapter 11 Verse 28

"*Concerning the gospel they are enemies for your sake, but concerning the election they are beloved for the sake of the fathers."* Before Paul himself became a

Christian, he was a fierce enemy of the early Christians. He arrested many of them; he even helped to kill some of them. However, this same Paul was the man whom God had chosen, even before his birth, to declare God's good news to the nations. While this is strange to our way of thinking about things, it is true. You and I may not have picked Paul for the job, but God did. You and I may not think God has picked us, but He has. He's just waiting for us to transition from who we are to who He wants us to be.

While Paul's experience was very extreme, the same principle is true about all God's people. God chooses His enemies to become His friends. By our evil deeds, we all have made ourselves enemies of God; by the death of Christ, God forgives us and makes us His people. He just asks that we learn the truth, develop a biblical worldview, and change; in essence, conform to His Son's image. He even gives us the instrument of change, His Spirit. Friends, we're not going to get a better offer or plan anywhere else.

In this verse Paul is not writing about Christians generally, but about the Jewish people. God loves the Jewish people for a very particular reason. It is not that they deserve His love. God's grace is a free gift and not something that we can earn. Paul says that God loves them because of "the fathers." Paul means Abraham, Isaac, and Jacob from whose family the Jewish people came. God made promises to these men about the future of their family, and He will certainly carry out all of His promises. He has chosen the Jewish people to be His special people, and therefore, he loves them. We can imagine that some Christians from other nations might protest against Paul's words. He was not just telling them to love their enemies now. He was urging them to recognize God's love for the entire nation from which many of their enemies came.

Perhaps Paul could have made that lesson easier. He could have spoken only about the many Jewish people who had accepted Christ. However, Paul was not trying to make his lesson easier. Rather, he wanted to show how great and wonderful God's wisdom is. God loves the Jewish people; he will forgive them upon their repentance, and he will give them a right relationship with Himself.

God loves you. He will forgive you upon your repentance. He will give you a right relationship with Himself. But the formula is faith in Jesus Christ. It is to admit who you really are, believe in who He really is, and turn from "you" to Him. It's that simple. But God has a bigger plan for you than just getting you out of hell at some point in the distant future. He wants a daily relationship with you. He wants to bless you, grow you, and make you more and more like His Son Jesus. It's a lifetime process, but it is a process, and He wants to do this work in you and me just as He did in Paul. But it requires knowledge of the truth, a changed heart, and a desire to please Him daily. Do you have that? Do you want that? Is life mediocre? Where are you in the process since you accepted Him and have been baptized? Not much further along than the day you got baptized? How mediocre is that?

Chapter 11 Verse 29-30

"*For the gifts and the calling of God are irrevocable.*" Praise God that this is true! When I was struggling with God calling me to the pastoral ministry, I ran away from God for six years. Once I learned that a calling is irrevocable, I surrendered. God called me; I was disobedient. But no matter what I was doing, the call on my life remained. I eventually came to my senses and surrendered. I can honestly say that God has never failed me since. Was it evil of me to run and hide, fight the call, and act like a petulant child, not wanting to do what God was calling me to do? Was it evil of me to be disobedient and rebellious to God's plan for my life? Of course not! At least it wasn't from my perspective. But from God's perspective, it most certainly was, yet here I am serving Him as a pastor. Amazing, huh?

Look, a person might hinder or even ruin his or her own relationship with God because of his or her evil deeds (Remember the story of Saul and David?). However, that person's evil deeds do not change the work that God has given that person to do. When God has chosen someone,

He does not change His mind. That person still has the duty to do what God wants him to do. And trust me, it's far easier, and much more pleasant, to surrender and do it, rather than run and hide. That's mediocrity at its finest, and I should know. Read on for more clarity on this!

"*For as you were once disobedient to God, yet have now obtained mercy through their disobedience.*" In Romans 11:30-32, Paul describes the two great periods of human history: the time before and the time after the death of Christ. He discusses the two groups of people who are called God's people: the Jews and the Christians. He explains their two different reactions to God: the choice not to obey God and the choice to accept His help. It's the same choice we face every day.

At a former time, the people who are now Christians did not obey God. This is true about each Christian's life before they accepted Christ into their lives. It was true about entire nations before the death of Christ. However, God had a plan to show His mercy, even to people who came from those nations. God's mercy is the help that He gives because of His great kindness.

If God's people, the Jews, obeyed Him then God would have used them to show His kindness to people in other nations. In fact, many of the Jews did obey God, and God did use them for this purpose. All the first Christians were Jews, and, through them, God's message, called the gospel, spread across the world.

However, many Jews did not believe the gospel. God used the fact that they did not believe as an opportunity to show His mercy to people from the other nations. He knew that people in every nation were not obeying Him. However, He wanted to show His mercy to people from every nation. So, even when God's own people were not obeying Him, He was actively helping other people to know Him. His work in the lives of those other people would help His own people to return to Him.

If you have rejected Him, but there are people in your life who have accepted Him, maybe He has used you to help others make a decision for Him. Perhaps others have seen in my mediocrity a reason to not want to be like me, and this has caused them to seek something better, leading them to choose Jesus.

Chapter 11 Verse 31-32

"*even so these also have now been disobedient, that through the mercy shown you they also may obtain mercy.*" Paul does not mean that none of Israel's people were obeying God. Rather, he is describing the present age (the period from Christ's death until His return) by the most important things that are happening. That is, what is the most important in God's opinion. People's opinion about what is most important differs much from God's opinion. Don't you agree? And God's opinion of mediocrity is that it needs to stop.

When these verses were written, many of the Jews were serving God loyally. From them came the first Christians. However, at the present time, most of the Jews are behaving in the same way as most people in other nations (including Christians), and that's mediocre at best. Why? They are not obeying God, although God is eager to show them His mercy. In other words, because of His great kindness, He wants to help them go from mediocrity to magnificence, from carnality to Christ-likeness. Would the world be a better place if this happened? Absolutely. Can it happen? Absolutely.

Even to this day many Jews are not accepting God's mercy, but He is showing mercy to people from other nations. However, by that act He is not neglecting the Jews; He has not forgotten His promises to them. Rather, God wants them to see His great love for the people from other nations. He wants the Jews to desire that love for themselves. Then they, too, will turn back to God. God will forgive them, and so they, too, will receive God's mercy. What an amazing God! Certainly a God like this deserves to be known and loved.

"For God has committed them all to disobedience, that He might have mercy on all." In Galatians 3:22-23, Paul describes all people to be like prisoners. The cause of this sad situation is their own evil attitude: they refuse to obey God. That was the first evil act that people ever did in Genesis. The same evil attitude is the reason for much of our evil behavior today. That is why God's law declares His judgement against us.

Sometimes a judge could order the death of a criminal, but instead, in an act of mercy, he sends the criminal to prison. So, although the judgement is severe, it actually gives hope to the prisoner. He has hope because, in the future, he may again become a free man. God could have destroyed all human life on earth at the time of Noah. However, He did not do that because of His mercy. His mercy is the help that He gives because of His great kindness. So, although He punished the wicked people, He saved Noah and his family.

At the present time, people are like prisoners, because their own evil behavior controls their lives. However, in His mercy, God is making people free. He does this for those people who accept His good news, the gospel. They turn from their evil behavior to invite Christ into their lives. Once this is done, it is never okay to return to the evil behavior! Can you accept Christ and then start making excuses for your evil behavior, as if that's okay? You could, but it would be a lie. And a lie is something the devil is known for.

CHAPTER 11 VERSE 33-36

"Oh, the depth of the riches both of the wisdom and knowledge of God! How unsearchable are His judgments and His ways past finding out!" God has a gracious plan for the world, but it never has included, nor ever will include mediocrity and excuses for sinfulness. I'm sorry, but that's really the gospel truth of it.

God's plan is based upon His wisdom and knowledge, which means He knows how to do everything perfectly. These attributes of God are said to be "deep and rich". Why deep and rich? Because they are *spiritually* deep and rich and important. God knows how to create everything, but He also knows how to keep order and govern everything, so that all things work out perfectly. The world is shallow, poor, and honestly unimportant from an eternal perspective. Of all the things shallow and poverty ridden, sin is the worst. It kills, steals, maims, and destroys. There is very little wisdom in sin. However, there is knowledge. But knowledge without wisdom is useless.

"For who has known the mind of the Lord? Or who has become His counselor?" Paul refers to God's words in Job 41:11. God cannot owe us anything. Whatever we might give to Him has come from Him. David realized this: *"Everything comes from you. We have given to you only what comes from you"* (1 Chronicles 29:14).

God created everything. God spoke, and the world and everything in it started to exist. Everything was for God. He was the beginning, and He will be the end. Glory belongs to God alone. People should not be proud. They should not behave as if they do not need God. They should stop making excuses for living a life full of unrepentant sin. So Paul prays that people will always praise God. They should praise Him because of who He is. And they should praise Him because of what He has done. He is holy and sinless. He has made a way for Himself to see us as holy and sinless through His Son's sacrifice and resurrection. Why we are so compelled to sin and attracted to it is simply proof we neither truly understand who God is and what He has done, nor who we are and what we are doing.

"Or who has first given to Him and it shall be repaid to him?" Paul next asks a question about a subject that is very important in the Book of Romans: "Who has the right to demand anything from God?" In other words, can a person give anything to God that God must repay? The short answer is no. The longer answer is absolutely no.

What could we possibly give God anyways? Could we even find a suitable gift for that purpose? After everything God has done for us, could we really do anything for Him to make Him indebted to us?

No. This is because everything in heaven and earth already belongs to God. In our gifts, we only give back to God what He first provided to us. All He asks is we live biblically for Him. And we even mess that up most of the time.

So, we can never pay God in order to receive His kindness. We cannot pay for His kindness, and we cannot earn it. God's kindness is a free gift that we do not deserve. God owes nothing to us. The reason why God helps people is not because of debt, but because of His great love. He works on behalf of those people who believe and trust Him. He saves them; He rescues them, from their own evil deeds, and from the power of the devil and death.

"For of Him and through Him and to Him are all things, to whom be glory forever. Amen." For several chapters, Paul has been explaining the wonderful plans that God has for His people. In chapter 12, Paul will start to explain how Christians should live at the present time. However, first he praises God, which is a good start and a good ending.

12

Chapter 12 Verse 1-2

"I beseech you therefore, brethren, by the mercies of God, that you present your bodies a living sacrifice, holy, acceptable to God, which is your reasonable service." We're not going to find a higher thought than these two verses in the Bible. In my opinion, these two verses are the zenith of Christian teaching and living. But we must consider these verses carefully. I will tell you exactly what the verses mean; it'll be up to you what you do with it. But choose wisely.

In the Bible, God demanded the living to die for the guilty. There had to be a payment for sin. Only a living, spotless, unblemished animal would suffice for the sacrifice for all of man's sins. Because man's sins were many, many sacrifices had to be made. The best solution was a sacrifice so powerful that it only needed to happen once. Enter Jesus.

Because of the mercies of God and the once-and-for-all sacrifice of God Himself, Paul is now begging that the person who calls out to God for forgiveness of his or her sins via Jesus' sacrifice might also present themselves, not as a dying sacrifice, but as one who would sacrifice and live for Jesus. The saved person should, at the very least, present his or her body as alive to Christ and now be willing to sacrifice the sin, not the Savior. In essence, the true believer is to be devoted to God now, not sin. Anything less than total devotion to God is short of God's glory. Anything short of God's glory is by definition, sin. Without equivocation, Scripture urges total devotion to God. If you have been reading this book since the beginning, I am sure you must see this now. Do you?

Now I realize this may be a new and challenging concept to many people. So many churches today focus on how to raise kids in the 21st century or what to do when you lose your pet, but when you study God's Word, you see things differently. Why? Because the concept isn't what God should give to you or be to you; the concept is what God has done for you and now what He expects from you. I hope you see this. I hope we all see it.

"And do not be conformed to this world, but be transformed by the renewing of your mind, that you may prove what is that good and acceptable and perfect will of God." Well, we're not supposed to be conformed to this world; we're supposed to be conformed to the image of God's Son. If we accept His offer of heaven, in essence we are offering our lives back to Him. If we are offering our lives back to God, then our lives must change. We cannot still live the way we lived before our conversion. We cannot still live in the way that so many people live during this present age. We need to have new thoughts, new desires, and new attitudes. Therefore, we need God to change even the way we think. This is accomplished by the renewing of our thinking which transforms us.

How? Love for God and His Word must replace love for our self, which is our biggest problem. Selfish attitudes are destroying us. The true believer must learn to trust God for those things that we truly need. Our attention should be upon heaven, where we belong, and not merely on the things of this world. But most importantly, we must be conformed to the image of His Son.

When we first invite Christ into our lives, the change in our relationship with God happens at once. We cannot always expect all our attitudes and thoughts to change so suddenly. So, we do wrong things that we should confess to God. However, as Christians we should at some point desire to live in the way that pleases God continuously, not just on Sundays. We must learn from the Bible about how God wants us to live. This is why I have written this book. I'm tired of all the selfish mediocrity, including my own. I honestly believe God is, too. Are you?

Chapter 12 Verse 3-5

"For I say, through the grace given to me, to everyone who is among you, not to think of himself more highly than he ought to think, but to think soberly, as God has dealt to each one a measure of faith." After looking at the subject of the believer and God, the believer needs to look at the subject of him or herself. The true believer needs to see what the exhortation of God is to him or her personally. We must deal with truth. Here, God directs a very forceful charge to the true believer personally.

It is okay to think highly about yourself because you are God's creation, and He is in you. But, don't think too highly of yourself; at least not to the point of prideful arrogance. The true believer is to work on his or her own humility. Everyone is equal, and by that I mean spiritually dead. If God lives in you, praise Him. But it's God that makes the difference, not anything about us. In other words, the believer can think good of him or herself (and should), but he or she can't be puffed up thinking he or she is better than others. To think soberly is to think rightly and from a balanced perspective. The best balance perspective is the biblical one. And the biblical perspective is that God loves everyone equally and does not play favorites. Because Jesus is in us we are special, and we should live that way.

"For as we have many members in one body, but all the members do not have the same function, 5 so we, being many, are one body in Christ, and individually members of one another." God has designed the parts of the human body differently from each other because they all carry out different tasks. We do not expect our hands to do what our feet do; our eyes cannot do what our ears do. However, no part of the body operates for its own benefit; all the parts work together for the benefit of the whole body.

That is how God wants Christians to live, too. God has brought together people from different nations, and they all have different skills and personal qualities. God has also given all of them the Holy Spirit; but the Holy Spirit works in them in many different ways. Therefore, Christians should never be selfish. In other words, they must not use what God has given them solely for their own benefit or to increase their own importance. Nor should Christians refuse to meet with other Christians, as in corporate worship. God has placed them together because they need each other.

Mediocre living is found in the lone wolf mentality. The lone wolf mentality stems from thinking too highly of ourselves. The lone wolf (in this case sheep) is an easy target for the master wolf (Satan) to hunt and devour. If the enemy can affect enough "hands" and "feet" of Jesus at the local church, we're left with only a torso which can't operate. We can sing; we can eat; we can gripe; we can complain, but we can't function properly. How mediocre and common, is that?

Chapter 12 Verse 6-8

"*Having then gifts differing according to the grace that is given to us, let us use them: if prophecy, let us prophesy in proportion to our faith;*" *God* gives every believer at least one spiritual gift. A gift is a special ability given to them for spiritual purposes. It is not a talent. Here, Paul lists a few of the gifts.

The gift of prophecy is mentioned first, and I think it is the most important from an eternal perspective. Prophecy is the gift of proclaiming and exclaiming the will of God. In the Old Testament, it included foretelling future events. In the New Testament, it changes dramatically. The New Testament prophet proclaims and exclaims what has taken place in the Lord Jesus Christ and what has been revealed by Jesus concerning future events. This proclaiming and exclaiming would now also include the duties of a biblical pastor.

"*or ministry, let us use it in our ministering; he who teaches, in teaching;*" Here, we are given the word ministry. "*Ministry*" means "*the way that a true believer acts as a servant."* As the believer serves, his or her principal duty is to serve God but also humbly to serve the people of the church too. He or she must not use the gift for his or her own benefit or as an opportunity to increase his or her own importance. Instead, as God's servant, he or she must do the work that God has given him or her to do.

Teaching is defined as "*to teach the Bible.*" A true believer must always be careful to teach God's Word and not his or her own ideas. Teaching is the ability to explain and ground people in truth. The Word of God must be proclaimed by the preacher, but it also must be taught by gifted teachers (who are often pastors but also include lay people).

"*he who exhorts, in exhortation; he who gives, with liberality; he who leads, with diligence; he who shows mercy, with cheerfulness.*" Exhortation is the ability to motivate and warn people with a sense of urgency. It is counseling to stir people to make a decision for Christ and to grow in Him. It is warning people with the truth. The gift of giving is the ability to give of one's resources generously and willingly. The gift of ruling is the ability of leadership, authority, and administration. The gift of mercy, as seen in a person is forgiveness and compassion towards others. It is always with a cheerful heart.

I have always found it very interesting the order the gifts are listed in. Have you noticed it? Let me list the order in today's vernacular: preaching, serving, discipling, counseling, giving, leading, encouraging. Do you see a connection? Do you see a pattern here? Is there any mediocrity or things leading to mediocrity mentioned here? What is really going on?

Chapter 12 Verse 9

We've seen how true believers are to respond to God and to themselves and if they're not responding as the Bible has described, there needs to be some soul searching. I think that is a fair statement. In these verses, God tells true believers how to relate to others. We could also say it this way: if a believer is not responding to others in the manner the Bible describes, some soul searching should occur. If one is a true believer, one will respond to God, themselves, and others as the Bible teaches. A person will behave like a Christian if the person really is a Christian. The Holy Spirit will see to it.

"Let love be without hypocrisy. Abhor what is evil. Cling to what is good." Here, Paul reminds us how Christ taught us to live. His instructions remind us of such passages as Matthew chapters 5 to 7 and John chapters 13 to 16. This is how Christians can and must live in an evil world. The truth is there can be no proper place in their lives for sinful behavior. Instead, an attitude of true love must guide all their actions.

True Christians should be very aware of the difference between right and wrong behavior. If they are under the leadership of the Holy Spirit, the ministry of the local church, and the spiritual gift packages of the people within the church, they should firmly refuse to do any evil thing. They should make a strong decision only to do what is good. Spiritual mediocrity should never be in their lives.

So the question now is, how does a true believer love others? Scripture gives us four practical ways. First, the believer is to love others by hating evil. The word "*abhor*" means "*to hate with intense feeling, to loathe, to look upon with horror.*" What is the believer to abhor? Evil! What is evil? What God says is evil. What does God say is evil? Glad you asked.

Evil is that which is morally wrong, sinful, or wicked; however, the word evil can also refer to anything that causes harm, with or without the moral dimension. The word is used both ways in the Bible. Anything that contradicts the holy nature of God is evil. The Bible labels these actions and activities as "sin". Sin is evil according to God. So why would the true believer be okay with his or her sin? Does that attitude really make any sense? Once again, of course not.

Those who fall into evil behavior usually start slowly. Paul shows the tragic progression into more and more evil in Romans 1 as we have studied. It starts with refusing to glorify God or give thanks to Him (Romans 1:21), and it ends with God giving them over to a "depraved mind" and allowing them to be "filled with every kind of wickedness" (verses 28–29).

Those who practice evil are in Satan's trap and are slaves to sin: "Opponents [of the Lord's servant] must be gently instructed, in the hope that God will grant them *repentance leading them to a knowledge of the truth, and that they will come to their senses and escape from the trap of the devil, who has taken them captive to do his will*" (2 Timothy 2:25–26; see also John 8:34).

The second way to love others is for the believer to cling to that which is good. The word "*cling*" means "*to attach or glue yourself to something.*" The believer is to hate evil and glue himself to good. The best "good" I know is Jesus and His Word. Want to know how to love? Start by hating evil through cementing yourself to Jesus and His Word. Only by the grace of God can we be set free. And I am praying this book is helping too.

Chapter 12 Verse 10-11

"*Be kindly affectionate to one another with brotherly love, in honor giving preference to one another;*" In contrast to loving others by hating evil and clinging to good, the world and our flesh want us to believe we can love and cling to evil, and everything will still be okay. As we have seen, this is not biblical, practical, or appropriate for the true Christian.

The other two ways a Christian can love others is by being kind and affectionate to them. The word "*affectionate*" means "*the love between family members.*" We are to love our church family as the Lord does. Many people today only know love as a kind of emotion that attracts people to each other. That is not the kind of love that the Bible is referring to here. Rather, true love shows itself in a genuine desire that good things will happen in other people's lives. We do not need to like another person in order to desire that good things will happen for him or her. If they are a member of the church where we belong or the church body at large, we should at least hope and encourage good things towards them.

The fourth way is found in the last part of the verse. The word "*honor*" means "to respect." We are to respect and give preference to other believers. It's not all about us; it's all about Him. Once that is learned, it becomes all about loving others for Him. Imagine a church full of people who truly love others out of a desire to love God. Imagine how much divisiveness could be eliminated if more people would be more biblical and less mediocre in this concept?

When we show that kind of love, it sometimes causes us to act in an extraordinary manner. Normally people desire honor for themselves; they want other people to respect them. However, the person who shows true love does not need anyone to give him or her honor. Instead, he or she cares more that other people should receive honor. He or she does not believe that only famous and important people deserve honor. A good person whom nobody respects deserves honor too, and the person who truly loves would gladly suffer shame in order to give honor to that person.

"*not lagging in diligence, fervent in spirit, serving the Lord.*" A Christian should never be mediocre in his or her walk with the Lord. You can be mediocre in sports, fishing, or academics, but never in your desire to love the Lord and His people. One should have a fervent spirit, or a passion and a fire to serve God. That fire means a Christian's eager desire to serve God, that is, to work for God. That desire should never stop. Rather, a Christian should have, deep inside him, a continuous desire to do what God wants. That desire should constantly direct his or her thoughts, words and actions.

Chapter 12 Verse 12-13

"*rejoicing in hope,*" The next five phrases help us to understand better how we are to serve the Lord. First, the true believer is to rejoice in hope. We do not usually expect people to have joy during their troubles.

However, God's people can and should be different. They do not, of course, have joy because of their troubles. Their joy is because of the good things that God is doing in their lives, even during their troubles. In other words, their joy is because of their hope, and their hope is Jesus.

In the Bible, hope does not mean something uncertain, like luck or chance. God's people put their hope in God, in the certain knowledge that he cannot disappoint them. In the end, He will certainly do all that He has promised to do for them. So, their joy does not depend on their present circumstances; their joy depends on the promises of God.

"patient in tribulation," However, God's people may still suffer great troubles at the present time. The proper reaction to those troubles is not despair but patience. Specifically, even during the worst troubles, God's people should stand firmly, and they should continue to trust God. How do we learn to trust in God more? Through the successful completion of trials and tribulations of life.

"continuing steadfastly in prayer;" Even God's people will be weak if they constantly allow doubts and fears to fill their minds. Their strength must come from God and not from themselves. That is why Paul taught Christians to pray much and often. God acts powerfully when His people pray. A "prayer-less" Christian will soon be a mediocre one. A church full of them will soon be mediocre too. A country full of mediocre churches will soon become mediocre itself. Can you see where I'm going with this?

"distributing to the needs of the saints, given to hospitality." God's people should not live their lives as if nobody else matters. Instead, they should be ready to share both their homes and their possessions with other people. This is exactly what "*distributing to the needs of the saints*" means. The word "*saint*" means "*God's holy people*," in other words, other Christians. Every true and genuine Christian is holy because of his or her relationship with God. Therefore, God will reward anyone who helps one of them (Mark 9:41). God accepts such acts of kindness as if they were for God himself (Matthew 25:40).

The second idea is "*hospitality*" and means *"kindness to a guest*" or "*showing love to strangers*." A stranger is someone whom we do not know, especially someone from another country. That was an especially important instruction for Rome's Christians to whom Paul was writing. Many people travelled to Rome, and their journeys were very dangerous. They might arrive in Rome in a desperate situation, without any friends or family there who could help them. So God's people, who are themselves living as strangers in this world, have a special duty to help them.

Chapter 12 Verse 14-15

"*Bless those who persecute you; bless and do not curse.*" I'm sure you have noticed that God has changed the focus since the beginning of chapter twelve to teach primarily on the believer's responsibility on how to live and behave. God's Word will continue on with this theme for the next three chapters. This is the practical application of the spiritual lessons we have learned from chapter one to chapter eleven. God is so good to His true followers that He doesn't just tell us the spiritual issues, but He explains how we are to live since we have been made spiritually alive now through Jesus. As you have surely learned, God is not content with our mediocrity. He equips and expects much more from all of us. Let's not be fooled into thinking complacency is natural and normal. It isn't. Never has been; never will be. Conforming to the image of His Son is what's important to God, not conforming to the world or other misinformed people.

Paul has just said that Christians should show kindness both to other Christians and to strangers (12:13). Now he adds an extraordinary statement that scolds mediocrity. Christians must not only be kind to good and grateful people; they must also be kind even to their enemies!

This is hard for us to comprehend though. Even the disciples preferred to see God's judgment against people who opposed them, and I often do too. But Jesus's attitude was different. Even at His death, He was praying for people who had dealt with Him so cruelly. Jesus was beyond phenomenal.

Some people, for various reasons, will just not get along with true believers. That's perfectly alright as long as the true believer doesn't become bitter and angry with them. It's okay to decide not to associate with people who cause us grief, but we should always be concerned with God showing them mercy as He has shown us. We do not desire that wicked people will succeed in their evil plans, but we should desire that God will save them from their sins.

"*Rejoice with those who rejoice, and weep with those who weep.*" Here's some more teaching that goes against our nature. Isn't it a wonderful thing that the true believer has received a new nature at their salvation? One of the reasons why is so we can live as these verses tell us.

Life is not all about you, or me, or anyone. It's about God. It's about serving Him faithfully. To serve God faithfully, we must develop a biblical worldview and see things the way He sees them. Then, as we become informed, we can allow the Holy Spirit to transform us more into the likeness of Christ. This is part of the transformation process of conforming to His image.

When we can truly rejoice with others as they have been blessed, without the jealousies and desires for God to do the same for us, we are stepping out of mediocrity and stepping into the footprints of Jesus. When we can weep with those who have been hurt or damaged, or treated wrongly, we can better relate to His ministry and minister to others. If we can do all of that without becoming bitter and angry against God, then we are demonstrating sanctification. Mediocrity cannot live in a world of true rejoicing and empathy.

Chapter 12 Verse 16-18

"*16 Be of the same mind toward one another. Do not set your mind on high things, but associate with the humble. Do not be wise in your own opinion.*" A Christian should not try to prove that he or she is superior to other Christians. Such an attitude only causes arguments and troubles. It spoils the love that Christians should show to each other. Instead, a Christian should think about how he or she can serve other people. In particular, he or she should try to help other Christians, and he or she should not be afraid to do even humble tasks. Those are the tasks that other people do not want to do. Nobody except God may notice them, but God will reward the person who does them. When Christians have that right attitude towards each other, they can work together to make each other stronger. That is how God wants churches to operate.

"Repay no one evil for evil. Have regard for good things in the sight of all men." All people have done wrong and evil things. In fact, their wicked behavior even brings God's anger against them. However, people have not lost all knowledge of what is good.

People still understand that certain kinds of behavior are noble, honorable, and right. They may not themselves be honest or sincere, but they still consider an honest, sincere person to be a good person. They may themselves be very evil, but they would not trust an evil person. They know that they can only really trust someone good. So, Paul urges Christians to test their own behavior by those standards. Christians have the responsibility to show God's true nature to the world, not mediocre religion. Part of that is living biblically, and that must include the notion that two wrongs don't make a right.

"*If it is possible, as much as depends on you, live peaceably with all men.*" When these verses were written, people hated true believers simply because they belonged to Christ. Not much has changed. In such circumstances, Paul urged Christians to be very careful how they lived. If a Christian always behaves in a good and moral way, then his or her enemies will have no proper reason to hate him. They might accuse him of many wrong things, but their own conscience will declare their words to be lies. A Christian should not allow his or her own behavior to be the cause of bitter feelings or anger for other people.

It is not possible to be friendly with everyone. People who hate Christ will hate Christians too. We cannot change what God declares to be holy, true, or right; we cannot agree to do any evil act. That is insanity.

We must grow and mature as followers of Jesus and show respect for people. That is our duty.

Chapter 12 Verse 19-21

"19 Beloved, do not avenge yourselves, but rather give place to wrath; for it is written, "Vengeance is Mine, I will repay," says the Lord." God's people should never be vengeful or feel they have a right to personally punish someone. God's people should have a different attitude: they forgive. They cannot of course deny that evil things have happened. However, they recognize God to be the perfect judge. So, they hand over all their rights in such matters to Him. They appeal to Him to deal with the matter instead of them. With such an attitude, they have no bitter feelings because it is not still their right to punish the guilty person. It is a matter for God alone to deal with, and all His judgements are right and good. This is a spiritual discipline and takes desire and practice to accomplish.

"20 Therefore "If your enemy is hungry, feed him; If he is thirsty, give him a drink; For in so doing you will heap coals of fire on his head." This is not what the world teaches or what we come out of the womb programmed for. Again, it's why God has given us a new nature. Look, doing good towards a person who is at enmity with you will do more to them than doing bad. Kindness will affect all but the staunchest of evil people. Nobody expects a person whom he or she hates to care about him or her. So it is not surprising if the enemy feels a deep sense of shame in that situation. That shame only becomes worse as the Christian continues his or her kind and generous acts. To the enemy, it feels like a burning fire: he or she is ashamed of his or her cruelty, his or her bad words, or evil actions. While there are people who absolutely will not be affected by this, many will be. I've seen it happen.

"Do not be overcome by evil, but overcome evil with good." Christians choose to live in a good, honest, and truthful manner because that kind of life pleases God. In fact, God, who is good and perfect in every way, can

approve of no other kind of life. But it's not easy. And it's counterintuitive to the world and the flesh.

God's people will certainly overcome all their troubles in this world, but they cannot behave as many people do in this world. They cannot allow hate, cruelty, or bitter feelings to direct their actions. Christians overcome their troubles, not by evil acts, but by good acts. Often, they find it very difficult to do the right things in such circumstances because it is against their natural feelings. So, they must depend on God to help them and to give them strength. They themselves are often weak, but Christ gives them the power to live in the manner that pleases God. And that's the secret to conforming to His image.

13

Chapter 13 Verse 1-2

"1. Let every soul be subject to the governing authorities. For there is no authority except from God, and the authorities that exist are appointed by God." God is now turning the teaching towards the true believer and the state, or governmental authority over the believer. We are all under someone's authority whether we like it or not, and whether we believe it or not. Unfortunately, rulers and governments often use their power in a wrong, evil, or even cruel manner. Many people, therefore, argue that governments should have as little power as possible. Nobody should have authority over anyone else they say. But that is not what the Bible teaches. It says that governments do important work in this world. They organize our cities and our societies. They deal with and punish criminals. They make laws to try to stop certain kinds of wrong behavior. When governments do these things properly, they are doing God's work in this world.

We might think that our governments gained their power by political skill or military strength. That may be correct, but in reality their authority comes from God. So, Christ told Pilate that all his power in fact came from God. Pilate would have no authority if God had not given it to him (John 19:10-11). That means that rulers and governments are responsible to God for their actions. That is a very serious matter because God will be their judge too (Psalm 2: Psalm 110:5-6).

That also means that Christians should respect their rulers. Of course they cannot obey any laws that tell them to do evil things or to go against what the Bible teaches. Of course they try to help the weakest people in their country. They care about those people who suffer because of their government's actions. However, usually most laws are not for an evil purpose but for a good purpose. Therefore, Christians must obey the laws of their country. They should be good citizens, not just because of the power of their government, but also because of their duties to God.

"*Therefore whoever resists the authority resists the ordinance of God, and those who resist will bring judgment on themselves.*" I know it's not a popular concept, but it is biblical. The true believer should not be rebellious and resistant. If we don't like what's going on in our country, we get out of mediocrity and vote or run for office. But we deal with the hand that is given to us. God has designed and allowed the offices of government to be established and filled. The three institutions which exist for the betterment of people, the family, the church, and the government are all set up so we have structure and order in our lives. The best life for any of us is to be a biblical family serving in a biblical church in a biblical nation. That being so, is there any wonder the enemy attacks all three institutions? If the enemy can be successful in degrading and devaluing these three institutions, chaos, ineffectiveness, and eventually physical and spiritual captivity will soon set in. What are the signs this is getting close? Well, mediocre Christian families serving in mediocre churches will, within a generation or two, spawn a mediocre country, at least spiritually. Do you see this happening in our country? I do. What's causing the decline? It could be a variety of things, but in my opinion and as I have stressed throughout this book, it's because we have become complacent with God and turned to spiritual apathy and mediocracy. Am I wrong?

CHAPTER 13 VERSE 3-4

"*For rulers are not a terror to good works, but to evil. Do you want to be unafraid of the authority? Do what is good, and you will have praise from the same. 4 For he is God's minister to you for good. But if you do evil, be afraid; for he does not bear the sword in vain; for he is God's minister, an avenger to execute wrath on him who practices evil."* Here, Paul describes rulers and government officials as "servants of God." To us today, that seems an unusual use of that phrase. We would expect the "servants of God" to mean loyal Christians. They serve God by their prayers, by good works, and by declaring His message. However, many rulers and officials do none of these things. Sometimes they use their power in a cruel or evil manner. Many of them do not know the true God; however, Paul still calls them God's servants.

God works powerfully in our world (8:28). God has the right to carry out His plans by means of anyone whom He chooses (9:17). In Isaiah 44:28 to 45:6, God appointed the powerful foreign king, Cyrus, to carry out His (God's) work in the world. Cyrus did not know the true God, but God used him to return Israel's people to their own country (Ezra 1).

A judge may not know the real God, but that judge's authority to punish criminals still comes from God. Our governments may not respect God, but their power to make laws still comes from God. The purpose of those laws is to make evil people afraid because there will be judgment of evil acts. Government officials have real power to punish guilty people, which Paul expresses in his reference to their "swords."

With so many evil governments in the world, we may ask whether good people should also be afraid of their power. Christ's answer was that we should not be afraid of them. God is the judge of all people. A powerful person might be able to kill someone's body, but he cannot send that person to hell (Matthew 10:28). Governments may deal cruelly with God's people, but God will always support His people (8:35-39). God will protect His people; he will bring them safely to heaven (John 14:1-3).

Do you know why we have government and laws in the first place? Government and law are a restraint upon evil. The power of evil and corruption are so strong that when people are without law, they often get out of control with selfishness and sin. So laws are good, and the government that enforces them are too. It's when the law is lax and there's no governmental enforcement that society starts to break down. God's law and enforcement are good too for the very same reason.

So, why do we fight it? Because we are natural-born lawbreakers, and we rebel against authority. This is why we drive 80 mph when the speed limit is 70 mph. And we convince ourselves "10 mph over" the speed limit is acceptable and okay. But, it's breaking the law. It might not be enforced and we get away with it, which makes it easier to break other laws, but it is still illegal. And most people are good at pushing the limit. We do the same with God's Word.

Chapter 13 Verse 5

"*Therefore you must be subject, not only because of wrath but also for conscience' sake.*"

Since the beginning of the Christian religion, some people have tried to change God's message of spiritual life into a message about freedom. They say that Christ has given them both moral and political freedom; therefore, they oppose any kind of authority. They want to be free to behave in any way that they wish. Namely, they had rights. But Jesus commands us to deny ourselves (our rights) and follow Him. Following Him includes being under the laws and governmental authority of those in authority. Jesus told His followers to give Caesar what is Caesar's, remember? If you don't like who's in office, vote. Until then, we are under those in authority over us.

Paul had seen this kind of rebellious behavior in the church at Corinth. There, people were saying that they possessed the rights of kings (1 Corinthians 4:8). One church member even believed that he had the right to have sex with his father's wife. Even people who were not Christians were not behaving like that (1 Corinthians 5:1). At church meetings, Christians were behaving in ways that would cause shock to other people (1 Corinthians 11:20-22). Often, people will use their so-called "faith" to justify their actions. However, we should have actions that prove our faith.

Paul could see how much trouble this kind of behavior would cause with the government. If Christians would not even obey God's law, they would not respect the laws of their country. Therefore, Paul urged Christians to respect God's authority. God had permitted the government to rule their nation, so they should respect its authority too. The enemy is constantly trying to lead you and me to new heights of rebellion against authority. Our politicians see it; our police officers see it; our pastors see it. People are growing more and more rebellious to any type of authority in their lives, whether it be political, legal, or spiritual.

Can we get away with it? Can we hide under the "I'm just a sinner saved by grace" mode of living? No. Governments will punish people who refuse to pay their taxes. People who do not obey the law will go to prison. And people who disobey pastoral and biblical leadership in their lives will suffer the consequences. Government officials, law enforcement officers, and pastors owe a duty to God to make sure that they are obedient to their calling to authority. So of course Christians should obey the law, and they should pay their taxes. Otherwise, they will suffer the same punishment as anyone else who does not obey the law. Even a Christian who cannot obey an evil law will often suffer punishment for it (1 Peter 4:15-16). Christians are not free from these matters. We should all be law-abiding citizens and not rebellious troublemakers.

A true Christian has freedom from sin and its final penalty, which is eternal separation from God, not freedom from being a good citizen. But make no mistake, you and I are not independent. We are dependent upon Jesus.

Chapter 13 Verse 6-7

"*For because of this you also pay taxes, for they are God's ministers attending continually to this very thing.*" Because of the earlier verses we have studied, we now see the reason we pay taxes. Let me help to take this idea of taxes to its simplest form.

We start with the concept of money. What is money? It is not really wealth. Money cannot pay for the things that are truly good, even in this life. We cannot buy a good family or a happy life. In fact, when a country has political troubles, money itself can lose its value. No, money is a way that governments show their authority over us. They pay us with money, so they control our power to buy and to sell (Revelation 13:16-17). For that reason, each government puts its own mark on the coins and notes that it provides for our use. That mark shows us to which country the money belongs.

Because the money belongs to a country, its government has the right to demand its payment (Mark 12:13-17). That is what taxes are. The government provided the money for our use, so it can demand its return. Christians should pay their debts (Mark 13:8); they should also pay their taxes. They do not do it merely because they are afraid of punishment. They do it because they consider it the right thing to do (13:5).

Paul makes a surprising statement about the work of people who collect taxes in this verse. We know how much other people often dislike tax collectors, but God calls them ministers. However, in the collection of taxes, governments are using the authority that God has given them (13:1). Therefore, the people who collect taxes are carrying out a public service on God's behalf. It impressed Paul how well they carry out this special work for God. They do not neglect their work; they constantly carry out the tasks that God has given them. From their attitudes, as from so many other things in this world, Christians can learn an important lesson.

"Render therefore to all their due: taxes to whom taxes are due, customs to whom customs, fear to whom fear, honor to whom honor." Christians are citizens of heaven, so they might argue that they do not need to respect people in authority in this world. However, Paul insisted that the opposite is true. In fact, Christians are people who respect God's authority. Therefore, they should be able to understand more clearly than other people what authority really is. It is God who chose to give authority to governments

in this world. He did it in order to place a limit on the power of evil people.

Therefore, Christians should respect the power of their government. They should give its officials whatever is rightly due to them. That often means the payment of money, specifically, taxes. Paul mentions two kinds of taxes here. One of these most likely means a tax on people and their property. The other probably refers to a tax when people buy and sell goods.

Nevertheless, there are other ways by which we show respect to people in authority. There is a proper sense of fear that we should show our judges. That sense of fear should cause us to avoid wrong behavior and to do what is right. Also, we should show honor to people who carry on important and responsible work. In Acts 26, we see how politely Paul himself spoke to powerful and important people. He showed great respect to them.

It is interesting to compare Paul's words in Romans 13:7 with the answer that Christ gave in Mark 12:13-17. Christ too insisted that God's people should pay their taxes. Even so, he then reminded the people that we all owe a much greater duty to God, and mediocre living isn't big enough to hide us from our responsibilities. Pay what you owe, Christian, and this must include loyalty and obedience to God.

Chapter 13 Verse 8

"Owe no one anything except to love one another, for he who loves another has fulfilled the law."

In financial matters, Christians are like other people in this world. They may have homes, families, and businesses. They have people whom they must pay; they have duties that they must carry out.

In all these things, Christians should be honorable. Christians should pay their debts; they should carry out their duties. They should be people whom other people can trust. When we have paid our debts, there is nothing more to pay. When we have carried out our duties, we are free from those duties. How does this work out in everyday life? There are three things we must know.

First, nothing should be purchased by a believer that isn't really needed, no matter how alluring it is on the advertised commercial. Next, nothing should ever be purchased unless the believer can meet the obligation to pay for it. Lastly, if a believer does make an expensive purchase, he must be able to afford the payments.

Still, there is a larger duty that Christians will always have towards other people. It is the duty to act in love towards other people. That kind of love is not an emotion, for our emotions change so frequently and for so many various reasons. No, this kind of love is based on the decision to offer help and kindness, as much as is possible, to everyone that God places in our lives. Sometimes that help will require money. If a believer is up to his or her ears in debt, it is extremely difficult to assist someone.

It is by our acts of love that we truly carry out God's law (13:9-10). Expressly, the law of God in the Bible is teaching us to show love to other people. A person might obey some of the rules in the Bible but still have an attitude of hate towards other people. That person would not truly be obeying God's law because he is not showing love. Yet, by means of love, a person does what the rest of God's law is teaching him to do. It is that person's desire to show to other people the same kind of love that God has for them. There can be no better attitude than that towards other people; that person is doing what God wants him to do.

Being deep in debt is living in mediocrity and helps to destroy the believer's witness. It helps to dramatically squelch the believer's ability to love others by having a lack of resources. The point is this: a believer is to owe no man anything. If he does, the believer is to pay his or her debts and fulfill his or her obligations; otherwise he can damage the name of Christ.

Chapter 13 Verse 9-10

"For the commandments, "You shall not commit adultery," "You shall not murder," "You shall not steal,""You shall not bear false witness," "You shall not covet," and if there is any other commandment, are all summed up in this saying, namely, "You shall love your neighbor as yourself." Love does no harm to a neighbor; therefore love is the fulfillment of the law."

The list of commands that God gave to Israel's people appears twice in the Bible: Exodus 20:1-17 and Deuteronomy 5:6-21. Those commands are not, of course, the whole of God's law, although they do sum it up quite nicely. They are a series of lessons to teach people how God wants them to live.

The commands are in two parts. The first few commands are lessons about a person's relationship with God. The other commands are about a person's relationships with other people. That is how Christ could explain the lessons even more simply in Mark 12:28-31. People should love God, and they should love other people. Those are the most important lessons that God's law teaches.

In that passage of Mark, Christ was not in fact teaching a new lesson. He was simply repeating words that already appeared in the Bible in both Deuteronomy 6:5 and Leviticus 19:18. Paul repeats only the last of these passages in Romans 13:9 because his subject here is relationships between people. He is teaching how Christians should deal with other people. As I stated earlier, this is the practical part of the book of Romans. This is what conforming to the image of His Son looks like.

Christians should act *in love*, and therefore they should offer kindness and help to other people whenever possible. That is how God's law teaches people to behave, and that is how God wants His people to behave. In 1 Corinthians 13:4-7, you can read Paul's description of the nature of true love. That kind of love is entirely good because it comes from God himself. The point here is people who offend by going against God's commands are not showing true love. The reason for most of these wrong acts is people's selfish and evil desires, which are the manifestations of a mediocre spiritual life. When people behave in a selfish manner that is the opposite of true love, they are actually living out their true beliefs in front of everyone. You see, biblical love is when we care about other people; we are selfish when we care too much about ourselves.

What does this have to do with anything? Once again I'm glad you asked, so stay with me on this. A true believer should love God with all of his or her heart, mind, and soul to the point that he or she will love others enough to forbid adultery, killing, stealing, false witnessing, and covetousness. In addition, this love should keep a believer from working to do wrong to a neighbor, which would be all the citizens of the world. Why? Think about this very carefully. Because God so loved the world He gave His only begotten Son, and He didn't commit adultery, murder, theft, lies, or selfishness to do it. He just did it. Out of love. And if He truly lives in us, we should be like Him.

Chapter 13 Verse 11-12

"And do this, knowing the time, that now it is high time to awake out of sleep; for now our salvation is nearer than when we first believed."

We often use the word "salvation" to mean the time when a person first believes in Christ, but it can also mean rescue and safety. Christ is coming to rescue all true believers from all their troubles in this world. Under His rule, they will always be safe. That is also a correct use of the word because God's work in a person's life is both certain and immediate. God will certainly carry out all His promises to His people, but that has not happened yet (1 Corinthians 15:12-19). It will happen only when Christ returns to rule all things.

So, as we wait for Christ's return, we must not become lazy, or (you guessed it) mediocre. We must not behave like people who do not care about Christ's return. We must not be like servants who are not ready for their master's return. The time of Christ's return becomes nearer every day. In fact we are all one day closer to His return than we were yesterday. We have believed Christ; we must continue to believe and trust him. We have put our hope in Christ; we must allow our hope to become stronger. We are the people of God; we must live our lives as God's people should live in this world. We must not always be like children; we must allow our relationship with God to develop and to become mature. If you are truly a born again believer, it is now high time to awake out of sleep. It is high time we dispense with the mediocre living and start living as God has provided for and intended.

"*The night is far spent, the day is at hand. Therefore let us cast off the works of darkness, and let us put on the armor of light.*" Paul's words seem to describe the camp of an army. That army hopes to surprise its enemies with a sudden attack, early in the morning. However, by night the soldiers are pleasing themselves with foolish and wild behavior. Doesn't that sound ridiculous if the soldiers are really serious?

The Bible often uses darkness as a symbol for people's evil deeds. Many people who are now Christians once cared only about pleasing themselves. However, God changed their lives in the most powerful manner. The knowledge of Christ changed them completely, like a light that shines in darkness. Why all the fuss about this? Well, the darkness of people's evil deeds must end because Christ will return suddenly. He will defeat all that is evil in this world. Here, Paul compares Christ's return to the beginning of a new day. The beginning of the new day has an astonishing effect on the soldiers in the camp. Long before dawn, they are all awake, and they are preparing themselves for the battle. Now none of them care to please himself; their only desire is to carry out their tasks well and to win.

The knowledge of Christ's imminent return should have a similar effect on the lives of Christians. Christians should not desire to please themselves. Instead, they should loyally do the work that God has given them to do. They should not behave like those foolish soldiers in the darkness. Instead, they should make themselves ready for the day of Christ's return.

A mediocre army is an ineffective army, and an army exists to fight the battle. You can rest assured the enemy's troops are battle tested and anything but mediocre. Do you fully understand what that implies?

Chapter 13 Verse 13-14

"*Let us walk properly, as in the day, not in revelry and drunkenness, not in lewdness and lust, not in strife and envy.*" It's time to walk straight, Christian! The word "*properly*" means "*decently and honorably.*" A believer is to walk honestly before the Lord and other people. He or she is not to hide from God or mankind. When a person claims to be a believer but never goes to worship God with other believers, I have always felt they were AWOL. All true believers should be consistent in their walk with God and others, which would include corporate worship.

Most Christians understand quite well how God wants them to live. Perhaps they behave well during the day when they are busy. However, in the evening when they start to relax, they do many wrong things. When people start to relax, they often try to please themselves. It is that kind of attitude that Paul warns against. Christians should not try to please themselves; that is a selfish attitude. Rather, their desire should be to please God always.

We are all instructed to walk honorably. We do not live with unrestrained indulgence (revelry), take intoxicating drinks or drugs (drunkenness), or run wild with our sensuality (lewdness/lust). No, our pattern is the life of Jesus, and He did not live this way. If we are to truly follow Him, then we must follow His leading by example. To live worldly as above and claim to be following Jesus is impossible. And it's at best mediocre. I ask you to once again to seriously think this through.

"*But put on the Lord Jesus Christ, and make no provision for the flesh, to fulfill its lusts.*" We are all aware of the weakness of our physical bodies. That is why we put on clothes: to cover our nakedness. We choose clothes to deal with our weaknesses. So, we wear warm clothes when we are cold. We wear cool clothes when we are hot. We choose clothes to protect us from the sun or the rain. In battle, soldiers wear armor: strong clothes that defend the weak parts of their bodies.

However, we have no clothes to deal with our inner weaknesses: our wrong desires, ambitions, emotions, and fears. To deal with these weaknesses, we must depend on Christ. He alone frees us from these weaknesses to live in the manner that pleases God. So we are taught to put on the Lord Jesus Christ. In Galatians 3:26-27, Paul again uses the expression to "put on Christ." There, he refers to the beginning of the Christian life, when a person first trusts Christ. However, we cannot stop then; we must continue to trust Christ through our whole lives. So, here, Paul urges people who are already Christians to "put on Christ." Particularly, they must trust Him every day, even as we put on our clothes every day. We need His help continuously. We constantly need to accept His strength in order to overcome our weaknesses. We need to conform to His image.

We also must not make provisions for the flesh by giving in to the flesh or our lusts. Impossible? Not according to God. Not only is it quite possible, it's expected.

Chapter 14 Verse 1-4

God has just explained how we should deal with our own weaknesses (13:14). His next subject is how we should deal with the weaknesses of other Christians, and He now shifts our attention to the law of liberty. The issue of Christian liberty versus license is always confronting the believer and the church. What can a believer do and not do socially and personally? Chapter 14 addresses some of the more important things.

"Receive one who is weak in the faith, but not to disputes over doubtful things." The question is how can a Christian be weak in faith? There are two main reasons. Some Christians are weak because they allow wrong desires and feelings to direct their actions (Romans 6:12-23). They do many wrong things simply because they want to do those things. They are not trusting God properly; they are not allowing His Holy Spirit to direct their lives. Other Christians are weak because of a wrong attitude. This too stems from not trusting God

"For one believes he may eat all things, but he who is weak eats only vegetables." Both the weak Christian believer and the strong Christian believer thought the other one was weak, and they were both criticizing and condemning each other. (Sounds mediocre and all too familiar to me). God simply says their relationship with Him does not depend on food but on faith: belief and trust in God.

"Let not him who eats despise him who does not eat, and let not him who does not eat judge him who eats; for God has received him." The picture here is that believers were arguing over eating and not eating. Is it just me, or do you find this ridiculous too? I like Key Lime pie, and I understand if someone else prefers carrots. I don't like to eat just before I teach or preach, but I understand if someone else is okay with doing so. Seems to me believers have better things to argue about than eating or not eating. I can't think of a better example of mediocrity than this. Imagine visiting a church where the people are arguing over something like the worship style or the color of the new carpet for the Sanctuary. Unbelievable. But I've seen it happen many times.

"*Who are you to judge another's servant? To his own master he stands or falls. Indeed, he will be made to stand, for God is able to make him stand."* It is wonderful for us to know that God approves of His servants. Of course He does not approve of their wrong deeds or their foolish actions. He approves of them because Christ died for them. He approves of them because of their faith in Him. He approves of them because they truly are His people. He has begun a great work in their lives, and He will certainly complete it. Our Master is Jesus, and if He's okay with us, it really doesn't matter what other people think or say.

Chapter 14 Verse 5-6

"*One person esteems one day above another; another esteems every day alike. Let each be fully convinced in his own mind."* As a pastor, I don't like to celebrate holidays very much during the worship hours at church. I know this goes against the vast majority of what people want from churches. Most churches use the worship hour to celebrate and recognize all sorts of people and events at the expense of actually worshipping God. I just don't think that is appropriate. This verse is one reason why.

Let me give you an example. Christmas day is a very joyful occasion for those Christians who choose that day to remember Christ's birth. However, we cannot say that the origins of December 25th are truly Christian. In fact, many of its traditions come from ancient false religions. That fact sometimes causes disagreements among Christians. And disagreements are not from the Holy Spirit.

Not all Christians agree even about the right day for church meetings. Most meet on Sundays. Some still meet on Saturdays. In addition, God gave to Israel its sacred holidays, and Paul considered them important. However, Paul had to warn the Christians in Galatia that some teachers were using those holidays as a means to control them. I'd rather just worship Jesus.

In Romans 14:5-6, Paul refuses to say whether he believes it right or wrong to have special sacred days. Christians give their whole lives to God, so, for them, every day is holy. However, many Christians still consider it helpful to have special holy days and sacred holidays. Paul refuses to argue against them. God can guide different people to do different things. Therefore different Christians, who have different opinions about these matters, may all be obeying God loyally. They do not have to agree about such things. Each person only needs to do what God has directed him or her to do. And for me, God has directed me to keep the church's worship hours holy unto Him.

"He who observes the day, observes it to the Lord; and he who does not observe the day, to the Lord he does not observe it. He who eats, eats to the Lord, for he gives God thanks; and he who does not eat, to the Lord he does not eat, and gives God thanks." When Christians eat, they should thank God for His goodness. It is God who provides food, both for people and for every living thing. We cannot in reality obtain food by our own efforts however hard our work may be (Psalm 127:2). Rather, our food is the kind gift that God, our Father in heaven, provides for us (Matthew 6:11; Matthew 6:31-33).

Therefore, for a Christian, even a simple meal provides both an opportunity and a reason to praise God. Sometimes a Christian might refuse to eat certain foods because of his or her beliefs. He or she makes that decision because he or she cares about his or her relationship with God; he or she is only doing what his or her conscience declares to be right. Therefore, in that decision, that Christian is also giving honor to God. He or she must not make that decision with a proud attitude but rather with a grateful heart. So, he too must thank God for His goodness. He may not eat the food, but he has both an opportunity and a reason to praise God.

Christians should be careful to give honor to God in *all* their decisions, especially in decisions about their religion. When they choose to have a special day, for example Christmas or Easter, it must not be just an opportunity for parties. They might have those happy activities, but the main purpose of the day must be to give honor to God.

It is possible for Christians to have different opinions about various matters. In their decisions about these things, Christians should be careful always to give honor to God. It's been my experience that holidays and fellowship opportunities can quickly become opportunities to honor anything but God. Have you seen that too?

Chapter 14 Verse 7-10

"For none of us liveth to himself, and no man dieth to himself. For whether we live, we live unto the Lord; and whether we die, we die unto the Lord: whether we live therefore, or die, we are the Lord's." You might think that your life and death are private matters for you alone. In life, your greatest desire is probably to please yourself. At its end, you alone and nobody else will suffer when you die. Other people may care about you, but, in the end, these things only really matter to you. Such may be your attitudes. But the truth is there will be a meeting we all will be summoned to. The alive in Christ will spend eternity with Him; the dead in Christ will not. This is what the Bible has taught for over six thousand years.

The Christian is a servant, and a servant cannot say that he or she has his or her own life separate from the life of his or her master. Rather, he or she gives his or her whole attention to his or her master, or at least a good servant does. A mediocre one may not, but we all know that would be displeasing to his or her master. His or her only desire is to do what his or her master wants, and to do it well. At the death of such a good and capable servant, the master himself feels great loss, and His loss is real. In life or death, the servant's desire is to please his or her master. The Christian servant uses his or her life to do the work that God directs him or her to do. Christians know that even death cannot defeat them. Its effect will only be to take them to be with God always. Those who are conformed to His Son know this and live it.

"*For to this end Christ both died, and rose, and revived, that he might be Lord both of the dead and living. But why dost thou judge thy brother? or why dost thou set at nought thy brother? for we shall all stand before the judgment seat of Christ. For it is written, As I live, saith the Lord, every knee shall bow to me, and every tongue shall confess to God. So then every one of us shall give account of himself to God.*" Jesus is the Lord of all living believers but also all those believers who have gone on from this world. This is exactly what verse nine means. He is Lord whether they are still living on this earth, or whether they are deceased and passed on to heaven. The Word of God proclaims this as truth.

Since it is true, we should leave the judgement of all true believers (brothers and sisters) to God. When the Bible says every knee shall bow and every tongue confess, it means everyone will bow down to Jesus; everyone will confess to God, for we will all stand before the judgment seat of Christ. Everyone will be judged by *Christ*, not by each other. And yes, our mediocrity will be judged there too.

But don't mistake this to mean everyone will have the opportunity to be saved at this time . No, this is the judgement seat of Christ, and it won't be a pleasant experience for many people; actually most people. During this event, Jesus will judge from perfect holiness and not average mediocrity. It would benefit all of us to know the difference and pattern our lives on what we should do biblically, and mediocrity isn't acceptable. You and I and everyone who has ever lived will be judged for what we have and haven't done. I think those of us who have chosen and been satisfied with being mediocre servants will be quite ashamed, and it will be costly for us. I need you to really reflect upon this because it's of eternal importance.

Chapter 14 Verse 13-15

"Let us not therefore judge one another anymore: but judge this rather, that no man put a stumbling block or an occasion to fall in his brother's way." Are you ready for this one? Believers are not to judge others; they are to judge themselves. As I think about this, I wonder what society would be like if just the people who claim to be followers of Christ actually did this regularly. If we judged ourselves and how we negatively impact other believers by what we do and say, and then stopped doing it because it caused our brothers to stumble in their faith, what would our society look like then? Would mediocrity morph into excellence at some point? I think there's a very good chance that would happen.

I know some Christians drink alcoholic beverages. I have had more than a few conversations with new believers who struggled with seeing more "mature" believers doing things they felt were inappropriate. I was once one of them. I wish believers would stop doing these things. My vocation would be much easier if Christians would practice these verses more (including me). Look, the grape is pure, but man makes an intoxicating drink from it. Vegetation is pure, but man takes it and makes it harmful to the body. Does this sound like God's will for the believer's body and well-being? Isn't drinking, smoking, and partying just excuses to live mediocre lives as Christians? Let's just be honest and admit it.

"I know, and am persuaded by the Lord Jesus, that there is nothing unclean of itself: but to him that esteemeth anything to be unclean, to him it is unclean." I may think taking drugs (or drinking or whatever) is absolutely fine, and it's my body, but the Bible teaches that as a believer, I shouldn't do it. As a believer I do not need to do anything which causes another believer to stumble. And it's the other believer's opinion of it that should be important to us. And we should certainly know God's opinion on issues and live our lives to please Him. Shouldn't we?

Our bottom line here is we need to care for those Christians whose relationship with God is weak. So, we should not do anything that might spoil their relationship with God. In particular, we should not urge them to do something that they believe to be wrong.

"*But if thy brother be grieved with thy meat, now walkest thou not charitably. Destroy not him with thy meat, for whom Christ died.*" Suppose that I believe a certain action to be wrong. In other words, I believe that it would offend God for me to do that thing. My opinion about that matter may, of course, be either right or wrong. However, if I then carry out that action, I have certainly done something wrong. Even if my action has not offended God, my attitude certainly has offended Him. I would have done something on purpose that I believed to be wrong and evil.

God wanted to separate Israel's people from the other nations, so that they would be His holy people. He taught them by His law to live differently from how other people lived. For example, He gave them careful rules about various animals that they should not eat. But mediocrity set in. People's attitude was they could do whatever they wanted, and if their neighbors didn't like it then they could move. Not very loving, right? But God reminds the reader that our neighbors are "someone for whom Christ died." God has shown such great love for all people, not just believers. Consequently, of course Christians must also show love to people; in fact, it is their duty to do that.

In both Rome and Corinth, some Christians were not showing that love. Their reason is quite astonishing. They cared more about their choice of food than about the people whom God loves so much. They wanted the freedom to eat any kind of food, and that attitude was upsetting weaker Christians. In Corinth, that attitude was even causing some weak Christians to do things that their conscience did not permit. Good old mediocrity. It's been around for a long time. When will it end? Will it ever end? It will when His people surrender daily and continue to conform to the image of His Son.

Chapter 14 Verse 16-18

"*Let not then your good be evil spoken of*:" Often, the result of bad and evil acts by Christians is that other people say wrong things against God. So, God's holy name does not receive the honor that is due to Him. When we live the way we want to and others think God is okay with it due to a lack of knowledge on their part, we discredit God and His offer. I, for one, do not want to be in front of God one day guilty of that.

The freedom that Christ gives to His people is certainly something good. If we use it for God's honor, then that freedom will bring honor to God. However, if we use that freedom to satisfy our own desires, weaker Christians may (and often do) suffer. It's too high of a price for everyone to pay. The point is this: the true believer is to be concerned with people, their relationship with God, and with himself or herself, not with the right to eat, drink, party, socialize, or howl at the moon. His or her primary purpose in life is to reach and build mankind up, not to grieve them and cause them to stumble.

"*For the kingdom of God is not meat and drink; but righteousness, and peace, and joy in the Holy Ghost.*" These are the issues we should be asking questions about and seeking diligently: righteousness, peace, and joy. I can't recall anyone ever asking me if a Christian should be experiencing these things. But I have had untold numbers asking me if a Christian could drink, have premarital sex, live with someone (and you know why), or use drugs, and a host of other ridiculous questions. Can you see how not conforming to the example of Jesus is causing us to focus on the wrong things?

"*For he that in these things serveth Christ is acceptable to God, and approved of men.*" I'm going to get very specific here and add Scripture reference to my commentary. Hold on to your hats.

Look, true religion is not merely a matter of food and drink, or anything like that, as we saw in verse 17. By now you surely have come to realize that it does not please God if we care only about the desires of our bodies. Nor do other people often approve of that kind of attitude. They consider it selfish and greedy. And if you really think about it, you do too.

Right religion is when we serve God in our spirits (John 4:24). We can only do that in the power that comes from His Holy Spirit (8:4-5). So you must be truly saved, or you're wasting your time (Acts 4:12). God is completely good (James 1:13-17); His Spirit causes us not to live for our own selfish benefit (Galatians 5:16-21) but to do what is truly good (Galatians 5:22-23). In other words, we cannot find in ourselves the power to do what is truly good in this world. Rather, we need to receive that power from the Holy Spirit.

So, Christians need to have an attitude that depends completely on God (2 Corinthians 12:9-10). They need His power to live in the way that truly pleases Him. They need to show in this world the kind of love that only comes from Him (1 John 4:7-11). Without that kind of love, their best efforts achieve nothing (1 Corinthians 13:1-3).

Yet, with that power and that love, Christians can achieve things that are truly good (James 1:27). They overcome their selfish attitudes, and they are genuinely able to help other people (Luke 10:28-37). Everyone who thinks in a right and proper manner approves of that kind of Christian behavior. Even their enemies can see that their acts are good (12:14-21).

That, my friends, blows mediocrity out of the water. I can hear it whimpering now. That, my friends, is also the sign of a Christian who has conformed to the image of His Son.

Chapter 14 Verse 19-23

"*Let us therefore follow after the things which make for peace, and things wherewith one may edify another.*" This is the very purpose for believers here on earth: to bring peace to men and to build them up. People must secure peace with God first and then with other people. The problem is too many Christians are content with mediocrity and being at peace with no one, or at least only those who look, act, and live like they do.

"*For meat destroy not the work of God. All things indeed are pure; but it is evil for that man who eateth with offence.* Do not destroy the work of God in another person's life; it is a sin. A man, woman, or child is worth far more than a person's right to anything, including the right to eat, drink, or whatever. We are to get our priorities straight. And our rights are not real priorities when it comes to leading others to Jesus. They have the most important rights. It's all about perspective and the worldview we have. A true, biblical worldview will allow us to see this.

"*It is good neither to eat flesh, nor to drink wine, nor any thing whereby thy brother stumbleth, or is offended, or is made weak.*" Again, do nothing to cause a brother or sister to stumble. Can it get any clearer than this? Nothing is worth losing a soul for the kingdom. Not food, nor alcohol, nor inappropriate music or television, nor improper relationships, nothing. But few people see this. Why? Well, they either don't realize this is biblical, or they don't really care. Both positions are the pinnacle of mediocrity.

"*Hast thou faith? have it to thyself before God. Happy is he that condemneth not himself in that thing which he alloweth.*" Friend, if you have faith, I mean real faith, you must have faith in yourself as you stand before God. The only way that can happen is you have faith in Jesus as He stands with you. Here, God's Word tells us that if a believer feels he or she can do something, he or she should do it *only before the Lord* if it causes another to sin. If God allows it, the believer should be happy he can't be condemned. But the believer should remember to keep it private before God.

For example, a glass of wine at dinner in the privacy of your own home alone before God might be okay for you, but to do it in front of a person who might sin because he saw you "drinking" is wrong. It's wrong because it is something that might cause another believer to stumble. And as a believer, we shouldn't commit a sin and say we thought God would be okay with it. That would be wrong now, wouldn't it? Why? Because a believer, with a true biblical worldview, should know right from wrong, and this knowledge should lead to the appropriate lifestyle.

"And he that doubteth is damned if he eat, because he eateth not of faith: for whatsoever is not of faith is sin." Again, it can't get any clearer: whatsoever is not of faith is sin. If a believer can't do whatever it is he wants to do (in this case the Bible says eat or drink) in faith, or knowing it is acceptable to God, then he shouldn't do it at all because doing it is a sin. Which is why we must know God's Word. Otherwise we will live in and accept mediocrity out of sheer ignorance. This is why I have written this book to help us understand better. And I hope it's helping.

Have you noticed God is being repetitive? Can you figure out why?

15

Chapter 15 Verse 1-3

These verses are a continuation of the former chapter. It clearly continues the marks of a strong church. Once we study this, a believer can never claim he did not know his or her duty within the church. Every true believer's part in making the church strong is clearly spelled out in this chapter, and helping to make the church strong is part of conforming to the image of His Son. Studying this chapter will do all of us some good!

"*We then that are strong ought to bear the infirmities of the weak, and not to please ourselves.*" In a strong church, the spiritually strong and mature believer bears the weakness of the spiritually weak or immature believer. The weak believers are described in chapter 14. These are the ones who judge, grumble, complain, murmur, and criticize. They are the ones who exhibit the wrong attitudes and behaviors. They disobey God's Word and commandments. This would be a good time to do some self-assessment and ask ourselves which category we belong in. It's been my experience that most churches are far more populated with immature believers than mature. This is truly unfortunate.

The word "*bear*" does not mean to overlook their actions; it means "*to love and teach them the errors of their ways.*" As a pastor, I try to do this as I preach and teach each week. It is an attempt to share the Word of

God to everyone present so any weakness that is present in the people's lives can be identified and dealt with. Why? So the person can become a stronger follower and the church body at large can be strengthened. How can this happen? Read on.

"Let every one of us please his neighbor for his good to edification." If our hearts are in the right place, we will put a premium on doing for our neighbors. We will be very sensitive and considerate to the needs of our brothers and sisters in Christ. We will not put the emphasis on pleasing ourselves, but on ministering to the needs of our church folk. The things we eat, drink, visit, buy, and see should be placed on the back burner of our lives if it causes a weaker brother or sister to stumble, as stated earlier. If it causes them to stumble in their walk with Jesus, we put those things aside and please our neighbors. When this concept is operating efficiently in the church, it makes a huge difference in the strength of the church. Conversely, when it is not operating, it weakens the church and her ministry and mission. Why should I do this, preacher? Well, again read on.

"For even Christ pleased not himself; but, as it is written, the reproaches of them that reproached thee fell on me." The greatest pattern in the world for a true believer is Jesus. The Bible clearly teaches Jesus did not do His will, He did the Father's will. Jesus was never concerned with His well-being; He trusted His Father for that. Jesus lived to call people out of mediocrity and death into extraordinary life. We should and could follow His example. I mean, after all, if we say we are followers of Jesus, shouldn't we actually follow Him? Shouldn't we follow His example? Shouldn't we live to be like Him?

What a glorious spirit would prevail in the church if this was really practiced by the members, or as Scripture says "every one of us." The true believer no longer asks if questionable behavior is right and moral, but if it is good for his or her brother and sister. There's mediocrity in finding excuses to live as one wants; there's excellence as one lives to please others and God.

Chapter 15 Verse 4-6

If the previous verses teach that the strong should bear up the weak by putting weaker people ahead of ourselves, then these verses teach us the next two things we need to learn about being less mediocre in our spiritual walk as it relates to our relationships with others.

"*For whatsoever things were written aforetime were written for our learning, that we through patience and comfort of the scriptures might have hope.*" In the context of strong people making a strong church, the idea here is we must read Scripture. Weak people, to become strong, need to know God's Word. Weak churches, in order to become strong, must have more strong people in it than weak. The more strong people there are, the stronger the church will be. Any team can be strong if the team's players are strong. It's conversely true too. Weak teammates will make the team weak.

"*Now the God of patience and consolation grant you to be likeminded one toward another according to Christ Jesus:*" *In* all strong teams, especially churches, everyone should always work for harmony. How can a church, with so many different and diverse personalities, achieve a harmonious reality? The only possible way is to become like minded. Well, who's mind will win out? Yours? Mine? The highest tither? No, the common denominator and only true hope of success any of us have is to have the mind of Christ as our guide. How do I get to that point? Read your Bible and surrender to its truths. Be Spirit led and not fleshly led. Surrender spiritual mediocrity and its desire to have its way, and follow His way. Conform to the image of His Son! When everyone begins to take this seriously and live it, the church becomes incredibly stronger, the cause of Christ incredibly more important, and the Holy Spirit's control and influence over all of us incredibly more powerful. That's when mediocrity fades into oblivion and excellence takes its proper place in our lives. What does that really look like? Read on.

"*That ye may with one mind and one mouth glorify God, even the Father of our Lord Jesus.*" The purpose for harmony among believers and within the church is striking: that we might glorify God. All of us. Together. At one time. In harmony. When is the last time you really saw this in practice? Unfortunately, I'm not sure I've ever seen it.

Since this is biblical and true, I would suppose the enemy would have this idea on his radar screen to try to disrupt and destroy. So he attacks us, and we get frustrated, angry, mad, or whatever. His intention is to destroy our ability to be in harmony, so we cannot possibly bring glory to God. Simple, yet effective. And since we don't read Scripture like we should and allow our emotions to dictate how we will respond to our brothers and sisters, little, if any, glory is given to God. Mediocrity at its finest.

Chapter 15 Verse 7-10

"*Wherefore receive ye one another, as Christ also received us to the glory of God.*" In a strong church, everyone accepts one another. There is no discrimination whatsoever in a strong church. The word "*receive*" means "*to take for oneself.*" We are to be caring and kind to all of our brothers and sisters in Christ. Are we? Are you?

"*Now I say that Jesus Christ was a minister of the circumcision for the truth of God, to confirm the promises made unto the fathers:*" Well, I'm not perfect we say. This is true. We struggle with all of this. This is why we need Jesus to not just get us to heaven someday, but to indwell in us every day until heaven. Look, by God's standards, we are all guilty people (3:23). That is why God sent Christ into the world (John 3:16). He died to suffer the punishment for our evil deeds (5:6-8). We must turn from our evil deeds and accept Him into our lives by faith (trust in God). God accepts all who turn to Him in faith, from every nation (3:29-30). Therefore, people from every nation can now receive a right relationship with God because of Christ's work.

Christ did not carry out that work separately from God's promises to Israel. Rather, Christ did it because of God's promises to Israel. Christ himself belonged to Israel (9:5). So, he brought the knowledge of God to all the nations on behalf of the rest of Israel. God's kindness, both to Israel and to all the nations, is a great reason to give thanks and honor to God as seen in the next verse.

"And that the Gentiles might glorify God for his mercy; as it is written, For this cause I will confess to thee among the Gentiles, and sing unto thy name." He has been proclaimed to Jews and Gentiles alike. That includes you and me. Shouldn't we have a song in our hearts because of what Jesus has done for us? Shouldn't we glorify Him all the time in all we say and do? Shouldn't our lives be infinitely different than what we see happening in the lives of so many so-called "believers"? Shouldn't we be followers of Jesus all week long rather than following weakly in a long service at church? Shouldn't our hearts long for Him more and more as we know Him more and more? Shouldn't we praise His mercy for us and understand His grace better? Shouldn't we desire to read and study His love letter to us? Shouldn't we seek advice from those who are more spiritually mature than we are and not fight them when they tell us the truth? Shouldn't our lives demonstrate the most extraordinary living patterns that glorify God and attract others to Him? I'd say we'd be at the height of foolishness and hypocrisy to live any other way. But mediocrity is a strong deceiver. Mediocrity has a massively strong gravitational pull, and many people are out of their orbit around the Son, and their world is chaotic. Do you recognize this in the life of anyone you know?

"And again he saith, Rejoice, ye Gentiles, with his people." I don't think it can be any plainer. If you can spare a few more minutes, please continue to read.

Romans 15:10 repeats a line from Deuteronomy 32:43. That line is near the end of the song that God told Moses to teach to Israel's people (Deuteronomy 31:19-22). That song is a sad song. Its subject is the people in Israel who did not want to be loyal to God. The song records the great kindness that God had shown to their nation. It describes how some of Israel's people would choose to serve false gods and to follow evil behavior. We can compare this with Paul's reference to the same people (10:19-21), in which he repeats other words from the song (Deuteronomy 32:21).

In the song, the people become so evil that God wants to destroy their nation completely. However, God declares that, for His own honor, He would not do that (Deuteronomy 32:26-27). Instead, He would permit them to suffer great troubles, and their enemies would attack them fiercely. Sounds like what's happening in our country.

Through all their troubles, God is waiting for the time when His people will no longer depend upon themselves (Deuteronomy 32:36). Then, at last, they will be ready to trust Him, and God will act powerfully on their behalf. That is the time when God will save the whole of Israel.

So, the song urges the inhabitants of both earth and heaven to praise God with great joy. Of course, the nations or Gentiles of Romans 15:10 are not the enemies who hate Israel, but the idea is the same. True joy is for the people from every nation who themselves trust in Israel's God. They have great joy because Israel's people are returning to the true God. We should have great joy too.

Joy has another name: Jesus. This name can get you back into a right orbit if you will allow Him to do so. Even black holes of mediocrity will bow before Him soon. Don't wait or take chances.

Chapter 15 Verse 11-13

"And again, Praise the Lord, all ye Gentiles; and laud him, all ye people." Why? Because He is faithful and true all the time. His promises endure forever. His Word endures forever. His way endures forever. He endures forever. Those who have been crucified with Him and are under the protection of His blood covenant will endure forever with Him. The question really isn't why should we praise Him. The question is why *don't* we?

"And again, Esaias saith, There shall be a root of Jesse, and he that shall rise to reign over the Gentiles; in him shall the Gentiles trust." People called Christ

"the son of David" because He came from the family of King David, Israel's ruler. However, the Bible also refers to Him as the "root of Jesse" who was David's father. It is the root that supports the plant; the plant does not support the root. Christ did not receive His authority to rule from David; instead, David's family received their authority to rule as kings from Christ.

The rule of Christ, the king of Israel, will be wonderful news for the whole world soon. In fact, His rule is already wonderful news for the Christians from every nation who have accepted His rule over their lives. Christians from every nation should join with Israel's people to praise God with great joy.

"*Now the God of hope fill you with all joy and peace in believing, that ye may abound in hope, through the power of the Holy Ghost.*" Here, Paul ends the long speech or sermon that he began in Romans 1:16. In it he has fully explained the gospel (God's message about Christ), so Paul ends with a message of hope. In the end, the gospel is always a message of hope to everyone who accepts it. It is God's good news for the world. I have always felt God's Word to us was a love letter for those willing to accept it and a condemnation report to those unwilling to accept it. But God wants to offer hope to everyone.

For Christians, the word "hope" has special meaning. It is not something uncertain, like luck or chance. "*Hope*" means "*the fact, or certain knowledge, that God will do good things in the future.*" In fact, He is already doing these things, even when our circumstances seem to show the opposite.

That knowledge gives joy and inner peace to God's people. Paul knew that joy even when he was in prison. He also knew that inner peace, an attitude that caused him to be content even in the most difficult circumstances (Philippians 4:11-12). Rome's Christians would have very serious troubles a few years later. Paul prayed that they would know that same joy and peace. That joy and peace would come to them as they trusted God more. As they believed God's promises, their troubles in this world would matter much less to them. Instead, their attention would be upon the wonderful things that God was doing in their lives. It's all about perspective, and the wrong perspective will always lead us to mediocrity.

Chapter 15 Verse 14-15

"*And I myself also am persuaded of you, my brethren, that ye also are full of goodness, filled with all knowledge, able also to admonish one another.*" God, through the pen of Paul, begins one of the most descriptive passages dealing with ministers here. You can see Paul's heart in these verses as he describes the audience for whom he writes. Paul knew that Rome's Christians were capable people with good church leaders. And that's a key element to having a strong church and minimum mediocrity.

We see in Romans 1:8 that Paul recognized they were a good church, mostly because the members were able to teach and correct each other. Even though Paul had never visited them, he wrote boldly enough to probably offend some of them. So Paul urges Rome's Christians not to allow that to upset them. Paul was just doing what a good minister would do: he was carrying out the work that God had given to him. Ministers, especially pastors, carried out their work for God so that other people could have a right relationship with Him. For Paul, that work was among the Gentiles, people from nations other than Israel. They belonged to nations that had not previously known God; God was making them into His holy people (1 Peter 2:9-10). Paul was not trying to achieve that wonderful change by means of his own words. Instead, he declared the gospel, and he depended not on his own strength but on the power of the Holy Spirit.

"*Nevertheless, brethren, I have written the more boldly unto you in some sort, as putting you in mind, because of the grace that is given to me of God.*" The first Christian churches had a serious problem with certain men who wanted to be leaders. These men spoke in an impressive manner, but they were not declaring the truth about Christ (2 Corinthians 11:4). They acted with great authority, but their authority did not come from the Holy Spirit (2 Corinthians 11:20). They claimed to work for God, but they were actually serving the devil (2 Corinthians 11:12-15). They had been especially active at Corinth from where Paul wrote the Book of Romans. Their kind, it grieves me to report, are active in churches today, too.

Since Paul had written very boldly to the Christians at Rome, he needed to show that he was not behaving in a proud and power hungry manner like those wrong leaders. Paul himself refused to be proud about anything except what God had done in his life. Still, it was his duty to speak clearly and boldly about the gospel. All good ministers do this.

In particular, Paul knew that he had a special work to do for God (as seen in 11:13). He mentions that work in Romans 1:5 too, and he repeats the same phrase here. It was to help people from the Gentile nations to obey God. The Gentile nations are all the nations except Israel, Paul's own nation, although Paul was eager to help Israel's people, too (11:13-14). However, in all the Gentile nations, people were serving false gods. Therefore, it was an important and difficult task to bring knowledge of the true God to those nations.

When Gentiles became Christians, Paul was still careful not to be proud. Paul knew that the honor for that success belonged to Christ: Christ had done this wonderful thing through Paul's work. It was Christ, and not Paul, who died for them. Christ had sent Paul to them with His message. Paul did not send himself. Christ had worked in their lives by the power of His Holy Spirit. Paul had simply obeyed Christ. If more ministers would do that, maybe we'd have less mediocrity in the pulpits.

Chapter 15 Verse 16-21

"*That I should be the minister of Jesus Christ to the Gentiles, ministering the gospel of God, that the offering up of the Gentiles might be acceptable, being sanctified by the Holy Ghost.*" Again, Paul never considered himself superior to anyone. He just accepted and was obedient to the call God had upon his life. This attitude produced great results; it always does. And true biblical sanctification is the cure to mediocrity.

The minister of God should be called by God and be obedient to God. The calling is the easy part; the obedience is infinitely harder. But all ministers should be bold in reminding people of the great truths of the gospel. If you were to re-read this book from the beginning, you would see how Paul did this. You see, the true minister, and ultimately that includes all believers, exists for no other purpose than to proclaim Jesus to a lost and dying world. That includes the church whose members have settled for heaven someday when in reality they should all be experiencing a little heaven on earth today.

"*17 I have therefore whereof I may glory through Jesus Christ in those things which pertain to God.*" The minister of God talks about the things of God. In the next verse, we see Paul saying he spoke by words and deeds (I'll have more on that later). Here, Paul talked about glorifying Jesus and Him alone. The minister may truly boast, but not about worldly things or fleshly things. The true minister boasts in Christ alone for God alone to receive the glory due Him. I pray I am more of a boaster of Jesus than of myself. But I know I have failed numerous times. I think we all have. But our Lord simply bids us to learn and press on and never, ever, settle for average service.

"*For I will not dare to speak of any of those things which Christ hath not wrought by me, to make the Gentiles obedient, by word and deed 19 Through mighty signs and wonders, by the power of the Spirit of God; so that from Jerusalem, and round about unto Illyricum, I have fully preached the gospel of Christ.*" Paul now tells us about the converts he has been involved with and how it was Jesus working through him and not himself which made the difference. As you study this verse deeper, you will find Paul is referring to the miracle of God's Word causing conversion in the hearts of sinners. These are miracles wrought by God only. If you are saved, and you have fond memories of the pastor who led you to Christ, that is fine. But it was God who called you and saved you. Do we follow men who God used or God Himself?

"Yea, so have I strived to preach the gospel, not where Christ was named, lest I should build upon another man's foundation:" I like what I do for the most part, but I love preaching and teaching the Word of God. I think all truly called ministers must. Paul took the hard road in his calling, as he went where no man had gone before. His ministry was a difficult one, to say the least, but he was obedient. He's in heaven right now, and nineteen hundred years after his death I am still talking about him. Pretty impressive, huh? Yet, he's nobody compared to Who he served.

We are all called to be "ministers" (2 Cor. 5:11-21). Are we faithful? Are we obedient? Are we prepared and willing? What will people say nineteen hundred years from now about each of us? Anything? Mediocrity stamps out our potential for anything of significance. Why would we allow that?

"But as it is written, To whom he was not spoken of, they shall see: and they that have not heard shall understand." Believe it or not, there are people in the world who still have never heard of Jesus. There are people in the United States who have never heard the name Jesus Christ except in the form of profanity. It's hard to fathom, but it's nonetheless true. It takes a special someone to go and tell the truth to a lost area. If you have a pastor, you really have a missionary sent to a mission area. In being obedient to their calling and to the Lord, they often sacrifice greatly so people can hear God's truths. It's typically low pay and low thanks, but they do it. The vast majority of people would never put up with what a pastor puts up with. They couldn't. As a people, maybe we should all be a little more grateful and a little less selfish.

Chapter 15 Verse 22-25

"For which cause also I have been much hindered from coming to you." All of God's people, whether a pastor, teacher, witnessing believer, church member, or deacon are under the same descriptive teaching. We are all required to stay and finish the job despite obstacles and hindrances. This is the "cause" Paul is referring to. He wanted to go to other places, and he did, but for now he knew God had him where he was for a reason.

There are three basic choices for all "ministers" including me, you, and everyone else. First, a minister can pull up and leave before his or her time is over in an area. Many ministers do just that; they leave too soon. I am sad to say I have done that in ignorance too, and I regret it. The second choice is to stay too long. It seems fairly common that many stay too long in an area. They get comfortable, lazy, content, or scared to leave, but they stay too long as their time in an area is over. This is often just as damaging as not staying long enough.

The third option is to stay as long as necessary, then leave when God calls you on to other areas of ministry. How does one know when it's time? All I can say is that one will know. Whether or not one will be obedient is another issue.

"*But now having no more place in these parts, and having a great desire these many years to come unto you,*" Paul knew his time was up after he fully completed his mission. His desire was to continue his mission in an area that would benefit from it. And the area was the entire world.

"*Whensoever I take my journey into Spain, I will come to you: for I trust to see you in my journey, and to be brought on my way thitherward by you, if first I be somewhat filled with your company.*" During Paul's life, the western regions of Spain were considered the outposts of the civilized world. Paul knew if he could evangelize the outermost part of the civilized world, the uncivilized would be evangelized too. If you and I evangelize our neighborhood, the rest of the city will soon be evangelized.

Interestingly, Paul was consumed with reaching every man, woman, and child with the gospel of Jesus Christ. Why? Why was he so passionate about that? Why was mediocrity not in his vocabulary? It's because Paul had a powerful meeting with the resurrected Jesus. Anyone who has had a true meeting with the resurrected Jesus will never be mediocre in his or her service to the Lord. This is a true statement, friends. Mediocrity is the offspring of a life based on thoughts and feelings about Jesus but not the truth of His resurrection. If you truly think about it, you'll see the truth in the statement. Paul had allowed himself to be conformed to the image of God's Son.

"*But now I go unto Jerusalem to minister unto the saints.*" Let's learn a little more historical facts. The Book of Acts records three long journeys that Paul travelled in order to declare the gospel. The first of these, which he travelled with Barnabas, is in Acts 13:1 to 14:28. It ends with the meeting of the apostles in Jerusalem in Acts chapter 15.

Paul's second journey, with Silas, is in Acts 15:36 to 18:22. During that journey, Paul stayed in Corinth for 18 months while he established the church there. That journey ends with Paul's return to Antioch, which was Paul's own church. It is believed Paul wrote Romans during his time at Corinth.

The third journey is in Acts 18:23 to 21:19. During this journey, Paul spent two years in Ephesus and he established a large church there. While he was still in Ephesus, he encouraged Corinth's Christians to collect a gift for the poor Christians in Judea (1 Corinthians 16:1-4). Paul then went through Macedonia into Corinth. There, Paul joined the men who were taking that gift to Jerusalem.

Through it all, Paul's heart was to minister to the spiritual needs of the people he came in contact with, wherever they were. Why? Again, because Paul had a life-changing experience with the resurrected Jesus. Have you? Is there fruit to prove it? If not, why not? Is mediocrity present in your life? If so, why?

Chapter 15 Verse 26-27

"*For it hath pleased them of Macedonia and Achaia to make a certain contribution for the poor saints which are at Jerusalem.*" The church at Jerusalem was the first Christian church in the world. Since its beginning, many of its members were very poor. So the first Christians there gladly chose to share their possessions with each other. Not long after that, they made special arrangements to provide for the poor widows in their church. This is our example for today too.

The Christians in Jerusalem were the first to suffer for their belief in Christ, and Paul (then called Saul) was personally responsible for many of their troubles. Many of them lost their homes and their jobs; several had to go to prison. Yet they still converted. Why? Because when you are around someone who has been with the resurrected Jesus, you typically get truly converted too.

After Paul became a Christian, he desired very much to help the poor Christians in Jerusalem. His opportunity to do that came when he established the church at Corinth in Achaia. The new Christians in Corinth were eager to do God's work, and many of them could afford to give. So Paul encouraged them to collect a gift for the poor Christians in Jerusalem. After he returned to Corinth, he would be able to take the gift to Jerusalem (1 Corinthians 16:1-4).

On the way back to Corinth, Paul passed through Macedonia. There, something happened that Paul had not expected. Macedonia's Christians were very poor, and Paul had not asked them to give. Even so, they heard about the gift that Paul was taking to Jerusalem. They urged Paul to take their gifts, too (2 Corinthians 8:1-5). They were eager to give; they considered it an honor to be able to help the poor Christians in Jerusalem. They trusted God to provide what they themselves needed. What an amazing testimony for these believers as well as a great conviction to modern day Christians who never give to the needs of the church.

"It hath pleased them verily; and their debtors they are. For if the Gentiles have been made partakers of their spiritual things, their duty is also to minister unto them in carnal things." Paul has written much in his letter about the love that Gentile Christians should have for the Jews. The world today wants Christians to turn their backs on the Jews but we are called to love and support them.

The Jews are Israel's people from the family of Abraham, Isaac and Jacob; the Gentiles are people from the other nations. In Romans 13:8, Paul describes love as a debt that Christians owe. They show that love when they act to help other people.

Christians have a general duty to show love to other people, and they should not expect anything in return. However, Gentile Christians have a particular duty to love the Jews because they have already received much in return. It was to the Jews that God originally gave the Bible and so many other good things (9:4-5). By means of Christ, they have now shared these benefits with the world (15:8-10). Gentile Christians receive these benefits as they join with the Jews as the people of God (Ephesians 2:11-19). In addition, all the first Christians were Jews; it was them who originally taught God's message about Christ, the gospel, to people from other nations.

The Christians in Macedonia and Achaia showed their love in a very practical way. They were mainly Gentile Christians. They collected a large gift to help the poor Christians in Jerusalem, who were Jewish Christians. They gave gladly; in fact, Paul did not even ask them to give. Each person gave what he himself had chosen to give. They considered it a wonderful opportunity to be able to help the Jewish Christians in this way.

CHAPTER 15 VERSE 28-29

"*When therefore I have performed this, and have sealed to them this fruit, I will come by you into Spain.*" Paul kept his world-wide vision of evangelism even in the face of the pressing needs of the Jerusalem believers. Their plight was desperate, and Paul knew it, but he was still intent on reaching the world. I'm reminded of how many conversations I have had with church folk who see no reason to be concerned with foreign missions when there's so much need here in their own backyard. Both are necessary according to Paul. Here's an interesting fact: for the first time in the history of the world, America has become the number one mission field for churches from other countries. Think about that!

"And I am sure that, when I come unto you, I shall come in the fullness of the blessing of the gospel of Christ." Why do missions at all? Because it is the blessing of Christ; namely it's reaching people with the gospel. There is no other truth or message that can meet the desperate need of mankind for life. Paul knew this and he was gripped with the burning desire to share the resurrected Lord with everyone he met. Does this describe anyone you know? Can you name three people who do this on a regular basis? Can you name one? I struggle too. But I can think of hundreds of names who reside in mediocrity. This may sound mean and hateful, but it's true.

"Now I beseech you, brethren, for the Lord Jesus Christ's sake, and for the love of the Spirit, that ye strive together with me in your prayers to God for me;" Paul is begging for prayer, not for selfish reasons but for the sake of the Lord. Paul's one ambition for his life was for Jesus Christ to be praised, worshipped, and served by all humanity. Again, I am longing to know why. I am convinced that the experience he had with Jesus on the road to Damascus was so personal and powerful that it changed him totally and eternally. This same experience should happen to all who say they have decided to follow Jesus, but I don't see it, even in myself some of the time. Do you see it in you?

Paul next listed four things he asked for prayer over.

"That I may be delivered from them that do not believe in Judaea; and that my service which I have for Jerusalem may be accepted of the saints;" Paul was seeking deliverance from those who would mock, scorn, reject, and abuse him. There are some people who will not simply say no to the message; instead they will try to destroy the messenger.

Paul then asks for prayer for his acceptance by those who do believe. Why in the world would he need prayers for that? Well, because too many believers do not accept the ministry of all of God's servants. Why? Because so many believers accept mediocrity and believe this to be the norm; they can't tolerate the minister who is passionate and on fire for God. Why? Well, because carnal believers are typically selfish, sinful, and don't really want to live in truth; they just don't want to go to hell. Look, Paul was constantly being opposed by carnal believers. I don't know of any ministers who aren't. This is both unfortunate and tragic. Mediocrity usually is.

"*That I may come unto you with joy by the will of God, and may with you be refreshed.*" Another prayer was for Paul to be able to visit and minister to them in joy. This would include everyone everywhere. And his ministry would be refreshing spiritually for those he touched. Paul had the right motive and methodology. And he had tenacity. He knew for an absolute fact Jesus Christ was alive from the dead. This conviction makes all the difference in the world. If you're not absolutely convinced Jesus is the Son of God and is alive from the dead, you'll always struggle with biblical things and spiritual mediocrity. Everyone does. Think about what it's going to take to get out of mediocrity, because if Jesus really is alive, we've got some explaining to do.

"*Now the God of peace be with you all. Amen.*" Paul now prays for us. Amen.

16

Chapter 16 Verse 1-2

The Book of Romans ends in an unusual manner. Normally, as seen in his other letters, Paul simply blesses his readers, and then the letter ends. However, Paul blesses the Christians in Rome four times (15:5-6; 15:13; 15:33; 16:20), but still the letter does not end. It's as if Paul doesn't want to say goodbye. I'm struggling with it too.

God had given Paul a great love, even for Christians whom he had never met. It is right and good for a church leader to have an attitude of love towards the people whom he serves, and it certainly helps if they help him by being friendly and caring. Nonetheless, there were probably more practical reasons why Paul wrote like that.

It seems that a Christian lady called Phoebe took Paul's letter from Corinth to Rome. She sailed from the port of Cenchrea near Corinth. Her sailing boat could not leave the port until the wind was in the right direction. While the sailors waited for the wind, Paul would have more time to complete his letter. This is what he wrote.

"*I commend unto you Phebe our sister, which is a servant of the church which is at Cenchrea:*" There are several things about Phoebe that are surprising. She is travelling to Rome, probably unescorted, and Paul gave her the responsibility to take this, perhaps the most important of all Paul's letters, to Rome. So she must have had Paul's trust.

Then, Paul's description of her is surprising. He calls her by a word that he used for a church leader in 1 Timothy 3:8-13. Paul could perhaps mean that she was the wife of a church leader. Yet, he says nothing about her husband. Again, it is clear that Paul respected and trusted this lady very much.

Cenchrea, from which Phoebe came, was very near Corinth. In Corinth, some women had tried to take authority over the church. They were eager and bold, but Paul could not approve of them. They were not helping people to trust God, and the Holy Spirit was not guiding them. They were taking authority over the men; they were behaving in ways that offended people. Phoebe too was a strong person, but she was not trying to control other people. Instead, she used her strength to help many of God's people, including Paul. Paul very much approved of her. Thank God for the women of the church who have the right attitudes and support and serve the church appropriately. I have been blessed with many such women in my ministry.

"*That ye receive her in the Lord, as becometh saints, and that ye assist her in whatsoever business she hath need of you: for she hath been a succourer of many, and of myself also,*" The word "*succourer*" gives us insight into this woman. Paul gives her an honorable title that means "*someone who protects other people.*" In ancient Greece, some rich and important people accepted the responsibility to protect people who were not citizens. It was their duty to protect the rights of these people in court. That is the true meaning of the title that Paul gives to Phoebe. It's interesting that Paul mentions Phoebe first and I suppose we are all to be Phoebes for the sake of those in need. Phoebe probably was a powerful woman, and that gave her opportunities to help other people with their problems. For example, she could speak to important people on their behalf. She had the skill to make arrangements for them; she had the knowledge to advise them wisely.

Today's Christians might not respect people with such skills. They might be jealous of them, or they might ask them to do more practical tasks. However, the Christians at Cenchrea near Corinth gave honor to Phoebe. They knew how often they had needed her help. The first Christians had many powerful enemies who tried to stop their work. Those enemies often used the legal system and the courts, as they did against Paul in Corinth. Paul was very grateful to have Phoebe's help in such a situation.

As a pastor, I am indebted to many women of the church who have served with great distinction and have been a great help to me. These women help to keep the church alive and active and are needed now more than ever. They help keep mediocrity at bay.

CHAPTER 16 VERSE 3-5

"*Greet Priscilla and Aquila my helpers in Christ Jesus:*" Aquila and Priscilla were a husband and wife team who helped Paul in several places. In the Bible, Priscilla's name always appears with her husband's name. That is unusual, and it probably shows the great importance of her part in their work: establishing new churches.

The most important churches that Paul established were the churches in Corinth and Ephesus. In those cities, large numbers of people who had formerly lived very wicked lives became Christians (they went from mediocre to extraordinary). For that reason, Paul continued to work in those places for longer than anywhere else. He stayed for 18 months in Corinth, and 2 years in Ephesus.

Aquila and Priscilla helped Paul to start both those great churches. When Paul arrived at Corinth, he stayed in their home. He also worked with them; he, like them, made tents to help support his financial needs. When Paul left Corinth, they travelled with him to Ephesus. At that time, Paul was just passing through Ephesus, but Aquila and Priscilla remained there. There was no church there yet, but they continued to speak to people about Christ. After some time, they established their own small church there, which met in their home. Later, they returned to Rome, where they also established a small church in their own home. However, Paul still encouraged the Christians in the first church to be friendly towards Aquila, Priscilla, and their church. Paul asked those Christians to greet Aquila and Priscilla on his behalf.

"Who have for my life laid down their own necks: unto whom not only I give thanks, but also all the churches of the Gentiles." So what's the big deal with these two? Why are they mentioned in God's Word? Well, Paul was writing about 25 or 30 years after Christ's death. At that time, the churches with the largest number of Gentile Christians were probably those at Rome, Corinth and Ephesus. Who are the common denominators, other than Paul, with these three churches? Yep! You guessed it.

These two had provided Paul with a home, work, and protection. They helped him in church planting and church growth. Every pastor needs an Aquila and Priscilla. What a blessing they are.

They really were a great blessing, but it was a dangerous thing to do because Paul had many enemies. It's still often dangerous for a couple to be so supportive of their pastor, but Paul gave them personal thanks and mentioned every church should too. Not bad for a lay couple.

"Likewise greet the church that is in their house. Salute my well-beloved Epaenetus, who is the first fruits of Achaia unto Christ." In Romans 16:3-15, Paul sends his greetings, mostly by name, to 25 of Rome's Christians and to 5 groups. Paul had not yet been to Rome. So he would only know the names of the leaders and of people whom he had met elsewhere. It seems likely, therefore, that there were several hundred Christians in Rome, or perhaps even a few thousand. This again was about 25 or 30 years after Christ's death.

As mentioned above, the first group that Paul greets is the church in the home of Priscilla and Aquila. Probably, many of the first Christians churches began to meet in ordinary houses. Priscilla and her husband Aquila worked at home, as most people did at that time. There was constant activity and probably many guests in their home. They were pleased to invite other people to join their prayers and Bible study. They were constantly available to discuss Christ with those people (Acts 18:26). So, a group of Christians gathered, and they became a church. Perhaps, like the first Christians in Jerusalem, they chose to eat together and to share their possessions (Acts 2:44-47).

In biblical times, the first person who becomes a Christian in any region has acted very bravely. In the region then called Asia, which is now part of Turkey, that person was Epaenetus. Many people in that region would oppose the Christians (2 Corinthians 1:8). By his decision to trust Christ, Epaenetus was risking the loss of his home, his job, and perhaps even his family. However, Epaenetus believed that, in Christ, he had found something much better: a right relationship with God.

Epaenetus may have lost many friends, but he found Paul to be a true friend and Christ to be the best friend of all. He probably loved to study the Bible with Paul, who had such a strong relationship with Christ. They had plenty of opportunity to do that during the two years that Paul spent in Ephesus (Acts 19:8-10).

By the way, can you discern how Epaenetus went from ordinary to extraordinary? We're almost through with our study of the book of Romans, and by now you should be able to clearly see and identify the issues. Can you?

Chapter 16 Verse 6-12

"*Greet Mary, who bestowed much labor on us.*" The Bible mentions several women with the name Mary. It was clearly a popular name at the time of the first Christians. It is the same name as Miriam, which was the name of Moses' sister. This is important when you think about it.

Paul mentions how hard Mary worked. Paul's word for her "work" may perhaps also express the idea that she suffered much. It is the same word that Christ uses for hard work in Matthew 11:28.

In addition to being a hard worker, this Mary seems to have also suffered the loss of her husband. That seems likely because there is no mention of him here. If he was with her, we would expect Paul to greet him too. Perhaps Mary was a widow, or perhaps her husband left her because of her trust in Christ. Paul urged the churches to support those older widows who truly worked for God to serve His people. Paul respected women of this caliber. We should too.

"Salute Andronicus and Junia, my kinsmen, and my fellow-prisoners, who are of note among the apostles, who also were in Christ before me. Greet Amplias my beloved in the Lord. Salute Urbane, our helper in Christ, and Stachys my beloved. Salute Apelles approved in Christ. Salute them which are of Aristobulus' household. Salute Herodion my kinsman. Greet them that be of the household of Narcissus, which are in the Lord. Salute Tryphena and Tryphosa, who labor in the Lord. Salute the beloved Persis, which labored much in the Lord." From Paul's long list of names, it is not possible to identify the main leaders of Rome's church. Paul loves and respects all of these people, and he sends personal greetings for so many of them. He is eager to encourage all Rome's loyal Christians.

However, it seems likely that Andronicus and Junias (verse 7) were among the principal leaders. Paul knew them well, and he respected them greatly. They had long trusted Christ, and they had gained knowledge and experience in trusting Him. They had also suffered for their belief in Christ; in fact on one occasion they went to prison with Paul. That was a common experience in Paul's life (2 Corinthians 11:23). On such occasions, Paul did not allow his situation to upset him. Instead, he encouraged the Christians who were in prison with him to sing and to praise God with him (Acts 16:25; Matthew 5:11-12). Do you see any mediocre faith here? I don't either. I see someone who has conformed to the image of His Son.

Paul's personal greetings show his strong desire to encourage people in their relationship with God. All good ministers will do this. He frequently mentions the love that they share as God's people (verses 8, 9 and 12), or their work for God (verses 9 and 12). He reminds them that God has chosen them to be His special people (verse 13); God is pleased with them (verse 10). Most of the people in verses 7 to 14 are men, but verse 12 refers to three women.

An interesting greeting is to those Christians who belong to the houses of Aristobulus (verse 10) and Narcissus (verse 11). There were many great palaces in Rome, and large numbers of slaves worked at each of them. It may be, therefore, that Paul's greetings here are for Christian slaves. Paul cared about the slaves, and he was pleased to declare the gospel, the message about Christ, to them. It seems that many of them became Christians (1 Corinthians 7:21-22; Colossians 3:22-24).

Does any of this remind you of anyone in your life? I can't think of anyone, including myself, who is even remotely like Paul. What made Paul such a powerful man of God? He refused to accept and live a mediocre Christian life for Jesus. Why? Paul had a true, life-changing confrontation with the resurrected Jesus Christ, and mediocrity was unacceptable. Conforming to the image of God's Son was the only viable alternative for Paul. It's honestly our only viable option too.

Imagine a church full of Paul-like Christians! The community the church serves in would soon change, followed by the state, and then the nation. What we're seeing in our country is more like change from a spirit of Saul: unrighteousness, discord, violence, rioting, murder, and chaos. This is absolutely a clear indication that something is spiritually wrong with people.

Chapter 16 Verse 13-16

"*13 Salute Rufus chosen in the Lord, and his mother and mine. Salute Asyncritus, Phlegon, Hermas, Patrobas, Hermes, and the brethren which are with them. Salute Philologus, and Julia, Nereus, and his sister, and Olympas, and all the saints which are with them. Salute one another with an holy kiss. The churches of Christ salute you.*" We are looking at the long list of greetings that Paul sent to the church at Rome. Twice in the list, Paul refers to people as his "relatives" (verses 7 and 11; also in verse 21), and once to someone as his "mother" (verse 13).

There is only one definite reference in the Bible to a relative of Paul's. In Acts 23:16-22, the son of Paul's sister acted in order to save Paul's life. Probably that relative did not believe in Christ; his act of kindness was rare for a relative of the first Christians. Rarely did a whole family become Christians; more often, the message about Christ separated families (Matthew 10:35-37).

So the reference to "relatives" in Romans chapter 16 may mean that these men, like Paul, were Jews. All the Jews come from the family of Abraham, Isaac, and Jacob, so their whole nation is one family. Paul uses the word for "relatives" with this meaning in Romans 9:3. Although Paul's subject in many of these greetings is a person's relationship with God. All Christians are brothers and sisters in God's family (Mark 3:31-35); therefore, they are all relatives.

The reference to Rufus (verse 13), whose mother is also called Paul's "mother" is especially interesting. Perhaps this same Rufus was the son of Simon, from Cyrene, who carried Christ's cross (Mark 15:21). Perhaps that same Simon became a leader of the church at Antioch with Paul, then called Saul (Acts 13:1). Perhaps at that time, Rufus's mother looked after Paul, as if she was Paul's own mother. Unfortunately, that can only be a guess.

Rufus was said to be chosen *in* the Lord and not *by* the Lord. The emphasis is not on election but on tenderness and preciousness. Rufus is known as a saintly man, and he had a personal and intimate relationship with the Lord to the point where he was totally set apart for Him. Every church needs people like that. In fact, without people like that, the church will peak at mediocrity but rarely get any better. I'm afraid there are fewer and fewer people like this today. Why? Well, I guess if we really think about it we know why.

In verses 14-16, the unknown servants are listed. The stress here is on unity in the body of Christ. Not all believers are leaders, and many are content to remain that way. But all believers should be *doers* of the Word and have a real and growing relationship with Jesus. These people are mentioned because they demonstrated a life of belief and surrender to the Lord. Two conditions exist for a person to be a true Christian: receive Jesus as Savior (for salvation) and receive Him as Lord (for sanctification). To receive Jesus as Savior, one must admit their sins to Him, repent or turn away from those sins, believe in the death, burial, and resurrection of Jesus, and have faith in His promises of salvation. That's the "making Jesus my Savior" part. The other part, which is just as important, is to be faithful and obedient to Him as one learns and grows in their faith. That's the "making Him Lord" part. This is part of the fruit a believer is to have in his or her life as a true believer. It's a vital part of the process of conforming to the image of His Son. If Jesus is not a person's Lord, mediocrity will quickly set in and ruin everything.

At the end of Paul's list, he urges Rome's Christians to greet each other like a family (16:16). He wanted them to have true love in their hearts for each other (1 Corinthians 13). Therefore, they should be friendly; they too should greet each other.

How friendly are we to our brothers and sisters in Christ? Some "believers" make it very difficult to be friendly towards them sometimes. But those that are truly in Christ should be friendly and loving to the point where others want to be friendly and loving towards us. But there are times when it is appropriate to disengage with those people.

Chapter 16 Verse 17-18

"*Now I beseech you, brethren, mark them which cause divisions and offences contrary to the doctrine which ye have learned; and avoid them. For they that are such serve not our Lord Jesus Christ, but their own belly; and by good words and fair speeches deceive the hearts of the simple.*" A sincere Christian serves God because of his or her love and respect for God. That Christian helps other people because of the love that God has given him or her for those people. He or she does not care whether other people consider him or her a leader or not. He or she is not trying to increase his or her importance; he or she is not trying to gain an advantage for himself or herself from his or her work for God. Perhaps he or she earns wages as a church leader (1 Corinthians 9:7-11) but he or she would still serve God loyally, even without those wages.

On the other hand, there are many people who try to make themselves important by their work in the churches. Their method is to increase their own power and importance. They want people to trust them rather than to trust God. So, they start to replace the Bible's simple message with their own clever ideas. They try to separate people from the sincere leaders who would teach them the truth about God. They try to attract people to themselves with their fine words and impressive speech. The Bible teaches that we are to avoid these types of people because they are wrong and they lead us to mediocrity or worse. I've seen them in every church I have pastored. They are there and they are a real issue. Beware people who cause division and sow discord within the church. Beware people who talk about the pastor behind his back and try to usurp his authority. If that person is you, repent and seek forgiveness and restoration. Believe me, the pastor of the church knows who you are and what you are saying; God certainly does too.

Why should this be addressed? Such behavior is evil; it can and will cause severe problems. It can ruin a person's relationship with God. A few weeks before Paul wrote the Book of Romans, he warned Corinth's Christians strongly about such leaders (2 Corinthians 11:1-6 and 11:12-15). A few weeks later, he warned Ephesus's church leaders about this matter (Acts 20:29-31). These people fan the flames for mediocrity and can destroy the effectiveness of a church.

Many Christians try to protect themselves from those evil leaders. However, those Christians often choose foolish methods, which God has not provided. Some Christians refuse to go to church, but God wants Christians to meet in order to encourage each other in their relationship with Him (Hebrews 10:25). Other Christians refuse to learn anything new. They only ever want to hear the first lessons that they learned about God again. In that way, they are too afraid to develop in their relationship with God.

Still, God provides leaders to teach His people (Ephesians 4:11-13), from His Word (the Bible) and by His Spirit. The correct way for us to protect ourselves is with a close relationship with God. We should constantly pray and study the Bible. We should allow God to direct our lives by His Holy Spirit. And we should develop and protect our relationship with the pastor He has sent.

If a person ever causes discord in the church, especially against the pastor, that person should repent and seek restoration with both God and the pastor immediately.

Chapter 16 Verse 19-20

"*For your obedience is come abroad unto all men. I am glad therefore on your behalf: but yet I would have you wise unto that which is good, and simple concerning evil. 20 And the God of peace shall bruise Satan under your feet shortly. The grace of our Lord Jesus Christ be with you. Amen."* In the garden called Eden, the first people chose not to obey God (Genesis 3). That was how sin (wrong and evil thoughts, words, and actions) entered our world (5:12). Its results are terrible because sin brings death (6:23). And as we have discussed, death means separation from God. At your physical "death," your soul and body separate. If you have not become spiritually saved by Jesus before then, you will be separated from God for all eternity, which is called eternal death. You will remain alive and coherent, just not with God. And friends, it won't be pleasant.

What God is doing in the lives of Christians by His gospel (the message about Christ) is truly wonderful (1:16-17). People from all nations are choosing to obey God (1:5) - the opposite of what Adam and Eve did in Eden (Genesis 3:1-6). God is giving them a wonderful life that never ends (John 3:16).

Adam and Eve decided not to obey God because they wanted the knowledge of both good and evil things, and when you think about it, that's exactly what they received. Still today, wrong and evil desires constantly tempt us. For that reason, we must give our attention to what is good; in other words, we must learn what is right. Additionally, we must have a simple attitude towards what is evil: we must refuse to do any evil thing. That is true wisdom and the antidote to mediocrity in our lives.

God is the God of peace; He is the God who brings people into a right relationship with Himself. By the death of Christ, He makes us, who were His enemies, into His friends (5:6-11). Paul refers to the first promise in the Bible, Genesis 3:15. Satan (a name for the devil that means "the accuser") came in the form of a "serpent," and he persuaded Adam and Eve not to obey God (Genesis 3:1-4). God promised that another man, Christ, would come from Eve's family. Christ would destroy Satan's power completely, like a person who destroys the head of a snake beneath his foot. Satan is losing his power because of the honor that God is giving to His people. Satan cannot defeat them because God has given them a right relationship with Himself. And a real, biblical relationship with God is the antidote to all the mediocrity in our lives. It's true; it's doable and available.

God never intended for us to know about evil. In the beginning He made the universe, the world, all living things, and mankind. Then He called it good. Evil, sin, and corruption never entered the picture until Eve was deceived by Satan and made a wrong choice. The devil used Eve's curiosity about evil to trick her into thinking she would be better off if she knew what evil was. The result was disastrous for mankind. As Adam and Eve partook in the tree that God commanded them not to eat of, their eyes were open to the knowledge of evil. The rest is history. The result was the universe and everything within it had a working knowledge that both good and evil existed, and we were not the better for it. So, we can now understand Satan is the father of all mediocrity, friends. But we are the carriers of it. It is up to us to determine who we will listen to and follow.

In this verse, Paul is giving a wonderful key to living the Christian life. We are to be wise about what is good and innocent about what is evil.

He is saying the best defense against sin and corruption is a good offense. We are to be wise and knowledgeable about what is good. Meaning we should know "good" and live in that knowledge. In the same way, we are to be innocent or guileless to evil. In other words, we should stay away from it, having nothing to do with it. Living in truth is living abundantly; living in sin is living in evil, which manifests itself typically in its hidden form: mediocre living.

Chapter 16 Verse 21-23

"Timotheus my workfellow, and Lucius, and Jason, and Sosipater, my kinsmen, salute you. I Tertius, who wrote Thisepistle, salute you in the Lord. Gaius mine host, and of the whole church, saluteth you. Erastus the chamberlain of the city saluteth you, and Quartus a brother." Perhaps the main lesson to learn from these final greetings is the friendly attitude that the first Christians showed. We cannot say whether any of these people had been to Rome. Perhaps they did not actually know any of the Christians there. However, they had heard about the Christians in Rome (1:8), and they felt only love towards them (1 John 4:19-21). So when Paul sent his or her letter, the Christians with him wanted to send their greetings too.

Timothy is Paul's younger helper, to whom he wrote the Books of 1 Timothy and 2 Timothy. He assisted Paul at Corinth, where Paul probably wrote the Book of Romans.

In Acts 20:4, there is a list of the Christian men who travelled with Paul on his journey from Corinth to Jerusalem. They include Sopater, which may perhaps be a different spelling of Sosipater. Similarly, Lucius may be a different spelling of Luke, the author of the Books of Luke and Acts.

We think that Paul usually wrote his own letters (Galatians 6:11). However, on this occasion Tertius, who was perhaps a scribe (professional writer), wrote down his words. Tertius' name means "third" and he would probably have been the third son in his family. Quartus' name means "fourth" possibly he was Tertius' younger brother. When Paul first visited Corinth, he stayed with Aquila and Priscilla (Acts 18:1-3).

On Paul's return there, they had gone back to Rome (16:3), so Paul stayed with Gaius. Perhaps he is the same man whose name appears in 1 Corinthians 1:14.

In 1 Corinthians 1:26, Paul says that not many important people there had trusted Christ. However, here he mentions an important official in the city of Corinth, called Erastus. Erastus had become a Christian, and he too sent his greetings to Rome's Christians.

What's the point? Of all the Christians at Rome, of all the brethren that were with Paul, of all the saints who were members of Caesar's household, there was no one who shared so intimately Paul's heart as the one listed here, especially Timothy. They were equal in soul, but Timothy was in the truest sense a disciple of Paul.

When a disciple is fully trained, he will be like his or her teacher. And these men were just like Paul. Paul clearly teaches that believers are to follow the example of his life. We can't see Paul. We read about him and thus learn of his life. But you can see your pastor.

Are you becoming like the example of your pastor, or are you content with believing he's more spiritual than you because he's called to be so? That's so mediocre. We are all called to be spiritual and righteous, and your pastor should be showing you this in Scripture and by example. I may not be the best example, but I do try to lead my flock to a closer walk with Jesus, conforming to the image of His Son. Hopefully, if you become more like your pastor, you'll become more like Jesus too. That's the point.

Could your pastor write a farewell letter and mention you in it as one of the best of the best?

Chapter 16 Verse 24-27

"*The grace of our Lord Jesus Christ be with you all. Amen. Now to him that is of power to establish you according to my gospel, and the preaching of Jesus*

Christ, according to the revelation of the mystery, which was kept secret since the world began, But now is made manifest, and by the scriptures of the prophets, according to the commandment of the everlasting God, made known to all nations for the obedience of faith: To God only wise, be glory through Jesus Christ forever. Amen." Usually at the end of Paul's letters, Paul blesses the people to whom he writes. However, he has already done this several times in chapters 15 and 16. Perhaps he blesses them again in verse 24, although that verse does not appear in many ancient copies of the Bible.

So, instead, at the end of the Book of Romans, Paul praises God with a special prayer. His prayer is that God will always receive the glory (honor) due to him (verse 27). Of course, Paul prays that wisely. In the end, God certainly will receive all glory and honor. This prayer cannot fail. Is that our prayer?

In verse 25, Paul describes God as the God who is able to make his people strong (Romans 8:37; 2 Corinthians 12:9-10; Philippians 1:6). He does it by the gospel (the message about Christ), which God's people are even now declaring in every nation (10:9-18).

For so many ages, the gospel seemed a mystery or a secret (Ephesians 1:9-10). However, that secret was only waiting for the time when God had chosen to make it public. Long before Christ came, the prophets (holy men) had written about it in their books (1 Peter 1:10-12). Ancient passages like Psalm 22 and Isaiah 53 declare God's plan clearly. It is that Christ, by His death, brings people into a right relationship with God. Because of their evil deeds, all people have made themselves into God's enemies (3:23). However, because of Christ's death, people from all nations can become God's friends. They do not achieve this by their own works, but by faith: simple belief and trust in God (chapter 4). It is God who, by His Spirit, makes it possible for them to obey Him (8:1-11). So God, by His great power, will complete the work that He has begun in their lives (8:18; 8:28-30).

Far too often, we take all of this for granted. We allow mediocrity to replace abundance. One of the problems many churches face these days is that they're neither great at things or terrible at things because they're full of people who share that trait. It's sad, isn't it?

So the Bible talks about giving God glory and not living in mediocrity. There are various ways that we might give God glory. One is through our worship. Many of our hymns that are written have songs of praise to God. But we've gotten so mediocre in our worship that we argue over style and not substance. That's sad too.

Look, the most powerful way to give God glory is by living a Christ-like life. What does God want you to do with your life? Pattern it after His Son and stay there. That's it. That's all. Who you marry, the job you take, the place you live, all of those decisions can be made by you. Just live your life, wherever, and with whomever, the way Christ lived His: Holy, connected to the Father, and pressing forward for Kingdom work.

We now understand Jesus was never, ever, mediocre. We also now know we shouldn't be either. Live out your faith. Allow your life to be defined as one who is conforming to His image.

EPILOGUE

We have come to the end of our journey, friends. We started our journey with the premise all true believers should be conformed to the image of God's Son. This is the answer to weak and ineffectual Christianity. As we have seen, the concept of "ordinary" or "average" is seemingly acceptable in many other things people do, but it must not be acceptable in the Christian life.

I hope you have all benefited from this effort. I know at times it was probably hard and offensive; God's Word has a way of being that way. But for those of you who made the journey, I am sure you might see mediocrity in a different light.

I hope your walk with Jesus is real and growing and your eyes have been open to some of the things that cause all of us to live in spiritual mediocrity. As we have seen, this is not the biblical template God has given us nor is it Christ honoring. It is readily accepted, but it is not the real Christianity we all search for. I hope we will all strive to bring God more glory, especially me, as we have seen the ideal from God yet the actual for so many.

If you don't have a relationship with Jesus as your Savior and Lord, you can turn to the Romans Road for your assistance. The first verse on the Romans Road to salvation is Romans 3:23, *"For all have sinned, and come short of the glory of God."* We have all sinned. We have all done things that are displeasing to God. There is no one who is innocent. Romans 3:10-18 gives a detailed picture of what sin looks like in our lives. The second Scripture on the Romans Road to salvation, Romans 6:23, teaches us about the consequences of sin - *"For the wages of sin is death; but the gift of God is eternal life through Jesus Christ our Lord."* The punishment that we have earned for our sins is death. Not just physical death, but eternal death.

The third verse on the Romans Road to salvation picks up where Romans 6:23 left off: *"but the gift of God is eternal life through Jesus Christ our Lord."* Romans 5:8 declares, *"But God demonstrates His own love toward us, in that while we were still sinners, Christ died for us."* Jesus Christ died for us! Jesus' death paid for the price of our sins. Jesus' resurrection proves that God accepted Jesus' death as the payment for our sins.

The fourth stop on the Romans Road to salvation is Romans 10:9: *"that if you confess with your mouth Jesus as Lord, and believe in your heart that God raised Him from the dead, you will be saved."* Because of Jesus' death on our behalf, all we have to do is believe in Him, repent of our sins and trust His death as the payment for our sins. Romans 10:13 says it again, *"for everyone who calls on the name of the Lord will be saved."* Jesus died to pay the penalty for our sins and rescue us from eternal death. Salvation, the forgiveness of sins, is available to anyone who will trust in Jesus Christ as their Savior. And if you trust Him for your salvation, then make Him Lord too! Anything else is mediocrity in its highest form.

The final aspect of the Romans Road to salvation is the results of salvation. Romans 5:1 has this wonderful message, *"Therefore, since we have been justified through faith, we have peace with God through our Lord Jesus Christ."* Through Jesus Christ we can have a relationship of peace with God. Romans 8:1 teaches us, *"Therefore, there is now no condemnation for those who are in Christ Jesus."* Because of Jesus' death on our behalf, we will never be condemned for our sins. Finally, we have this precious promise of God from Romans 8:38-39, *"For I am convinced that neither death nor life, neither angels nor demons, neither the present nor the future, nor any powers, neither height nor depth, nor anything else in all creation, will be able to separate us from the love of God that is in Christ Jesus our Lord."*

Would you like to follow the Romans Road to salvation? If so, here is a simple prayer you can pray to God. Saying this prayer is a way to declare to God that you are relying on Jesus Christ for your salvation. The words themselves will not save you. Only faith in Jesus Christ can provide salvation.

"God, I know that I have sinned against you and am deserving of punishment. But Jesus Christ took the punishment that I deserve so that through faith in Him I could be forgiven. With your help, I place my trust in You for salvation. I repent of my sins and ask you to help me with my daily walk with you now. I pray you will assist me as I conform to the image of Your Son. Thank You for Your wonderful grace and forgiveness - the gift of eternal life! Amen!"

Now, go live beyond mediocrity into the abundant life Jesus died to give you! Find a church that understands Jesus and His Word, and grow in your faith. Be the person Christ has called and equipped you to be, and never forget He is alive forevermore! Praise be to the mighty Lamb of God! Amen!

Printed in the United States
By Bookmasters